THE ENCHANTMENT OF MODERN LIFE

THE ENCHANTMENT OF MODERN LIFE

ATTACHMENTS, CROSSINGS, AND ETHICS

Jane Bennett

PRINCETON UNIVERSITY PRESS   PRINCETON AND OXFORD

Library of Congress Cataloging-in-Publication Data

Bennett, Jane 1957–
The enchantment of modern life : attachments, crossings,
and ethics / Jane Bennett.
p. cm.
Includes bibliographical references and index.
ISBN 0-691-08812-8 (alk. paper)
ISBN 0-691-08813-6 (pbk. : alk. paper)
1. Ethics, Modern. 2. Civilization, Secular. I. Title.
BJ301 B46 2001
191–dc21   00-069283

This book has been composed in Galliard

www.pup.princeton.edu

Printed in the United States of America

10 9 8 7 6 5 4 3 2 1

10 9 8 7 6 5 4 3 2 1
(Pbk)

Contents

Acknowledgments

THIS BOOK owes its existence to a lively group of colleagues who believe that theory matters. Over the past five years or so, they have responded to developing versions of my story with provocative criticisms, thoughtful elaborations, and encouraging interest. I am very fortunate to be engaged with them. My thanks to Anne Brown, John Buell, Eloise Buker, Penny Cordish, Ned Curthoys, Joshua Dienstag, Thomas Dumm, Blake Ethridge (who also prepared the index), Chris Falzon, Kathy Ferguson, Kennan Ferguson, Richard Flathman, Michael Gibbons, Katherine Gibson, Judith Grant, Bonnie Honig, Barry Hindess, Steven Johnston, Ann Kaplan, Thom Kuehls, Alessandra Lippucci, Tim Luke, Mary Marchand, Lori Marso, Sid Maskit, Sara Monoson, Pat Moynagh, David Owen, Davide Panagia, Paul Patton, George Shulman, Andrew Seligsohn, Jon Simon, David Snyder, David Tait, Michelle Tokarczyk, Mark Warren, Fred White, Nathan Widder, and Harlan Wilson.

My special gratitude to Kathryn Trevenen, who met with me at the Daily Grind, enabled me to clarify my voice, and introduced me to Horkheimer and Adorno's work, and whose sensitive and insightful commentary has contributed so much to the book. I am grateful to Melissa Orlie for our animated conversations, her careful reader's report, and her thoughtful wariness of certain elements of my project. John Docker read much of the manuscript, charmed and inspired me with his wit and insight, and pushed me to say things straight out. Ann Curthoys helped me to think about the disenchantment tale as a historical event, and I thank her for all our serious and playful discussions. I am also grateful to Donald Bennett for reading the manuscript and liking it and for his and Constance Bennett's love and support.

Stephen White read the entire manuscript and I hope that this version responds to his perspicuous comments about the ethics of enchanted materialism. I am indebted to his thinking about "weak ontology" and am the beneficiary of his exemplary generosity. Wade Sikorski contributed much to my understanding of mind-body relations and I am lucky to have his friendship and his thoughtful commentaries on several chapters. The book also has profited from Bill Chaloupka's encouragement and his insights about contemporary political culture. My sincere thanks, as well, to Brian Massumi for his thinking about affect, for his acute reading of the entire manuscript, and for pressing me to think about the conception of power employed in my story.

Deborah Connolly helped me to figure out what enchantment is, and she provides a model of the engaged intellectual and caring friend. I am indebted to Mort Schoolman and Michael Shapiro for their ideas about aesthetics and politics and about how to do theory in interesting ways. The book has also benefited from Wendy Brown's thoughtful skepticism about commodity enchantment and from Robert Welch's thoughts on wonder and talent for practicing both philosophy and deanship. Rom Coles and Paul Saurette gave me their close and smart readings of several chapters and their provocative orientations to Kant. I am grateful to Lisa Disch for her helpful commentary and for reminding me that sometimes less is more. My heartfelt thanks to Moira Gatens for her thinking about corporeality and ethics, for her generous and astute reading of the manuscript, and for encouraging me to elaborate the relationship between a moral code and an enchanted sensibility.

I am grateful to Ian Malcolm of Princeton University Press for being a most supportive and effective editor. Blackwell Publishers Limited granted permission to reprint materials in Chapter 3 from "The Enchanted World of Modernity," in *Cultural Values*, volume 1, number 1, April 1997, 1–28, and Carfax Publishers, Taylor and Francis Limited, allowed me to reprint sections of "De Rerum Natura," *Strategies*, volume 13, number 1, 2000: 9–22, in Chapter 4.

Finally, I thank Bill Connolly, my partner in everything, for the inspiration of his *Why I Am Not a Secularist*, for his timely and thoughtful readings of the manuscript, for the seminars we taught together on Kant, Deleuze, Lucretius et al., and for the joys of our daily life.

THE ENCHANTMENT OF MODERN LIFE

1

The Wonder of Minor Experiences

Queasiness

"Tereza was born of the rumbling of a stomach."[1] That is how the novelist Milan Kundera describes the genesis of one of his characters. I take Kundera to be referring to his own affective state as he sat at his typewriter one day. Queasiness is something he felt, but it also participated in thought: the quivering sac in his abdomen helped to conceive the nervous, needy persona of Tereza. Indeed, a discomfiting affect is often what initiates a story, a claim, a thesis.

The story I tell is of a contemporary world sprinkled with natural and cultural sites that have the power to "enchant." It is a story born of my own discomfort in the presence of two images circulating in political and social theory. The first is the image of modernity as disenchanted, that is to say, as a place of dearth and alienation (when compared to a golden age of community and cosmological coherency) or a place of reason, freedom, and control (when compared to a dark and confused premodernity). For me the question is not whether disenchantment is a regrettable or a progressive historical development. It is, rather, whether the very characterization of the world as disenchanted ignores and then discourages affective attachment to that world. The question is important because the mood of enchantment may be valuable for ethical life.

The second source of my queasiness is the image of ethics as a code to which one is obligated, a set of criteria to which one assents or subscribes. In this picture, the affective dimensions of ethics are drawn too lightly. Codes and criteria are indispensable parts of ethics, and surely they will not work without a sense of obligation or subscription. But these last things are still not sufficient to the *enactment* of ethical aspirations, which requires bodily movements in space, mobilizations of heat and energy, a series of choreographed gestures, a distinctive assemblage of affective propulsions. Nor can they nurture the spirit of generosity that must suffuse ethical codes if they are to be responsive to the surprises that regularly punctuate life.[2]

This book tells a story of contemporary life that accentuates its moments of enchantment and explores the possibility that the affective force of those moments might be deployed to propel ethical generosity. It claims both that the contemporary world retains the power to enchant humans and that humans can cultivate themselves so as to experience more of that effect. Enchantment is something that we encounter, that hits us, but it is also a comportment that can be fostered through deliberate strategies. One of those strategies might be to give greater expression to the sense of play, another to hone sensory receptivity to the marvelous specificity of things. Yet another way to enhance the enchantment effect is to resist the story of the disenchantment of modernity.

For that story has itself contributed to the condition it describes. Its rhetorical power has real effects. The depiction of nature and culture as orders no longer capable of inspiring deep attachment inflects the self as a creature of loss and thus discourages discernment of the marvelous vitality of bodies human and nonhuman, natural and artifactual. While I agree that there are plenty of aspects of contemporary life that fit the disenchantment story, I also think there is enough evidence of everyday enchantment to warrant the telling of an alter-tale. Such sites of enchantment today include, for example, the discovery of sophisticated modes of communication among nonhumans, the strange agency of physical systems at far-from-equilibrium states, and the animation of objects by video technologies—an animation whose effects are not fully captured by the idea of "commodity fetishism."

To be enchanted is to be struck and shaken by the extraordinary that lives amid the familiar and the everyday. Starting from the assumption that the world has become neither inert nor devoid of surprise but continues to inspire deep and powerful attachments, I tell a tale designed to render that attachment more palpable and audible. If popular psychological wisdom has it that you have to love yourself before you can love another, my story suggests that you have to love life before you can care about anything. The wager is that, to some small but irreducible extent, one must be enamored with existence and occasionally even enchanted in the face of it in order to be capable of donating some of one's scarce mortal resources to the service of others.

In the cultural narrative of disenchantment, the prospects for loving life—or saying "yes" to the world—are not good. What's to love about an alienated existence on a dead planet? If, under the sway of this tale, one does encounter events or entities that provoke joyful attachment, the mood is likely to pass without comment and thus without more substantial embodiment. The disenchantment tale does reserve a divine space for enchantment; in my alter-tale, even secular life houses extraordinary goings-on. This life provokes moments of joy, and that joy can propel ethics.[3] I experiment in this book with a fable of everyday marvels in order to uncover and to assess the ethical potential of the mood of enchantment.

A Brief Phenomenology of Enchantment

As I'm using the term, *enchantment* entails a state of wonder, and one of the distinctions of this state is the temporary suspension of chronological time and bodily movement. To be enchanted, then, is to participate in a momentarily immobilizing encounter; it is to be transfixed, spellbound. Philip Fisher describes this as a "moment of pure presence":

> [T]he moment of pure presence within wonder lies in the object's difference and uniqueness being so striking to the mind that it does not remind us of anything and we find ourselves delaying in its presence for a time in which the mind does not move on by association to something else.[4]

Thoughts, but also limbs (to augment Fisher's account), are brought to rest, even as the senses continue to operate, indeed, in high gear. You notice new colors, discern details previously ignored, hear extraordinary sounds, as familiar landscapes of sense sharpen and intensify. The world comes alive as a collection of singularities. Enchantment includes, then, a condition of exhilaration or acute sensory activity. To be simultaneously transfixed in wonder and transported by sense, to be both caught up and carried away—enchantment is marked by this odd combination of somatic effects.

Fear, accompanying such an extraordinary state, also plays a role in enchantment. The thirteenth-century writer Albertus Magnus described wonder as " 'shocked surprise' . . . before the sensible appearance of a great prodigy, so that the heart experiences systole. Thus wonder is somewhat similar to fear. . . ."[5] But fear cannot dominate if enchantment is to be, for the latter requires active engagement with objects of sensuous experience; it is a state of interactive fascination, not fall-to-your-knees awe. Unlike enchantment, overwhelming fear will not becalm and intensify perception but only shut it down.

The mood I'm calling enchantment involves, in the first instance, a surprising encounter, a meeting with something that you did not expect and are not fully prepared to engage. Contained within this surprise state are (1) a pleasurable feeling of being charmed by the novel and as yet unprocessed encounter and (2) a more *unheimlich* (uncanny) feeling of being disrupted or torn out of one's default sensory-psychic-intellectual disposition. The overall effect of enchantment is a mood of fullness, plenitude, or liveliness, a sense of having had one's nerves or circulation or concentration powers tuned up or recharged[6]—a shot in the arm, a fleeting return to childlike excitement about life. Historians Lorraine Daston and Katharine Park note that, in early modern Europe, the terms for wonder and wonders—*admiratio, mirabilia, miracula*—"seem to have their roots in an Indo-European word for 'smile.' "[7]

One also notes that the word *enchant* is linked to the French verb *to sing: chanter*. To "en-chant": to surround with song or incantation; hence, to cast a spell with sounds, to make fall under the sway of a magical refrain, to carry away on a sonorous stream. The philosophers Gilles Deleuze and Felix Guattari describe the refrain as having a transformative or "catalytic function: not only to increase the speed of the exchanges and reactions in that which surrounds it, but also to assure indirect interactions between elements devoid of so-called natural affinity, and thereby to form [new] organized masses." In other words, the repetition of word sounds not only exaggerates the tempo of an ordinary phrase and not only eventually renders a meaningful phrase nonsense—it can also provoke new ideas, perspectives, and identities. In an enchanting refrain, sense become nonsense and then a new sense of things. The refrain, say Deleuze and Guattari, "turns back on itself, opens onto itself, revealing until then unheard-of potentialities, entering into other connections, setting [things] . . . adrift in the direction of other assemblages."[8] I emphasize throughout the book the ethical relevance of such "sonority." The last two chapters focus on the sonorous dimension of language, which makes possible plays on words, the spell-binding effect of stories told aloud, the enchantment power of chants.

Reuse and Recycle

Near the beginning of Franz Kafka's *The Trial*, it is mentioned that an old woman stands at the window directly across the way from Joseph K.'s room. A bit later, we are told that she peers in at K. "with truly senile inquisitiveness." Then, after K. has been informed of his arrest, we read that the old woman has "dragged to the window an even older man, whom she was holding round the waist." Finally, we learn that "the two old creatures . . . had enlarged their party, for behind them, towering head and shoulders above them, stood a man with a shirt open at the neck and a reddish, pointed beard, which he kept pinching and twisting with his fingers."[9] The old lady and her entourage are not mentioned again in the story; neither is there the slightest intimation of their relevance to the plot, which ostensibly concerns K.'s dogged pursuit of his accusation. Indeed, it was only after several readings that it occurred to me to wonder about them at all.

The onlookers are easy to ignore because they do not participate in the narrative quest—for justice, for someone in charge, for insight into the law—in which K. and I are caught up. The onlookers and their actions might be explained as red herrings, were it not for the fact that everything in Kafka's book is one, at least with regard to the mystery of K.'s crime.

Every decision, event, proclamation, project, and scene are described with precision, but each is ultimately as rheumy as the old woman's eyes.

It seems, then, that Kafka crafts his story of the trial from the bits of experience ordinarily discarded as irrelevant to such a story. Instead of recounting those events that contribute to the reader's narrative preoccupation, Kafka names other contemporaneous events that constitute other stories. *The Trial* is less a photograph of Joseph K.'s trial than its negative: "background" objects are vivid, while one strains to discern the slightest trace of the "foreground." You wake up one day and are arrested without cause; your indignation grabs you by the throat and motivates your quest for vindication. But even as the warders make the charge against you, even as your affect kicks in, even as you hurry to clear your name, someone across the street glances out of her window, and someone near that woman puts on his shirt, leaves it open at the neck, and twists the hairs of his beard. These acts fall into the shadow of your rushing, indignant body. You note them—they are within the purview of your experience—but you pass them by. But if you were to gather up these dark, discarded scraps and peer into them, you would be on a different path, the path of a Kafkan tale.

Kafka's stories might thus be read as a literary form of garbage-picking, or "reusing and recycling." What I try to do in this book is something similar: to pick up some of the experiences that lie in the wake of a familiar story—not the tale of a man wronged, but of a civilization somehow wronged because it has been "disenchanted." The disenchantment of modernity is, I contend, a powerful and rather pervasive narrative in contemporary politics and political theory. It goes something like this:

> There was once a time when Nature was purposive, God was active in the details of human affairs, human and other creatures were defined by a preexisting web of relations, social life was characterized by face-to-face relations, and political order took the form of organic community. Then, this premodern world gave way to forces of scientific and instrumental rationality, secularism, individualism, and the bureaucratic state—all of which, combined, disenchant the world.[10]

The disenchantment tale figures nonhuman nature as more or less inert "matter"; it construes the modern West as a radical break from other cultures; and it depicts the modern self as predisposed toward rationalism, skepticism, and the problem of meaninglessness. Its versions vary according to what is identified as the primary target of the disenchantment process: selves can be disenchanted with ideals once held or heroes once admired, and so disenchantment can name an unhappy psychological state; the culture can be disenchanted, in that collective life no longer operates according to the cyclical logic of premodern or traditional forms and instead organizes itself along the lines of a linear mathematics or rationality; or nature can be the object of disenchantment, in that a spiritual dimension once found in plants, earth, sky is now nowhere to be seen.[11]

There are more or less subtle, more or less convincing, versions of this tale, all of which posit some kind of absence or loss in the modern condition. The tale is flexible enough to accommodate both positive and negative valuations of the disenchantment process; it is told both by those who celebrate it as the fall of superstition and confusion and by those who lament it as the loss of contact with a meaningful moral universe. Even the celebrators, however, convey a sense of loss: the inevitable price for rationalization or scientization is, they say, the eclipse of wonder at the world. Max Weber makes this point when he says that life in a disenchanted world is stamped with "the imprint of meaninglessness."[12] In this world, "there are no mysterious, incalculable forces that come into play, but rather . . . one can, . . . in principle, master all things by calculation."[13] Weber and other griots of enchantment are the focus of chapter 4.

Surely the very prevalence of the disenchantment story, even if it can be resisted, reveals something about contemporary experience. Although I want to weaken its hold, I am less its critic than its trash collector. With Kafka as my inspiration, I dust off and shine up what it discards, that is, the experiences of wonder and surprise that endure alongside a cynical world of business as usual, nature as manmade, and affect as the effect of commercial strategy. The experiences that I recycle, like those of Kafka's three onlookers, are not invaders of the major tale but underground or background residents of it.

Kafka himself chooses not to give coherence to what Deleuze and Guattari might call the "minor tales" of these residents: he prefers them as fragments. Kafka also refrains from allowing the underground men to explain themselves: he prefers to let the scrappy onlookers stand silently as witnesses to the contingency of the plot that is getting all of the attention. Neither does Kafka explore the affect that their counterstory might spark, he does not allow the reader to take the flights that it might propel, and he does not experiment with how their minor story, with different affects and propulsions, might rewire the political or ethical circuitry. But I try to do these things. I weave the moments of enchantment that I find into an alter-tale, and I imagine the impact on ethical relations that such an alternative narrative might have.

My counterstory seeks to induce an experience of the contemporary world—a world of inequity, racism, pollution, poverty, violence of all kinds—as also enchanted—not a tale of reenchantment but one that calls attention to magical sites already here. Not magical in the sense of "a set of rituals for summoning up supernatural powers within a coherent cosmology," but in the sense of cultural practices that mark "the marvelous erupting amid the everyday."[14] I want to tell this story because I take seriously what geographer J. K. Gibson-Graham calls "the performativity of social representations," that is, the ways in which the cultural narratives that we use help to shape the world in which we will have to live.[15] As I emphasize throughout the book, the marvelous sites highlighted and exaggerated here don't fit neatly into either the cosmology of the Christian Middle Ages or the contemporary understanding of secularism.

Enchantment without Design

One day, Candide meets his beloved teacher Pangloss on the street. At first, Candide does not recognize him, for Pangloss "was covered with pustules, his eyes were sunken, the end of his nose rotted off, his mouth twisted, his teeth black . . . " Pangloss recounts the story of how he caught the venereal disease responsible for his disfigurement, and he also traces the source of the disease back to Columbus's encounter with the natives of the New World. Candide decries this as the work of the devil, but Pangloss argues to the contrary:

> If Columbus had not caught, on an American island, this sickness which attacks the source of generation and sometimes prevents generation entirely—which thus strikes at and defeats the greatest end of Nature itself—we should have neither chocolate nor cochineal. . . . It was all indispensable, . . . since private misfortunes make for public welfare, and therefore the more private misfortunes there are, the better everything is.[16]

For Pangloss the optimist, the outcome of every act is already assured: everything works out for the best. And because the world is already the best of all possible worlds, any ameliorative activity on our part is redundant. No need, for example, to help a drowning man:

> . . . the air grew dark, the winds blew from all directions, and the vessel was attacked by a horrible tempest within sight of Lisbon harbor. . . . [One] sailor lurched so violently that he fell head first over the side, where he hung, clutching a fragment of the broken mast. The good Jacques [an Anabaptist] ran to his aid, and helped him to climb back on board, but in the process was himself thrown into the sea under the very eyes of the sailor, who allowed him to drown without even glancing at him. Candide rushed to the rail. . . . He wanted to dive to his rescue; but the philosopher Pangloss prevented him by proving that the bay of Lisbon had been formed expressly for this Anabaptist to drown in.[17]

Voltaire, the teller of this ridiculous tale, is one of many critical theorists for whom an attitude of pervasive skepticism is the authoritative marker of a social conscience. For such thinkers, the face of social justice has an eyebrow cocked in disbelief, a nose poised to sniff out power, or eyes crinkled with satirical laughter. For them, the quest for enchantment is always suspect, for it signals only a longing to forget about injustice, sink into naivete, and escape from politics.

Sometimes this wariness of joy is expressed as the charge of elitism—that is, only effete intellectuals have the luxury of feeling enchanted, whereas real people must cope with the real world. It surely is the case that hunger and other serious deprivations are incompatible with wonder. But the claim that the capacity for wonder is restricted to the rich, learned, and leisured, or that it finds its most vibrant expression there, is more confidently asserted than established. Even if it were true, all the more reason for privileged intellectuals to develop that capacity. For, if enchantment can foster an ethically laudable generosity of spirit, then the cultivation of an eye for the wonderful becomes something like an academic duty.

The charge of naive optimism is more probing. It raises the question of the link between enchantment and mindlessness, between joy and forgetfulness. In the chapters that follow, I do not deny such a link or its dangers, but I also argue that, in small, controlled doses, a certain forgetfulness is ethically indispensable.[18] Occasions during which one's critical faculties are suspended and one is caught up in the moment can produce a kind of enjoyment—a sense of adequacy or fullness—that temporarily eclipses the anxiety endemic to critical awareness of the world's often tragic complexity. And, sometimes, even complexity can enchant, as I suggest in chapter 5. Under fortuitous conditions, the good humor of enchantment spills over into critical consciousness and tempers it, thus rendering its judgments more generous and its claims less dogmatic. I pursue a life with moments of enchantment rather than an enchanted way of life. Such moments can be cultivated and intensified by artful means. Enchantment, as I use the term, is an uneasy combination of artifice and spontaneity.

Embedded within the charge of optimism is a rejection, on moral grounds, of the idea of a designed universe. Voltaire ridicules such an ontology and shows how it can engender complacency in the face of cruelty and violence. Although the experience of enchantment is often linked to a belief in a designed universe, it need not be.[19] I identify sites on the contemporary cultural landscape that are capable of inspiring wonder, even an energetic love of the world. I call the effect of visits to these sites *enchantment* and draw connections between the experience of enchantment and cultivation of an ethic of generosity toward others. The fabulous world that I describe is not a purposive one, however, or, at least, it does not have to be interpreted through that lens. By choosing the term *enchantment* to describe this landscape, I contest the near monopoly over that term held by teleological perspectives, both of the traditional theological sort described by Voltaire and the New Age varieties in which some sort of divinity remains indispensable to enchantment. This teleological model of enchantment, discussed in chapter 3, is also the one at work in the story of modernity as *disenchanted*: proponents of disenchantment share with those who lament its loss the assumption that only a teleological world is worthy of our enchantment.

I contest that assumption. A world capable of enchanting need not be designed, or predisposed toward human happiness, or expressive of intrinsic purpose or meaning. It seems that there is musicological support for this kind of enchantment, for "chant is modal music, which means that it doesn't have the powerful drive that much of modern music has to arrive at a final harmonic destination."[20] Moreover, the world that I describe as enchanted is not confined to structures, entities, and events in nature; there are also literary, machinic, and electronic sites of enchantment.

Kant best revealed how hard it is to dislodge the teleological assumption. After criticizing the "dogmatic" metaphysics of teleology (which pictures a world enchanted with divine signs), he finds himself driven to replace it with another "subjective" teleology that gives point or purpose to human existence. According to Kant's discussion of teleological judgment, the very presence in our world of organized beings *forces* us to think in terms of purpose. Why? Consider what an organism is: it is a product of nature "in which everything is a purpose and reciprocally also a means."[21] In an organism, Kant says, "the parts of the thing combine into the unity of a whole because they are reciprocally cause and effect of their form."[22] What, for example, is a human lung if not an organ for breathing? The human mind resists the idea that the intricate interconnectivity that marks something as an organism can "be attributed to a blind natural mechanism."[23] For if the parts work as parts of a whole—if that is what an organism is—then each part must appear to us as serving a purpose in relation to that whole. It seems, then, that the idea of purposiveness is embedded in our very concept of organism, as well as in our experience of encountering complexly organized natural things. Hence, Kant's conclusion that "we must judge certain things in nature (organized beings) and their possibility in terms of the concept of final causes."[24]

The projection of purpose into the experience of effects is a hard habit to kick. But one of the legacies of Nietzsche is the idea that it is possible to counter the teleogical tendency of one's thought with genealogical strategies that call its necessity into question. Epicurus and Lucretius also resisted the purposive habit: they offered an enchanting but materialist explanation for how nature came to have its complexity and patterns, a materialism where matter (the "primordia") is animated but not designed. Says Lucretius:

Not by design did the primordia of things place themselves each in their order with foreseeing mind, nor indeed did they make compact what movements each should start. But because many of them, shifting in many ways throughout the world, are harried and buffeted by blows from limitless time, by trying movements and unions of every kind, at last they fall into such dispositions as those, whereby our world of things is created and holds together.[25]

Unlike Kant, the Epicureans did not think of a mechanistic universe as the only alternative to the subjective assumption of teleology. They were enchanted with a world without a transcendental design. More on this enchanted materialism in chapters 4, 5, and 6.

Joyful Attachment

The alter-tale that I tell first refigures what counts as enchantment and then explores its ethical potential. I think that both those who celebrate disenchantment and those who lament it remain too governed by a single model of enchantment. My quasi-pagan model of enchantment pushes against a powerful and versatile Western tradition (in the disciplines of history, philosophy, and literature) that make enchantment depend on a divine creator, Providence, or, at the very least, a physical world with some original connection to a divine will. But what is at stake in such a retelling? The answer for me has to do with the effect—always indirect—that a cultural narrative has on the ethical sensibility of its bearers.

I tell my alter-tale because it seems to me that presumptive generosity, as well as the will to social justice, are sustained by periodic bouts of being enamored with existence, and that it is too hard to love a disenchanted world. Affective fascination with a world thought to be worthy of it may help to ward off the existential resentment that plagues mortals, that is, the sense of victimization that recurrently descends upon the tragic (or absurd or incomplete) beings called human. These beings are caught in a variety of binds: they live by projecting an indefinite future for themselves, but they ultimately die; they suffer from undeserved and underdeserved punishments while harboring the indispensable idea of moral responsibility and personal accountability; they fail to live up to impossible ideals that alone can inspire them. Such is the generic human condition, which nevertheless feels as if it is directed against you in particular and thus provokes a personal sense of resentment or victimization.

According to Nietzsche's Zarathustra, goodness rarely issues from such feelings. A more powerful source of ethics, he suggests, is joy:

Verily, I may have done this and that for sufferers; but always I seemed to have done better when I learned to feel better joys. As long as there have been men, man has felt too little joy: that alone, my brothers, is our original sin. And learning better to feel joy, we best unlearn how to do harm to others and to contrive harm.[26]

Most commentators focus on Nietzsche's condemnation of pity as an engine of resentment. (I myself have reservations about this reductive account of pity.) But few of them note Zarathustra's positive ethical point, that is, that he endorses en-joyment over pity for the sake of an enhanced capacity to "unlearn how to do harm to others."[27]

I agree with the Epicureans that matter is wondrous, even without purpose; I agree with Nietzsche that resentment is integral to the human condition; I agree with Zarathustra that joy enhances the prospect of ethical engagement and that one of the tasks proper to ethics is to "en-joy" the world. I also fear that acceptance of the disenchantment story, when combined with a sharp sense of the injustice of things by the Left, too often produces an enervating cynicism.

How the Story Goes

Chapter 2, "Cross-Species Encounters," explores one contemporary site of enchantment: the encounter with beings, including ourselves, who morph from one category of being to another. Here I tell the stories of a variety of interspecies crossings, some of which move between human and animal, some straddle between organism and machine, some are intraspecies journeys, some live in novels, and some are out on the streets. Resources for the stories include Michel Tournier's novel *Friday*, Kafka's ape in "A Report to an Academy," a television magazine segment about a very smart parrot, and Deleuze and Guattari's experiment with becoming a "body without organs." This chapter begins to articulate an ethical sensibility that is extended to nonhumans as well as to humans.

In Chapter 3, "The Marvelous Worlds of Paracelsus, Kant, and Deleuze," I take a look at the teleological model of enchantment of the Renaissance physician Paracelsus, for whom the world was divine prose. This is the model that many have in mind when they lament or celebrate the dis-enchantment of modernity. I then describe two other pictures of an enchanted world. The first is Kant's, who invents an amazing interior world of reason and of mental faculties capable of harmonizing with each other. The second picture comes from Kafka and from Deleuze and Guattari, where the world's enchantments reside in its material capacity for ongoing metamorphoses. There is a tendency in theoretical and popular discourse to restrict the experience of enchantment to a world like that of late medieval or Renaissance Christendom. But what happens when you compare that cosmological model of enchantment with teleology-resistant models drawn from Kant or Deleuze? It then appears that a variety of enchanting sites continue to make their home in late modernity.

My emerging tale of enchantment exists only in dialogue with the better-known accounting of modernity as disenchanted. So I move next, in chapter 4, "Disenchantment Tales," to an examination of several versions of the disenchantment story. The first is Max Weber's account of how the world became "calculable"; the second is Hans Blumenberg's grand narrative of the secularization of modernity, which draws on Weber's account even as it celebrates secularization; the third is the version of the tale that inspires Simon Critchley's pursuit of an ethics of "finitude." I claim that, although the disenchantment story captures important features of contemporary life, it is also important to come to terms as closely as possible with enchanting events and affects residing within or alongside scientific calculation, instrumental reason, secularism, or disciplinary power. This seems advisable in order to induce a more visionary and expansive mood from the one that would be present if the disenchantment story held the whole field. Toward that end, I contrast an ethics built around finitude with an Epicurean picture of the world as a lively and endless flow of molecular events, where matter is animate without necessarily being animated by divine will or intent. I call this latter view an "enchanted materialism."

Chapter 5, "Complexity and Enchantment," continues to explore the category of nature and its place in the phenomenology of contemporary enchantment. According to both defenders and critics of a disenchanted modernity, a purposive nature unmarred by human culture is the best, if not the only, site capable of putting the experience of enchantment to ethical effect. Challenging that assumption, I argue that, in addition to the beauty and sublimity of nature, there also exist hi-tech, artifactual sites of enchantment. Here the work of Bruno Latour helps me to augment a Thoreau-like attachment to the Wild with technological enchantments, and the work of Ilya Prigogine (a founder of chaos theory) and Isabelle Stengers (a philosopher of science) helps me to think about material complexity as a site of enchantment. The chapter ends with a Kafkaesque consideration of the possibility that institutional complexity, in particular the encounter with bureaucratic forms, might also provoke a kind of enchantment.

In chapter 6, "Commodity Fetishism and Commodity Enchantment," I take on the question of whether the kind of orientation toward life that I endorse can survive the widespread commercialization of culture. I argue that Marx's notion of "commodity fetishism"—like Max Horkheimer's and Theodor Adorno's "culture industry" thesis—is not capacious enough to account for the affects and effects of exposure to mass-produced

entertainment. Can commodities enchant? I answer yes and examine the 1998–99 Gap advertising campaign for khaki pants to explore the link between enchantment and encounters with the mobility, even the agency, of matter.

Political and ethical dangers are associated with a project such as mine, in which I seek to narrate modernity in a way that heightens the experience of wonder within it. The term *enchantment* can name an uncritical cast of mind antithetical to reason and ethics alike. Such a concern has found thoughtful expression in recent debates about the aestheticization of ethics and politics. In a world construed as disenchanted, residual experiences of enchantment are slotted into two categories: the first is, as mentioned above, the religious or transcendental; the second is the sensuous, subjective realm of taste or aesthetics. In chapter 7, "Ethical Energetics," I examine the view that ethics ought to be protected from the onslaught of aestheticizing forces and, drawing on the different ethical models of Kant, Schiller, Michel Foucault, and Richard Flathman, make a case for the impossibility of divorcing the affective from the ethical. The goal of my dialogue with each of these positions is to provide the reader with a clearer picture of the model of ethics within which enchantment can function as a positive resource.

Chapter 8, "Attachments and Refrains," positions my tale of enchantment in relation to Stephen White's notion of weak ontology and its role in contemporary social theory. The term *weak ontology* refers to a style of theorizing that includes a set of claims about human being and the fundamental character of the world, even as these claims are presented as essentially contestable. White helps me to make a case for the value of such *onto-stories*, as I call them, to political theory, in particular, the onto-story of enchanted materialism. And his assertion of the need for such tales to emphasize finitude is the important other to my own approach, which pins its ethical hopes on a feeling of plenitude and generosity. I then return to Deleuze and Guattari in order to describe the role that sound or "the refrain" plays in an onto-tale of enchantment. The chapter ends by revisiting the sites of enchantment considered in the book and by surveying a variety of other candidates in the natural and cultural worlds—other places, things, and experiences that draw out our profound and often joyful attachment to existence.

To talk in terms of the narratives of disenchantment and enchantment is to talk some big talk, to paint with broad strokes. Rather than examine political culture through specific events, or by means of a history of the ideas that shape them, or by a study of the institutional arrangements (of government, class, law, race, gender, consumption) that support them, I focus on a register of experience—the register of a cultural imaginary—that, although implicated in these other registers, is more amorphous and less directly related to politics. But not, perhaps, less powerfully so. The story of disenchantment represents and sustains a specific range of aesthetic sensibilities; it enters into the moods, temperaments, habits, perceptual comportments, and somatic predispositions that find expression or resistance in political choices, alliances, and policies. Some portions of those sensibilities and comportments are so sedimented that they are highly resistant to reform, but there also seem to be others that are more susceptible to techniques of the self. My project is premised on those existence of those latter portions, the hope and target of my alter-tale.

2

Cross-Species Encounters

Crossings and Enchantment

I find myself responding with wonder to metamorphing creatures—for example, to the criminal fiend Catwoman; to the oceanic woman in Luce Irigaray's *Marine Lover*; to the strategic insects in the 1996 documentary *Microcosmos*; to the porcine star of George Miller's 1995 film, *Babe*; to Andoar, the goat-kite in Michel Tournier's *Friday*; to Deleuze's and Guattari's body-without-organs; to Deep Blue, the machinic-self who beat former chess champion Kasparov; to Rotpeter, Kafka's ape-man; to Alex, an African Grey parrot learning to use abstract concepts; to the technonatural creatures called fractals; to Dolly the cloned sheep. Strange bedfellows, them: a *cat* woman? a *deliberate* bug? an *aerial* goat? an *organless* body? a *computer* champion? a *brainy* bird? Such attractions are hard to fathom or anticipate. In chaos theory, a particle's motion is said to have a "strange attractor" if the path of its transits is always unpredictable, even though the sum of every unique path forms a recognizable butterfly shape.[1] If these wonderful creatures are like strange attractors, then each is always in a state of becoming; each is not simply a species crossing but a crossing species. One might picture them as molecular groupings within a magnetic field; the field is not smooth, but, instead, each point exudes differential degrees of energy in dynamic response to the other molecules entering and leaving its range of reception.

This chapter explores the enchanting effect of interspecies and intraspecies crossings and considers the implications of such enchantment for ethics. My strategy is to tell the stories of several of the metamorphoses named above.

To the extent that crossings have the power to enchant, what about them is responsible for this effect? I pursue the line of thought that their magic resides in their mobility, that is, in their capacity to travel, fly, or transform themselves; in their morphing transits (primate toward other primate, terrestrial toward solar, silicon toward carbon, living toward dead—and toward new formations exterior to the relation between each of these sets of terms.) Metamorphing creatures enact the very possibility of change; their presence carries with it the trace of dangerous but also exciting and exhilarating migrations. To live among or as a crossing is to have motion called to mind, and this reminding is also a somatic event. My hunch is this: hybrids enchant for the same reason that moving one's body in space can carry one away—think of dancing of or the quick intake of breath and the rush after a hard push on the swing.[2] Some of the political potency of the term *freedom* might be traced to its association with the pleasure of bodily mobility. It seems to me, for example, that the extraordinary popularity of Haraway's cyborg stems in part from its evocation of the free movements of a child at play: walking around like a robot, crawling into the playground tube and becoming concrete, barking like a dog, jumping like a kangaroo.[3]

But perhaps the best way to confront the enchantment potential of crossings is to have some close encounters with them. I turn to the tales of four such creatures: Andoar, the goat-kite; Rotpeter, the ape-man; Alex, the thoughtful parrot; and Deleuze and Guattari's body-without-organs.

Andoar's Transcendence

Andoar was born on a tropical island, the very one on which Robinson Crusoe was stranded, and, although Andoar ended up as a kite, he was of mixed human/goat heritage. The human side comes from Friday, whose own ancestors, we are told, were probably coastal Indians, inhabiting the central part of Chile, who had held the Inca invaders at bay and inflicted bloody defeats on the Spanish conquistadores.[4] Friday was playful, light, solar; he greeted everything with laughter, not a naive laughter but one sprung from a sophisticated form of acceptance: in his eyes, there "is always a hint of derision, a touch of mockery defeated by the drollery of everything he sees."[5] Friday was aerial; he had a passion, for example, for shooting arrows to see how far and long they could fly. As for the goat side of the mix, we know that Andoar's other parent was a powerful and fearless goat with startlingly green eyes and a terrible smell, which, we are told, could be detected from a great distance.

But to know Andoar, you have to know not only the elements of his crossing but also the circumstances of his birth. After several agonistic encounters between Friday and the goat, they engage in a great, final contest. At the end of it, entwined around each other's bodies, they tumble over a cliff and emerge as a new composite creature. Andoar consists of the man formerly known as Friday, now thoroughly impregnated with eau de goat and sporting an aerial accessory—the old goat's skin, now scraped, cured, and polished, is attached to a frame of twigs and connected by a vine to the old Friday's ankle. Andoar spends his days battling "with the tricks of the wind, diving to its sudden gusts, turning when it veered, sinking when it slackened, and in a soaring bound regaining the altitude it had lost,"[6] as the more terrestrial parts of his body dance alongside on the sand.

I am drawn to Andoar because of his talent for boundless flight, for lightness, frictionless, free mobility. Tournier's novel as a whole is a tale of how to become solar or "an angel of helium."[7] Robinson, portrayed as the heaviest, most cramped of Englishmen, undergoes a transformation akin to that achieved in Andoar. After the island civilization (of goat pens, wheat fields, storehouses, law books, and gunpowder armories) that Robinson had so arduously built was blown to bits by the (uncanny) carelessness of Friday, Robinson shaves his beard (which had oriented him downward), climbs a tree to "embrace the air" (in violation of Island Policy to refrain from simian behavior), and finally scales a sheer rock face (to see if Friday had survived his battle with the goat):

> There was earth and air, and between them, clinging to the rock like a trembling butterfly, was Robinson, painfully striving to effect his conversion from one to the other. . . . He realized that vertigo is nothing but terrestrial magnetism acting upon the spirit of man, who is creature of the earth. The soul yearns for that foothold of . . . granite. . . . whose distance at once terrifies and attracts, since it harbors the peace of death. . . . With his face now turned to the sky, Robinson felt that something stronger than the insidious appeal of those scattered gravestones might be found in that summons to flight of two albatross , companionably soaring amid the pink-tinted clouds.[8]

Andoar reactivates the childhood wish to fly; to extend the limits of one's current embodiment; to escape the confines of biography, culture, training; to expand the horizon of the conceivable. Andoar's mobility activates a longing for what Tournier calls "*something else*,"[9] a longing that has been at the heart of a variety of social and liberation movements. One can see how the fantasy of transcendence might have ethically laudable effects. But there is also cause to be wary of the pursuit of pure freedom, a wariness that our next crossing expresses.

Rotpeter's Way Out

Exit the island paradise; enter the lecture hall of a great university. A well-dressed, hairy male addresses us, the members of a learned society[10]: "Honored members of the Academy! You have done me the honor of inviting me . . ." (250–62). Our speaker, named Rotpeter, offers a firsthand account of a most remarkable event: his recent passage from apehood to manhood. Apehood to manhood, not ape to man, for he is both and neither. He is a hybridization, straddling (at least) two realms of being, not necessarily divided equally between them. He has added humanity but is not simply a man.

Kafka's "A Report to an Academy" is a recounting of a self-made metamorphosis from ape to ape-man. It is the story of becoming a new assemblage by rearranging old parts and adding some novel ones. It's also a tale of how this reconfiguration ameliorated a set of intolerable circumstances, that is, being captured on the Gold Coast and encaged on a ship. In that cage, says Rotpeter, one feeling dominated:

> . . . no way out. . . . I was pinned down. . . . I had no way out but I had to devise one, for without it I could not live. . . . I fear that perhaps you do not quite understand what I mean by "way out." . . . I deliberately do not use the word "freedom." I do not mean the spacious feeling of freedom on all sides. . . . No, freedom was not what I wanted. Only a way out; right or left, or in any direction; I made no other demand. . . . To get out somewhere, to get out! Only not to stay motionless with raised arms, crushed against a wooden wall (253–54).

The way out of Rotpeter's animal cage was to work his way into the cage of humanity by carefully performing humanity's distinctive set of movements. Not "freedom" or escape into uncontrolled, undemarcated space—which would only mean leaping overboard into the deep sea (255)—but a choreographed way out. Not a free fall into Andoar's transcendence but a scooting through the hole in the wall of one cage into another, new enclosure. If freedom is the transcendence of power and external to a system of constraints, Rotpeter desires it not, for such isolation spells death. Freedom requires the antisocial pursuit of autonomy; the way out, rather, lurks in heteronomy, in, that is, being closely attuned to the distinctive set of interrelations and interdependencies at work in one's life.

Rotpeter did not aim to be a human but to perform humanity, to add human bits to ape bits, stir the mix, and fashion a new aggregation.

> It was so easy to imitate these people. I learned to spit in the first few days. . . . I could soon smoke a pipe. . . . My worst trouble came from the schnapps bottle. . . . I would lift the bottle, . . . put it to my lips and—and then throw it down in disgust. . . . What a triumph it was then . . . when one evening before a large circle of spectators . . . I took hold of a bottle . . . uncorked it in the best style, . . . set it to my lips . . . like a professional drinker . . . and truly drank it empty; then threw the bottle away, . . . this time . . . as an artistic performer. . . . I repeat: there was no attraction for me in imitating human being; I imitated them because I needed a way out . . . (257).

Performance, not being, and yet over time the performance humanized his very flesh. But not, of course, thoroughly or eternally. Our speaker is no more permanently anchored to humanity than he was to apehood. True, the more he "spurred" himself onto manhood, the more the "opening" to his prior self "narrowed and shrank" such that "I should have to scrape the very skin from my body to crawl through" (250). Nonetheless, the "wind" through that hole continues to blow, "tickling at the heels."

That Rotpeter describes his metamorphosis as "the line an erstwhile ape has had to follow in entering and establishing himself in the world of men," (251) is significant, for lines are transversable in both directions. That he also speaks of an "archway" between man and ape tells us that the line is not an undifferentiated continuum but has nodal points or thresholds marking the boundaries between existential forms. These nodes are difficult passages, as our speaker makes clear: "With an effort which up til now has never been repeated, I managed to reach the cultural level of an average European. . . . There is an excellent idiom: to fight one's way through the thick of things; that is what I have done, I have fought through the thick of things" (258).

Perhaps the association of apehood with European civilization was designed to amuse his audience. I suspect, however, that their laughter underwent several transitions from the moment it left their throats to the moment it faded away. Initially self-congratulatory (Hear that, you pretentious fellows among us!), it became apprehensive (This co-mingling of human and animal may well live in me. . . .), and then, finally, appreciative (To become hybrid has both the dignity of labor and the allure of travel!).

Rotpeter insists that the pass to his past is still open—as a crossing he still participates in his former being. (He has, for example, a tendency to pull down his pants and proudly display his neatly groomed fur.) Even more important, however, is the fact that a breeze blows from openings to other, unknown forms. Once learned, techniques of self-propulsion—techniques devised under the pressure of a cage—surely can be used again. This interspecies crossing asserts that there is always a way out. What Rotpeter has won by his efforts is not the prize of being human and transcending animality but the gift of an enhanced capacity to identify exits secreted by any enclosure—be it animality, humanity, or the current configuration of one's hybridity.[11]

Alex Changes the Subject

On October 10, 1996, to an American television audience of millions, Alex, a parrot, also gave a report on a turning point in his life: his passage from birdbrain to abstract thinker. Alex displays for Diane Sawyer, the host of *Turning Point*, his ability to identify, in English, the color, shape, material content, quantity, or relative size of a variety of objects presented to him. When shown a green clothespin and asked, "What color?" Alex responds, "Green"; when shown a yellow block and asked, "What matter?"

he says, "Wood"; when shown a green keychain and asked, "Say the whole thing," he says, "Keychain"; when shown a red sheet of paper and a purple clothespin and asked "What color bigger?" he says, "Red." We are told by other speakers that, overall, Alex gives the correct answer 80 percent of the time.

Articles written about Alex by his partner and trainer, Irene Pepperberg, Professor of Ecology and Evolutionary Biology at the University of Arizona, reveal that not only can Alex distinguish similarities and differences along these lines, but he can also recognize their absence. For example, when presented with two different objects, each of a different color, shape, and material, and asked "What's same?" Alex can answer, "None." On tests using objects that he had never seen before, he responded correctly 78.4 percent of the time! In addition, 5 percent of the time, the examiner was wrong and Alex was right. To the unjust scoldings that he received in those cases, Alex would simply "repeat his correct response, despite procedures that encourage a lose-shift strategy."[12]

Pepperberg carefully designs the experiments so that they are capable of demonstrating that Alex is not merely parroting words but dealing in abstract concepts. In the "comprehension of absence" experiment, for example, Pepperberg took pains to prevent the possibility of Alex responding on the basis of his remembering what used to be there and is not now (or used not to be there and is now), as well as the possibility of "match-to-sample" and "oddity-from-sample" effects:

> He was not responding to specific instances or sets of objects, nor from a repertoire restricted to a limited number of responses, but rather was providing a description of the attributes, if any, that were shared by the two exemplars. In other words, he was discriminating accurately, by means of arbitrary symbols (i.e., English labels), either the presence or absence of . . . categories that these objects might have in common.[13]

The crucial point, the point that marks Alex's passage, is this: Alex does not simply discriminate between specific objects, for any bird can do that; he discriminates between abstract categories, even in the absence of any concrete instance of that universal!

This same emphasis on Alex as a manipulator of abstract categories is found in Pepperberg's account of her test of Alex's "numerical competency," or ability to count (to six). Counting, she notes, is "a slow, effortful process generally for numbers greater than 4 that requires spatial attention." Its less impressive counterpart is "subitizing," a "fast, effortless, perceptual apprehension of numbers" in which "number loses its abstract nature as a descriptor to become a holistic attribute, like color or shape." Counting is an indicator of "an ability to generalize abstract categories across domains"[14] and thus of human-like intelligence. Here again, Alex proves himself in transit to thinker; when "asked about the quantity of one of four subsets of items that varied with respect to two color and two object categories," Alex counted correctly 83.1 percent of the time.[15]

In fact, Alex performed with exemplary thoughtfulness in all but one of the experiments, the one designed to see whether his private speech, where he "played" with sounds when no one was in the room, functioned like the private speech of children, that is, was "a form of practice that . . . allow[s] a speaker to experiment with a communication code without experiencing the consequences of failure."[16] Alex did not so much fail here but, rather, produced inconclusive results.

In that same study, Pepperberg notes in passing that "Alex becomes restless during sessions devoted to a single task. He will cease to work, begin to preen, or interrupt with many successive requests for other items."[17] And, indeed, in the middle of his television performance, Alex employed just such a strategy. He *changed the subject*:

> Pepperberg: (holding a piece of green felt) What matter?
> Alex: Want to go back.
> Pepperberg: Not yet.
> Alex: I'm sorry!
> Pepperberg: Well, you're a good boy.
> Alex: Want to go eat dinner.
> Pepperberg: I know. I know. It's time to eat dinner, sweetie. I know it's time, but we have to do one more chore, okay?
> Alex: (restless) Shoulder!
> Pepperberg: Okay. All right. You can go shoulder.[18]

Alex's attempt to redirect the authoritative context is, like his use of concepts, one of the passages leading from bird to thinker. He tries to carve out a small space of self-direction within a context where he is the tutee, operating under the constraints of being an exotic show parrot, a freak of sorts. Alex does not simply flap his wings and fly to Pepperberg's shoulder—he first tries to reorient the group's attention. And then, like a friend who has just rather abruptly changed the subject on you, Alex acknowledges the disruption by apologizing—"I'm sorry."

The case for Alex as an interspecially and intersubjectively constituted being is strengthened by the pedagogical method, termed the *model/rival approach*, that is most effective in teaching him:

> In Alex's presence, one human acts as a trainer of a second human. The trainer presents exemplars to this human, asks questions about the objects, gives praise and reward . . . [or] scolds and removes the objects for incorrect answers. . . . The second human is both a model for the bird's responses and a rival for the trainer's attention.[19]

This approach is based on assumptions strikingly similar to those in Rene Girard's triangular theory of (human) desire:

> In all the varieties of desire examined . . . , we have encountered not only a subject and an object, but a third presence as well, the rival. . . . Rivalry does not arise because of the fortuitous convergence of two desires on a single object; *rather, the subject desires the object because the rival desires it.* In desiring the object the rival alerts the subject to the desirability of the object.[20]

Alex accomplishes his metamorphosis by moving through a series of social contexts whose contours he actively helps to shape. He seems to share the same structure of desire as humans, at least if Girard is right. Alex reminds humans that they don't have a monopoly on subjectivity, and he opens the door to an intersubjective ethics that is also interspecied.[21]

Body without Organs

On a mesa in the land of a thousand plateaus, there lives a fourth crossing. Andoar, Rotpeter, and Alex seem to transit between two apparently stable and smooth wholes (goat-kite, man-ape, parrot-speaker); such is not the case with our fourth exemplar who is best described as a "circuit of intensity" between fields or planes of becoming. What kinds of things can travel along such electrical circuits? It would be difficult for heavy, fixed commodities to join the flow but easier for sparks, insights, identifications, repulsions, allegiances, affinities, and winged thoughts. The speed with which such things circulate and spark along the wire makes it difficult to name the being who is the circuit. But let's follow Deleuze and Guattari and call that creature BwO, body-without-organs, or, even more formally, human body working itself out of its organ-ization as an organic whole. BwO is never an achieved state. It is a multispecied and ongoing project of becoming in which new links are forged among "things, plants, animals, tools, people, power, and fragments of all of these."[22] BwO is the weird science of self-rehybridization.[23]

BwO is a social creature—actually, the extent of its networks of implication go beyond the social to include alliances with nonhumans, the inorganic, the imaginary, and other "planes of consistency."[24] According to Deleuze and Guattari, BwO is a creature that hovers between human and nonhuman being, between who-ness and it-ness. It an assemblage who "takes and makes what she or he can, according to tastes she or he will have succeeded in abstracting from a Self, according to a politics or strategy successfully abstracted from a given formation."[25] BwO is not thoughtless or undisciplined or the effect of unconscious drives. It is a deliberate, carefully contrived self-experiment: "Find your body without organs. Find out how to make it. . . . This is not a phantasy, it is a program."[26]

To know BwO is to know its how: the techniques, exercises, postures, movements, and rituals through which BwO might (the outcome is surely not certain) come to pass. These practices of self-rehybridization are no more specific, no more difficult to perform, and, upon their initial introduction, no more weird than those that have forged what Deleuze calls the "stratified" and "organic" body of the average European. Norbert Elias has chronicled some of these practices as they were inculcated through books of manners from the fifteenth through the eighteenth centuries. He shows how human animals engaged in painstaking attempts to regulate their hand, eye, and mouth movements while eating, drinking, sharing a bed, urinating, spitting, defecating, and conversing. Other practices were concerned with partitioning of living space, with the aim of a more definitive segregation by age, degree of kinship, and species. The overall effects of these exercises were (1) to confine bodily movements to those that mimicked the delicacy of the courtly class and (2) to extend the psychological and phenomenological distance between human and animal.[27] It is useful to keep in mind these historically institutionalized techniques of becoming-European as you review the following counterregimen of BwO.

1. Inject Caution

BwO attempts to compose its body in a way not fully contained by the dominant form of organization (i.e., organism). It is a making strange, or "deterritorialization," of bodily experience, a disruption of its usual habits of posture, movement, facial expression, voice, etc. These habits form the "strata" that organize your body. And so, to play the game of becoming a body-without-organs is to twist and tweak those usual habits. To do so requires a whole regimen; it is to engage in a kind of scientific experiment. As such, it requires the utmost precision in planning, measurement, and implementation. Hence the first rule of BwO is to proceed with caution and to resist the lure of total freedom and wild disorganization.[28] To break this rule, Deleuze and Guattari warn, is to end up not with a robust, joyful, context-rich, rehybridized BwO, but with either the emptied body of the hypochondriac, the suicide, the paranoid, the junkie, or the cancerous body of the fascist state.[29] Moreover, if you want to induce BwO, it is better not to be motivated by a love of the new for its own sake. Such a passion encourages an overzealous dismantling of the organs: "The important thing is not to destroy . . . [the organism] all of a sudden. You have to diminish it, shrink it, clean it, and that only at certain moments."[30] The new must be administered in milligrams.

2. Mimic the Strata

BwO seeks to remorph its socially located body and to assemble a refreshed conglomeration of affiliations and stratifications. One way to do so is to use the organism as a model, but a model stretched by means of parody. Mimic the strata: place organism-strata alongside slightly altered copies of them; compose yourself in a way that's almost like your usual way, but with a twist; repeat yourself but with a difference; conjugate your body as you would a verb. Exploit the destratifying potential of the strata; locate and follow its "lines of flight." Such a task requires a great intimacy, with a "meticulous relation" to, the organism and its world. Again, Deleuze and Guattari: "Connect, conjugate, continue. . . . We are in a social formation; first see how it is stratified for us and in us and at the place where we are; then descend from the strata to the deeper assemblage within which we are held; gently tip the assemblage, making it pass over to the side of the plane of consistency."[31] A meticulous relation with the strata issues in a momentary escape from it; the very forces that form the body as organism also take flight as centrifugal vectors.[32]

What does that mean? It depends on who you are. For Rotpeter, it could mean identifying with your jailers, conjugating your primate hunger and thirst into lip-smacking seamanship and barroom congeniality, and continuing as a novelty for the stage circuit. For Kasparov, the chess master, it might entail wearing a headset for four hours daily, emulating Deep Blue's silence every other day, humming quietly to yourself on alternative days, having anonymous fingers touch your skin in patterned sequence, becoming-machine, and then writing a book about how humiliated you had once felt about defeat at the nonhands of a computer. For Alex, the parrot, it might mean engaging in apparently random acts of kindness and senseless acts of beauty, perching on a rail, sleeping under a tent, and doing it in the presence of a model/rival. To become is not to achieve a final state of being; it is to give more of a chance to that which rumbles in you, but you are not.

3. Becoming-Animal

Once you have identified lines of flight distinctive to your own (always already) hybridized body, you might experiment with specific techniques to induce a rehybridization, to enter into new alignments with, say, animals. You might or might not learn something here, Deleuze and Guattari suggest, from the case of a certain masochist who, "for two hours during the days, and in the evening as the master wishes," dons horse gear—bridle, bit, harness—and submits to carefully timed, systematic whipping. It is possible to interpret this regimen as an attempt to create a new circuit of intensities, a new flow-exchange among man, woman, and horse. In order for this circuit to form, the organ-ization of the man had to be dislodged, and the means toward this end are the very maneuvers, corporal punishments, and restraining equipment used to train horses:

> Horses are trained: humans impose upon the horse's instinctive forces transmitted forces that regulate the former, select, dominate, overcode them. The masochist . . . [has] the horse transmit . . . its transmitted forces to him, so that the masochist's innate forces will in turn be tamed. . . . The . . . mistress-rider . . . ensures the conversion of forces.[33]

Does the masochist's program suggest to you that subjectivity is mobilizable in a variety of ways? Does it demonstrate the possibility of magnetic realignments between a subject usually organized as an organism and the animals, gear, regimens, edibles, and other particles in its "field of immanence?" Does it tell you that BwO requires practices that intensify its uncanny sense that there are other bodies escaping in the wake of your body-with-organs, other bodies around the blind corner? Brian Massumi calls this impossible perception-of-escape "side-perception."[34]

Masochism is surely not the only way to rewire or place yourself in "molecular proximity" to other forms of being. The experience of having pets or of working with animals in dressage also comes to mind. Deleuze and Guattari acknowledge as much,[35] but privilege the masochism example because it reveals what they believe to be the centrality of "desire" to BwO. Desire is "a process of production without reference to any exterior agency, whether it be a lack that hollows it out or a pleasure that fills it." Through his willingness to suffer pain, the masochist allegedly "untie[s] the pseudobond between desire and pleasure as an intrinsic measure."[36] The masochist frees desire from organ-ization. But, in celebrating the liberation of an apparently unadulterated form of desire, Deleuze and Guattari here come dangerously close to breaking rule number one: inject caution and refuse complete destratification.[37] Paradoxically, they also risk the converse—the masochist might "free" desire only to substitute compulsion—the hyperorder of bridles, bits, and exactly enacted repetitions. Compulsion probably can function as a means of becoming otherwise. But I doubt that it has a place in the project of cultivating presumptive generosity. If BwO is a hybrid with the potential to enchant, its hybridity must transcend obsession and force. For the ethical value of enchantment resides in its ability to persuade without compelling, to structure experience without insisting that this structure is the one that must be duplicated again and again.[38]

My Wager

Andoar, Rotpeter, Alex, BwO. Different crossings, distinguishable on the basis of the kind of mobility that each strives to enact. Andoar rises above it all, flies to the sun, to the freedom of unencumbered, playful transcendence. Rotpeter's movement is a scanning scrutiny of the margins of one's specific situation in order to uncover its singular way out and thus be free to enter a different cage. Although Alex, like Andoar, is embodied in such a way as to be capable of flight, he eschews this form of mobility. He moves his feathered body only in conjunction with a liberating attempt to alter his intersubjective landscape. BwO mimics the quivering dynamism of electron flows. Like Robinson, Rotpeter and Alex, BwO attempts to realign the particles of its persona and enrich the mix of its assemblage. Here, freedom consists in making the experimental most of the limited agency available to subjects constrained and enabled by a human body, by social formations, by political regimes, and by historical locale.

Why would you want to become any of these (or other) crossings? For the same reasons that Robinson is drawn to Andoar, Rotpeter to man, Alex to concept-literacy, and the organic body to BwO. Isn't it the desire for mobility, for the space to become otherwise, to exercise your faculties, play around, shift the scene, shuffle the deck, change places, look forward to something, "have a small plot of new land at all times?"[39] Metamorphosis carries within it the lure of the new, the green of the grass on the far side, the pleasure of the feeling of movement, and the magic of transformation. As Rotpeter, Alex, and BwO show us, these enchanting effects are greatest under conditions of discipline and experimental reflexivity. Mobility is widest when it is not random, erratic, or too fast; space for becoming is greatest when it is not an accidental effect; and novelty is most valuable when it is not treated as an end in itself. As BwO puts it: "Staying stratified is not the worst that can happen; the worst that can happen is if you throw the strata into demented or suicidal collapse, which brings them back down on us heavier than ever."[40]

Crossings bear some resemblance to the wonderful, unlikely possibilities called miracles. One might even say that these figures have a spiritual effect, even though they are quite human-made, earthy, technological. The cultural historian Jackson Lears argues that American advertising, in promising a new body and a new self to the consumer, reinhabits the Augustinian "fascination with the ecstatic experience of conversion."[41] Perhaps my fascination with morphing admixtures participates in that longing to become-otherwise; perhaps I envy their mobile subjectivity[42]; perhaps that envy can inspire me to new rehybridizations with the other participants in the air that I breathe and the noise that I make. Although I include myself among those multiculturalists and hyphenated selves who proffer their hybridity in lieu of purist identities of ethnicity, race, gender, or nation, what I really want is to acknowledge a more radical permeability. Like Donna Haraway's cyborg, my crossings extend to nonhuman animals, the wind, rocks, trees, plants, tools, machines.

My concern with human-nonhuman relations is one way in which my after-tale diverges from postcolonial discussions of cultural hybridity. A second difference lies in the fact that, rather than conceive crossings from the perspective of marginality, my stories are addressed to those whose (contingently formed but sedimented) identities are, for the most part, beneficiaries of the received moral imaginary. It is important to inquire into the political pros and cons of hybridization as an ideal imposed upon or chosen by racialized, marginalized or diasporic groups."[43] But, it is also useful to think about what would happen if privileged constituencies were to embrace self-morphing. Might such a project render one more open to novelty, less defensive in the face of challenges to norms that one already embodies, and thus more responsive to the injustices that haunt both cross-cultural and cross-species relations?[44]

I think of ethics as requiring both a moral code and a deliberately cultivated sensibility. A moral code is insufficient to ethics. In addition to rules of behavior, one needs an aesthetic disposition hospitable to them, the perceptual refinement to apply them to particular cases, the energy or will to live them out, and the generous mood that enables one to reconsider them in the face of new and surprising developments. I take this to be the point of Henry Thoreau's use of the Wild (chapter 5) and Friedrich Schiller's and Michel Foucault's critique of Kant's model of morality (chapter 7).Thoreau, Schiller, and Foucault—each works hard to educate, discipline, or cultivate the sensibility appropriate to a set of ethical ideals. But, each also acknowledges that, if such training is to take, some catalyst unsusceptible to full understanding is also required—some potion strong enough to draw sensuous performances toward avowed purposes and vice versa. Thoreau found this magic in the Wild, Schiller in high art, and Foucault in the unthought and bodily regimens.

To think about ethics in this way, however, does not sit well with the story of modernity as disenchanted. Bruno Latour rejects this story—not only because it issues from the grandiose conceit that modernity is a radical break from the past, but also because it fails aesthetically. Latour is not moved by this narrative but by the very creatures exiled from it: "How could we be capable of disenchanting the world when every day our laboratories and our factories populate the world with hundreds of hybrids stranger than those of the day before?"[45] As I show in chapter 5, Latour suggests that the ethical magic that Thoreau, Schiller, and Foucault identified also might be found in the encounter with crossings. If crossings function as contemporary sites of enchantment, then they might play a role in cultivating an ethical sensibility. Their magic might generate what might be called presumptive generosity toward the animals, vegetables, and minerals within one's field of encounter.

Marvels and Monsters

Although I explore the ethical potential of the enchanting effect of crossing, not all crossings, of course, enchant. Their affect-effect will vary according to the context of the encounter and the significance of the categorical boundary that they confuse, not to mention the particular body and sensibility that have been affected. Lorraine Daston and Katharine Park, in their historical study of wonder in pre–modern Europe, testify to the wide array of emotional responses that unusual admixtures can provoke:

> [M]onsters in early modern natural philosophy and theology illustrate the intimate links between cognitive and emotional responses to such anomalies. As portents signifying divine wrath and imminent catastrophe, monsters evoked horror: they were *contra naturam*, violations of both the natural and moral orders. As marvels, they elicited wondering pleasure: they were *praeter naturam*, rare but not menacing, reflecting an aesthetic of variety and ingenuity in nature as well as art. As deformities or natural errors, monsters inspired repugnance: they were neither ominous nor admirable but regrettable, the occasional price to be paid for the very simplicity and regularity in nature from which they . . . deviated.[46]

Moreover, even those crossings that provoke wonder rarely do only that. Gerald of Wales, for example, linked the "unusual number of animal-human hybrids and defective births" in twelfth-century Ireland to the inhabitants' "shameful," "spiteful" and "horrible" practices of incest and bestiality. The section of his *Topographia Hibernia* devoted to woman-goat sex shows no sign of the marveling appreciation of Michel Tournier's account of Friday's intimacies with Andoar.[47]

Other crossings, such as cinema's *Fly* or *Terminator* or human clones, can provoke disgust, dread, or other negative emotions. But, in these latter cases, it could be that the negative affect stems more from the voracious character of these creatures than from their combo-form. One recoils at the thought of being swallowed up or consumed by them; one dreads the world they seem to seek, one in which all diversity is eliminated for the sake of the domination of one type. If their capacity to master and annihilate could be disabled, however, their offer to participate with them or in them in a world with many other crossings might not be received as loathsome.[48]

Some crossings invoke the exciting sense of traveling to new lands, to different planes, to postures not ordinarily associated with human bodies. Crossings bring new things into being. It's not just that a new combo of old parts is effected in their transmogrifications—new elements are themselves sporadically drawn into molecular proximity. And every new assemblage reverberates back upon the old atoms and changes them. Thinking in terms of hybridized cultural identities, Homi Bhabha argues that hybridization creates a space for novelty:

> [H]ybridity [is] . . . a process of identifying with and through another object, an object of otherness, at which point the agency of identification—the subject—is itself always ambivalent, because of the intervention of that otherness. But the importance of hybridity is that it bears the traces of those feelings and practices which inform it . . . , so that hybridity puts together the traces of certain other meanings or discourses . . . The process of cultural hybridity gives rise to something different, something new and unrecognizable, a new area of negotiation of meaning and representation.[49]

I use the image of crossings rather than hybrids in order to avoid the suggestion that the segments of the crossing had a previous life in tact. There is a danger that the word *hybridity* conjures up the image of static entities coming together to form a compound. As Brian Massumi argues, hybridity may be too easily "conceived as a space of interaction of already constituted individuals and societies." Within this frame, change is understood as the negation, deviation, rupture, or subversion of the established poles between which hybrids are figured as dwelling. Thus, the positivity of change, its being as the new, is lost from the articulation. "The interrelation simply realizes external configurations already implicit as possibilities in the form of the preexistent terms. You can rearrange the furniture, even move it to a new location, but you still have the same old furniture."[50]

Crossings bring new things into being. But again, it must be acknowledged that not all of these are desirable from a human point of view, as Marsha Rosengarten points out in her study of animal-to-human organ transplants. It is not only the case, she says, that such "medical alterations" pose a challenge to naturalistic or fixed notions of identity—which might very well be a good thing; cross-species encounters also allow deadly viruses to "jump the species barrier." That "all organisms are open systems which engage in transversal and intraspecies genetic exchanges as well as filial, species-specific genetic lineages" is a fact both liberating and dangerous to humans.[51]

There is also a troubling link between novelty and commodification. Advertising has become so efficient at deploying the appeal of the new for commercial purposes that it is tempting to conclude that kitschification and souvenirization have made it impossible to experience the new without simultaneously desiring to consume it. The same kind of temptation is provoked by the ease with which enchantment as wonder-at-the-world is channeled into the thrall of shopping. But, as I argue in chapter 6, commodification is not in full control of the effects of the encounter between human bodies and commercial artifacts. The new, even in commodified form, in some cases retains the power to open a window onto previously occluded lines of alliance, affiliation, and identification; it still harbors the potential to reconfigure political discourse in surprising and productive ways.

In this chapter, I explore and seek to strengthen whatever affinities might exist between crossings, the spirit of generosity and enchantment. Enchantment is not a moral code, but it might spark a bodily will to enact such a code and foster the presumption of generosity toward those who transgress or question it.[52] My wager is that if you engage certain crossings under propitious conditions, you might find that their dynamism revivifies your wonder at life, their morphings inform your reflections upon freedom, their charm energizes your social conscience, and their flexibility stretches your moral sense of the possible. It is important that each of these elements—dynamism-wonder, morphing-reflection, charm-conscience, flexibility-possibility—be mobilized in relation to all of the others, for, without the ensemble, you could end up with a ruthless commitment to your own mobility, or a merely spectatorial caring, or a homesick variant of romanticism.

Inter- and intraspecies crossings might function as one of the sites of enchantment within a high-tech world where God's presence, while available to many, is vague to others and absent for some. The world might or might not be a divine creation; that security might not be available for the practice of ethics. But this uncertainty does not mean that disenchantment is the only tale to tell. Crossings can show the world to be capable of inspiring wonder, with room for play and for high spirits. And crossings might just help to induce the kind of magnanimous mood that seems to be crucial to the ethical demands of a sociality that is increasingly multicultural, multispecied, and multitechnical.

3

The Marvelous Worlds of Paracelsus, Kant, and Deleuze

> . . . among wonders we are born and placed and
> surrounded on all sides, so that to whatever thing
> we first turn our eyes, it is a wonder and full of
> wonders, if only we examine it for a little.
>   (*Giovanni Dondi*)[1]

IN *Primate Visions*, Donna Haraway argues that the sound of the fall from
Eden still echoes in our cultural narratives.[2] In particular, she shows how
the science of primatology—with its cast of apes, African guides and habitats, and famous white women anthropologists—reenacts the drama of
Adam, Eve, and their expulsion from the garden. The outline of this plot
also can be discerned in political theory, insofar as it is taught as the progressive demise of communal forms of order and meaning in favor of modern, secular—and alienating—modes of government and society. This narrative is a tale of loss, though not always of woe: disenchantment is
sometimes decried as the destruction of a golden age when the world was
a home, sometimes celebrated as the end of a dark age and the dawn of a
world of human freedom and rational agency, and sometimes presented
as a mixed blessing.[3] But, in each of these cases, it is agreed that disenchantment describes the contemporary condition.

Just what is the enchantment from which we are purported to be
"dissed?" In this chapter, I examine the particular notion of enchantment
that the dis-enchantment story employs. It is an enchantment that requires a world with a telos or intrinsic purpose, something like the world
described by the Renaissance physician Paracelsus, for whom nature was
to be read as divine prose and for whom the mood of enchantment was
the sign of God's presence. My contention is that this (Christian cosmological) kind of enchantment is but one possible kind, and that there are
others that do not depend on a world construed as divine Creation. I
suggest, for example, that Kant invented and deployed a slightly different
image of enchantment. Though he repudiated the kind of "dogmatic teleology" espoused in one way by Aristotle and in another by Paracelsus,
Kant's world, too, includes fabulous elements—for example, the "facul-

ties" of the mind that can arrange themselves in a "spontaneous harmony," or a nonhuman nature that gives us a "hint" into the "supersensible" realm of freedom and rational ideas. A Kantian world too has its enchantments.

I then sketch a third, Deleuzean kind of enchantment, where wonders persist in a rhizomatic world without intrinsic purpose or divinity, or the "subjective necessity" (again, Kant's phrase) of assuming telos or God. Kant brackets the question of the telos of nature; Deleuze pictures a world without it. For him, enchantment resides in the spaces where nature and culture overlap: where becomings happen among humans, animals, and machines. Deleuze brings out the wondrous qualities of late modernity's admixtures and, in a different way than Kant, reminds us what a marvel human thinking is.

There's a tendency, perhaps especially in the human sciences, to restrict the experience of enchantment to a world like that of an idealized version of Renaissance Christendom. But, if you compare that cosmological image with teleology-resistant images drawn from Kant and Deleuze, it appears that a variety of wonders continue to live among us, that neither we nor the world is dis-enchanted. As I'm using the term, *enchantment* is a peculiar kind of mood, often induced by sound (the *chant* in enchantment). To be enchanted is to be both charmed and disturbed: charmed by a fascinating repetition of sounds or images, disturbed to find that, although your sense-perception has become intensified, your background sense of order has flown out the door.

I look at Kant and Deleuze with an eye toward the marvelous, which I understand to cohabit with secular freedom, rationality, alienation, anomie, and political cynicism. I spotlight sites of enchantment in order to intensify the experience of them and thus perhaps to erode the belief that an undesigned universe calls above all for a cold-eyed instrumentalism. Such ontological cynicism, it seems to me, is one of the streams that feed political cynicism—liberals who see disenchantment as clearing the way for reason and tolerance come to be cynical about a political sphere that refuses to realize its historical potential, and communitarians who decry disenchantment as the dawn of homesickness come to doubt the ability of politics to induce the kind of spiritual and cultural transformation required to restore the world as a home.[4] But what if the contemporary world is *not* disenchanted? Let me spin out a bit more of this tale.

The Satyrion Root

Let's look first at the teleological and theocentric kind of enchantment that the story of our disenchantment presumes. One interesting example of it is offered by the Renaissance physician and alchemist Paracelsus

Figure 1. The Satyrion Root. John Gerard, "Great Dogs Stones," in *The Herbal: The complete 1633 edition as revised and enlarged by Thomas Johnson* (1975), p. 205, used with permission from Dover Publications, Inc.

(1493–1541), one of a group of "preternatural" philosophers that included Giovanni Dondi, Marsilio Ficino, Giovanni Battista della Porta, and Girolama Cardano.[5] Paracelsus held a minority view during his time, but his model of enchantment has had a powerful impact on retrospective images of what has been lost in modernity.

Paracelsus was a kind of Christian animist, who combined the idea that plants and animals are powerful agents with the idea of a heavenly Creator who made each earthly thing for a purpose.[6] The purpose (or "virtue") of all creation was darkly inscribed on its outward form. According to the Paracelsian doctrine of "Signatures," nature "endows everything with the form which is also the essence, and thus the form reveals the essence. There is nothing that nature has not signed in such a way that man may discover its essence. . . ."[7] Nature was to be approached as a difficult book, to be read with the same hermeneutic care given to the Bible.[8] Behold, for example, the Satyrion (orchid) root:

> [I]s it not formed like the male privy parts? No one can deny this. Accordingly magic discovered it and revealed that it can restore a man's virility and passion. And then we have the thistle; do not its leaves prickle like needles? Thanks to this sign, the art of magic discovered that there is no better herb against internal prickling. The *Siegwurz* root is wrapped in an envelope like armour; and this is

a magic sign showing that like armour it gives protection against weapons. And the *Syderica* bears the image and form of a snake on each of its leaves, and thus, according to magic, it gives protection against any kind of poisoning. The chicory stands under a special influence of the sun; this is seen in its leaves, which always bend toward the sun as though they wanted to show it gratitude. Hence it is most effective while the sun is shining. . . . Why, do you think, does its root assume the shape of a bird after seven years? What has the art of magic to say about this? If you know the answer, keep silent and say nothing [to] the scoffers; if you do not know it, try to find out; investigate, and do not be ashamed to ask questions.[9]

If you don't know why the chicory root assumes the shape of a bird and, if by the grace of God, you have been given the capacity to do so, "try to find out; investigate." Which means, in part, listen to the chicory. For, as Walter Pagel explains, "in order to have full knowledge of the herb and its specific virtue," the naturalist must eavesdrop (*ablauschen*) on its inner mechanism. "In other words, there is an element inside the naturalist . . . which corresponds to this particular plant and must, by an act of sympathetic attraction, unite with it."[10] Once you have imaginatively discerned your affinity with the chicory and have caught a glimpse into why it is signed with a bird, "keep silent and say nothing to the scoffers"—no need to antagonize them. Among them, it turns out, will be Kant, who, along with some others, will form an Enlightenment that will reject Paracelsian notions of cosmos, Signatures, magic, and herbal virility; they will, at least according to the disenchantment tale, demagify the world for good and ill.

But does enchantment disappear with the demise of the ontology of divine prose? Must it share the fate of Paracelsian herbology? Or has enchantment—though not the divine-cosmos kind—endured alongside Enlightenment and later versions of biology, medical science, and physics?

Enchantment and Repetition

Sensuous experience is central to enchantment, but, of course, not all sensuous experience enchants. Enchantment seems to require, among other things, the presence of a pattern or recognizable ensembling of sounds, smells, tastes, forms, colors, textures. One could say, then, that enchantment functions by means of a kind of repetition. But what kind?

One kind of repetition is that practiced by Augustine in his *Confessions*. There, theological arguments about the problem of evil are interrupted by passages from Scripture, which one can imagine Augustine to have repeated out loud. Augustine's verbal litanies of faith (similar to recita-

tions of "The Catholic Profession of Faith" or the Rosary) work to overcome doubts about a benevolent God apparently tolerant of the suffering
of innocents—and these refrains do so not only intellectually (by explaining evil as part of a mysterious, divine plan) but also somatically (by
the calming effect of chanting magic words). Augustine says his prayers
in order to transfix his eyes and his thoughts upon an invisible and ineffa-
ble God. He sings himself to faith.

Augustine's repetitions, however, stop just short of the complex mood
I am calling enchantment because his audio-induced wonder is not accompanied by a heightening of sensuous or aesthetic experience.[11] Or perhaps
it is more precise to say that it probably was but that Augustine then deployed tactics to neutralize this very effect lest sense-experience contami-
nate the purity of his spirit. Paracelsus, more alchemist than ascetic, embraces the somatic effects of repetition. For him, enchantment is not only
a property of the natural world—it is also the joyful human mood that
results from a special way of engaging that world. Enchantment as a mood
requires a cultivated form of perception, a discerning and meticulous attentiveness to the singular specificity of things.[12] Practicing this discipline
of perception, Paracelsus could see how one thing mirrored another and
could experience this repetition as itself wondrous:

> The inner stars of man are, in their properties, kind, and nature, by their course
> and position, like his outer stars. . . . For as regards their nature, it is the same
> in the ether and in the microcosm, man. . . . Just as the sun shines through a
> glass—as though divested of body and substance—so the stars penetrate one
> another in the body. . . . For the sun and the moon and all planets, as well as all
> the stars and the whole chaos, are in man. . . .[13]

Paracelsus marvels at how the light of the stars repeated in the twinkle of
his eyes. In this example, the repetition is visual, but, at other times, Paracelsus describes repetition in sonorous terms: the knowledge possessed by
herbs (which enabled them to produce their medicinal effects) echoes in
our own bodies once we eavesdrop on the plant's wisdom.[14]

I think that many things are remarkable about Paracelus's theory of
microcosm-macrocosm relations, but I emphasize this one—the parties to
the repetitions that he describes are equal in status. This equality is the
result of each party's equidistance from an implied third term. According
to Paracelsus, all things—stars and eyes, herbal bodies, and human bodies—are expressions of the "Iliaster" (also called "Prime Matter" or primordial "semen"). Here, Paracelsus, like all interesting thinkers, feels free
to invent new terms of art. Iliaster is the basic "matrix" of being, the
general structure of possibility or potentiality of matter.[15] Iliaster, is the
structural analog to what Deleuze refers to as the virtual field.[16] According
to Paracelsus, it is at the "hem" (or "margin" or "border") of Iliaster,

where the matrix folds over on itself, that potentiality gives way to specific, real things. He names this hem the *limbus*," the ambiguous space of becoming, where "eternal principles become concrete."[17] Both Iliaster and limbus are themselves parts of a divine cosmological whole.

My point is this: Even though Paracelsus emphasized the wondrous diversity of creation and even though his medical practices required meticulous attention to the sensuous specifics of natural forms, any given particularity ultimately derived its existence and its marvelousness from the system of divine creation of which it formed a part. The singularity of things was thus compromised by the common status of all things as cosmological signposts. Every repetition referred back to what Daston and Park describe as a "metaphysical structure of the universe, conceived in terms of correspondences and emanations." Pagel, too, notes the "dualistic co-existence" in Paracelsus "between individual specificity and an ultimate unity of all objects in which specific differences are submerged."[18]

In *Difference and Repetition*, Deleuze gives a name to this kind of repetition, wherein the difference between elements in a sensuous pattern is the difference between "particulars" subsumable under a "universal." He calls it "bare repetition" and contrasts it with a kind of repetition, wherein singular elements enter into relations with each other but not as particulars to a universal. Rather, the singularities form alliances in a way that cannot be referred to a general concept under which each is "subsumed." Moreover, these "non-exchangeable and non-substitutable singularities"[19] themselves change as a result of their encounters with each other. They are always undergoing mini-metamorphoses.

The system of relations—the repetitions—that they form is more spiral than cyclical. The movement is not A to B, B to A . . . , but the more complicated series A to B, B^1 to A^1, A^2 to B^2 . . . (where B^1 = B + a nano-alteration produced by B's encounter with A.) From a Deleuzean perspective, both Augustine's movement between Scripture and prose and Paracelsus's movement between herb and herbalist are likely to entail spiral repetition. They can be conceived, that is, along the model of biological evolution or the mathematical figure of the variable curve:

> Even in nature, isochronic rotations are only the outward appearance of a more profound movement, the revolving cycles are only abstractions: placed together, they reveal evolutionary . . . spirals whose principle is a variable curve and the trajectory of which has two dissymetrical aspects, as though it had a right and a left. It is always in this gap . . . that creatures weave their repetition and receive at the same time the gift of living and dying.[20]

One can think of DNA replication as practicing both bare and spiral repetition. Most of the time, a DNA molecule repeats exactly in a bare repetition, but, now and then, a tiny alteration is somehow introduced "in link-

Figure 2. Spiral Repetition. Fractal image, four-
dimensional attractor, courtesy of Alan Norton,
Silicon Graphics Inc.

ing up the tens of millions of bases ('teeth') within" it. "And when the
DNA replicates itself and reproduces that alteration in the new molecule,
we have . . . a *mutation*."[21]

In this spiral repetition, things repeat but with a twist. And this twist—
or to use the Lucretian term, *swerve*—makes possible new formations (all
originally "mutants," but some of which will find a productive niche
within a larger network). In attempting to describe the kind of repetition that does not issue in perfect duplicates, Deleuze appeals to imagery
from mathematics, evolutionary biology, and molecular chemistry. But,
he also suggests that the mathematical, macrobiological, and microbiological are morphologically parallel to the sociopolitical. From the twists and
swerves of spiral repetitions are born new molecules and new viruses but
also new images, new identities, and new social movements.[22] Although
these surprises could be understood as part of the world with a telos, they
need not be.

One last distinctive feature of spiral repetition is the way that it operates not "extensively" but "intensively." This can be seen most clearly in the linguistic realm. Spiral repetition is not a matter, say, of calling for the same thing over and over—"Row, row, ROW! your boat" or "Hail Mary, full of grace! Hail Mary, full of grace!"—but of taking the singular object of one's attention to what Deleuze calls the nth power—of weighing down the unbearable singularity of the "row" or the "Hail!" by invoking increasingly intense versions of it to the effect that its meaning eventually dissolves and realigns.
Deleuze and Guattari note that children are especially skilled

> in the exercise of repeating a word . . . in order to make it vibrate around itself. . . . Kafka tells how, as a child, he repeated one of his father's expressions in order to make it take flight on a line of non-sense: "end of the month, end of the month."[23]

My point about spiral repetition is that sometimes that-which-repeats-itself also *transforms* itself. Because each iteration occurs in an absolutely unique context, each turn of the spiral enters into a new and distinctive assemblage—with the absolutely local chirps, odors, herbs, thoughts, whirs, images, breezes, light waves, viruses, animals, machines, and minerals in its milieu. Spiral repetition is an example of an enchanting phenomenon that need not be understood as part of a divine creation or as a *particular* instance of a *universal* will. Spiral repetitions are not best understood as parts of a larger, designed "matrix" (Paracelsus) but can be accidents that give birth to wondrous and unsettling—enchanting—new forms. In short, Deleuze's idea of spiral repetition allows me to introduce a non-teleological and perhaps neo-pagan image of enchantment. In this image, fortuity, contingency, and chance—like will, design, and intent—can repeat and enchant. Both of these trios can engender a repetition that stops time, freezes movement, heightens senses, and provokes wonder and unease.

But I'm getting ahead of myself. More on Deleuzean enchantment later. Let's look now at the kind of enchantment operative in Kant.

Kantian Wonders

There are significant differences between the natural world of Paracelsus and the appearances of nature according to Kant. For Paracelsus, nature has been prepared to receive its residents, whose relations of sympathy and antipathy form a dynamic but self-maintaining mosaic. Sympathy is what "drives the root towards the water, and . . . makes the great yellow disk of the sunflower turn to follow the curving path of the sun"[24]; antipathy explains why "the olive and the vine hate the cabbage" and why "the cucumber flies from the olive."[25] Kant's natural world does not play this game of sympathy and antipathy. (Though perhaps it does pose "antinomies" to challenge the wit of philosophers.)

In a Paracelsian imaginary, sensuous nature is an integral part of a harmonious cosmos. Foucault describes it this way: "[T]he universe was folded in upon itself: the earth echoing the sky, faces seeing themselves reflected in the stars, and plants holding within their stems the secrets that were of use to man."[26] For Kant, on the other hand, nature cannot be known to be part of a cosmos. It presents itself to us as an almost self-enclosed domain of the sensible, defined in contrast to a supersensible substrate "about which we cannot determine anything affirmatively, except that it is the being in itself of which we know merely the appearance."[27] Phenomena and noumena, or the natural and the supersensible realms, are not wholly unconnected, as we shall see, but our knowledge of how they are linked is extremely limited.

For Kant, the Paracelsian notion of signs exaggerates the scope of human understanding and thus leads to all sorts of error and evil. To be so confident (as Paracelsus often seems to be) in an objective harmony between knower and known is, says Kant, utterly "presumptuous":

> A judgment in which we forget to estimate the extent of our power (of understanding) may at times sound very humble, and yet it makes vast claims and is very presumptuous. Of that sort are most of those judgments in which we purport to exalt divine wisdom, by attributing the works of creation and preservation to divine intentions that are actually meant to give credit to the wisdom of the very person who does this subtle reasoning.[28]

Kant's critiques, which reveal the limits of our faculties, are designed to protect against this conceit, for Kant too is wary of what William Connolly has called "transcendental narcissism."[29]

Kant's exposure to Newton's work on the mechanism of nature (as well as, perhaps, Kant's own temperament) made him wary of the idea that an herb was signed with its divine purpose. But Kant did not reject wholesale the idea of an intrinsically purposive nature. He simply qualified it very carefully. First, he restricted intrinsic purpose to organisms only—an organism is an entity in which each part "*produces* the other parts" such that "if parts are removed" the organism will "replace them on its own . . . [or] . . . compensate for this [lack] by having the other parts help out . . . (374)."[30] Second, he reduced the epistemological status of any claim about the purposiveness of organisms to that of a "subjective necessity" only— we can "only say that the character of *our* understanding and of *our* reason is such that the only way *we can conceive* of the origin of such beings is in terms of final causes (426, my emphasis)." We must think in terms of final causes here because the model of mechanism is insufficient to account for the self-organizing character of organisms—an organism will always provoke the question: what is it there *for* (425)? We make sense of nature by reference to final causes, but we know nothing about its objective purposiveness. Nature merely allows itself to be treated *as if* it harmonized with our cognitive faculties.

Kant categorizes such judgments of purposiveness as "reflective" rather than "determinative." They reflect (today, one might say project) onto the object the knower's sense of *himself* as a purposive being (361). Likewise, the concept of intrinsic purposiveness in nature is a "critical concept": "We treat a concept . . . critically if we consider it only in relation to our cognitive power, and hence in relation to the subjective conditions under which we think it, without venturing to decide anything about its object" (396). As long as we remember its critical and reflective status, "we are right to bring teleological judging into our investigation of nature, at least problematically . . . (360)."

The key point, at least with regard to noting the wonders of Kantian philosophy, is that not only are we "right" to treat nature as purposive, we *must* do so. Reason demands it, and reason has what seems to me to be the magical power to get what it demands. Though we should try, says Kant, to "explain all products and events of nature . . . in mechanical terms as far as we possibly can; . . . our reason will still force us to subordinate such products . . . to the causality in terms of purposes (415)." Reason "forces" this "subordination" because that is the only way that all of the diverse particularities of nature can be "combined in a unified and hence lawful way" (404)—the concept of final cause brings "nature's appearances under rules in those cases where the causal laws of nature's mere mechanism are not sufficient to allow us to do so" (360).

Kantian reason, here as elsewhere, demands "absolute unity in the principle" of things. This reason is an unmistakable internal "demand" for finality, necessity, harmony or unity—and for action that treats others as one wishes to be treated oneself.[31] Kant himself is often presented as a model of sober punctuality, as a far less extravagant thinker than Paracelsus. But one of the most enchanting claims of modern ethics comes from Kantian lips: there exists an imperious voice of reason (the moral law) embedded in the very structure of human cognition. What a marvel this human reason is!

In Kant's world, reason possesses a fabulous degree of forceful and creative power. Not only does it compel the concept of nature as purposive, it also sires the concept of a divine intelligence behind nature. Reason produces the insistent idea of a divine intelligence by virtue of the fact that "its ultimate demand aims at the unconditioned."[32] Though our "understanding" tries to subsume all the particular organisms under a single universal, "the universal supplied" fails to "determine" them, for organisms continue to act independently and as self-sufficient wholes. The "variety of ways in which they may come before our perception" remains "contingent."[33] This is not good enough for reason, which demands that the subsumption be a necessary and determinative one. Reason thus commands into being the concept an understanding superior to our own, which *is* able to "determine" the particular. That superior understanding is a divine intelligence.[34] In like manner, reason inexorably generates the concept of a supersensible realm: the two principles for the investigation of nature (mechanical and teleological) "must" be unified in a single meta-principle, and "we must posit this further principle in something that lies beyond both . . . , namely, . . . in the supersensible"[35] (412).

I identify "reason," with its imperious, generative power, as the first wonder in a Kantian world. This reason never fails to create the concept of the supersensible. And this concept itself turns out to have a share in the fabulous power of its creator. The concept itself, says Kant, gives us an intimation, though not proof, of the inaccessible noumenal realm. The very "subjective necessity" of the concept of the supersensible gestures toward the supersensible. Though humans can never "form the slightest determinate and positive concept" of the supersensible, in the "subjective necessity" of conceiving of this transcendental site of unity, "we are assured that it is at least possible that objectively, too, both . . . [mechanical and teleological] principles might be reconciled in one principle" (413). Likewise, the inevitable idea of nature as purposive "does allow us to look beyond nature with some prospect that perhaps we can determine the concept of an original being more closely . . ." (437). The idea of the supersensible fortuitously "assures" us of the possibility of its objective existence, and the idea of a purposive nature affords the enchanting "prospect" of closer contact with an original being (437).

In making such claims, Kant finesses his fundamental distinction between the noumenal and the phenomenal. He seems to be aware of this finesse, for he immediately qualifies it: The idea of purpose in nature offers a "prospect" *even though* it "in no way helps us to explain [the actual origin of] natural things." We receive a prospect, not an explanation. But this rear-guard action does not fully restore the noumena-phenomena divide—for how can a "reflective" judgment of purposiveness foster any kind of "determination," even a "prospective" one, about an original being? What seems to be going on here is that Kant needs to weave a thin thread of communication between the two realms, so that sensible beings can have some intimation of the moral realm that ultimately sustains their existence. Without some such intimation, it might be psychologically impossible for humans to maintain faith in that higher realm.

Figure 3. Nature and the Prospect of the Supersensible. Rene Magritte's
"The Enchanted Forest," 1951, used with permission © 2001 C. Herscovici,
Brussels/Artists Rights Society (ARS), New York.

Another site of enchantment in Kant's world is nature, which, as we shall see, also "hints" at the supersensible realm. Though it is we who (must!) introduce purposiveness into nature, Kant assures us that there is "nothing wrong" with admiring nature for allowing itself to fit with our capacities for cognizing it. For this admiration" too "makes us suspect" the objective reality of the supersensible: "The agreement of that form of sensible intu- ition (called space) with our power of concepts (the understanding) . . . expands the mind; it makes it suspect . . . that there is something else above and beyond those presentations of sense . . . " (365). Or, again, Kant's claim that "nature gives us a hint . . . that if we use the concept of final purposes we could perhaps reach beyond nature . . . to the highest point in the series of causes" (390). Or, finally, his assertion that the experience of the sublime in nature "exhibits" the supersensible, without of course "our being able to bring this exhibition about objectively."[36]

In these passages, the link between phenomena and noumena consists in "suspicions," "hints," and "exhibitions." Nevertheless, even in a Kantian world, encounters with nature retain a fascinating but also unsettling power to throw us a tenuous line to an other-world. My point is this: nature for Kant is not altogether different from nature for Paracelsus. For neither of them is nature dead matter devoid of marvelous powers, for neither is the natural world disenchanted. Kant's nature speaks, though more haltingly and cryptically than Paracelsus's. But it utters enough to

Figure 4. Nature Gives Us A Hint. Rene Magritte's "Les graces naturelles," 1948, used with permission © 2001 C. Herscovici, Brussels/Artists Rights Society (ARS), New York.

assure us that, or at least give us enough hope that, the world is a coherent order.

A Kantian world has, then, its own sites of enchantment. These come to the fore in *The Critique of Judgment*, especially in the discussion of teleological judgment, even though they sit uncomfortably with Kant's ongoing project of critique. Why does Kant mess with teleology at all? Perhaps he wanted to save teleology in order to save a place for God.[37] Although Kant endorsed Newton's thinking about the mechanism of nature, he, like Newton himself, did everything in his philosophical power to retain the idea of purposiveness in nature. Kant sought to salvage teleology by rescuing it from its "dogmatic" form. Kant changed the epistemological status of teleological judgment and thus reduced both the robustness and the degree of certainty appropriate to it. But he was nevertheless careful not to render dispensable the idea of purposiveness in nature.

What, then, is at stake for Kant in teleological judgment? Why is it so important to retain some kind of purposiveness in nature, some sense of nature as animated or lively? Kant *says* that he does so in order to supplement the principle of mechanism, which appears to be inadequate to account for organisms: the principle of final causality

> allows us to consider natural things in terms of a new law-governed order by referring them to an already given basis [a purpose]. . . . Thus we expand natural science in terms of a different principle, . . . yet without detracting from the principle of mechanism.[38]

But Kant did not devote all those pages to teleology simply because of its heuristic value to science. Only a moral matter could warrant so much attention from him. And teleological judgment does indeed play a vital role in morality—in the very act of teleological judgment a faith in a beyond is engendered. Teleological judgment is the means by which humans are exposed to evidence that the link—*indispensable to morality*—between the sensible and the supersensible actually holds. This evidence is by its very nature indirect and mysterious—consisting only in hints, gestures, suspicions, and prospects. The beyond is by definition inaccessible to the senses; that is why our access to it must have something of the magical about it.

What is magic? It is a power to create whose mechanism can never be fully understood. For Paracelsus, the primary site of magic was external nature: there the Satyrion root and divine mingled and spawned the impossible reality of a materialized spirituality. Those humans graced with the requisite ability (the "adepts") participated in this process, but the scene or venue of enchantment was more external than internal nature. Things are different in a Kantian world. Kant saw how easily the naive theology of Paracelsus—which wove the natural, the divine, and the human too tightly and too smoothly—could be attacked on Newtonian grounds and, more disturbingly, how much this susceptibility to skepticism fostered religious disbelief. Kant's response to this moral danger was first to divorce the sensible world from the transcendental realm and then to allow only mini-encounters between them. Kant separated physics from metaphysics and tried to limit metaphysics to questions of the mind and its transcendental needs, but he did not give up on magic in doing so. Instead, he shifted its principal locale. Kantian magic occurs only fleetingly and ambiguously in nature itself—nature does offer tantalizing threads of connection to the supersensible, but they are fragile and thin. The primary venue of enchantment has become interior to the self, in an imperious "reason" and the "subjective necessities" it spawns.[39]

Kant's doctrine of the "harmony of the faculties" is, alongside the marvel that is reason, another example of this shift in emphasis from external to internal nature as the site of enchantment. Kant says that the harmony of the faculties is operative in the presence of beauty (i.e., when one is engaged in aesthetic judgment or the exercise of taste). In Kant's story, judgments of *any* sort entail some kind of "accord" among the faculties, but aesthetic judgment is the only one where this accord is not the result of one faculty determining or ruling over the others. Rather, in aesthetic judgment, the accord (between Imagination and Understanding[40]) is a free, spontaneous, and indeterminate one. In the presence of beauty, there is a "free play" of the faculties. Here is why: in taste, what is important is the *particularity* of a given beautiful thing, and so, in taste, the Imagination does not try to subsume the beautiful object under a *determinate concept*, for "our imagination is playing, as it were, while it contemplates the shape, and such a concept would only restrict its freedom."[41] The Imagination's reflections occasioned by an object of beauty are more spontaneous than any "determinate" concept could allow. But taste is not wholly devoid of Understanding: concepts are deployed, it's just that they are "indeterminate" or open-ended ones.

Because in taste the Imagination is self-referential or concerned only with the internal feeling generated by its own creative presentations, aesthetic judgments are "subjective."[42] They are also, says Kant, "disinterested":

> What matters is what I do with this presentation within myself, and not the [respect] in which I depend on the object's existence. . . . In order to play the judge in matters of taste, we must not be in the least biased in favor of the thing's existence but must be wholly indifferent about it.[43]

It is this disinterestedness that leads me (and you), despite the subjective quality of my taste, to the uncanny conviction that my taste is *universally valid*: "For if someone likes something and is conscious that he himself does so without any interest, then he cannot help judging that it . . . must contain a basis for being liked [that holds] for everyone."[44] Kant's major preoccupation in his discussion of taste is to explain this strong sense of universal validity.

It turns out that the basis of this sense is the enchanting idea that all humans do indeed share the same kind of free and indeterminate accord between Imagination and Understanding whenever each exercises his taste. What is common or universal is the free play of the faculties inevitably operative during aesthetic judgment: "We are justified in presupposing universally in all people the same subjective conditions of the power of [aesthetic] judgment that we find in ourselves."[45] Moreover, concludes Kant, the subjective conditions of taste turn out to be the very "conditions

Figure 5. The Free Play of the Faculties. Drawing by
Donald P. Bennett, 1999.

for the possibility of cognition as such"!⁴⁶ This is because any *determinate*
accord of the faculties presupposes the existence of a free *indeterminate*
accord.⁴⁷ In other words, there could be no legislation of one faculty by
another (as, for example, is required for the exercise of pure and practical
reason) if the faculties were not already of such a nature that spontaneous,
unhierarchical cooperation among them were possible. Taste makes visible
this primordial accord: the critique of taste reveals the good and upright
nature of the faculties in relation to each other.

Kant tells an intriguing fable about humans and their two worlds, one
experienced and the other (almost but not quite) beyond experience. In
his enchanting world, reason has awesome powers, and the human mind
has "prospective" insights into the supersensible as well as the capacity for
a "spontaneous" harmonization of its faculties. Kant's enchanted world
distinguishes itself from Paracelsus's teleological one primarily by means
of four related distinctions: (1) between a critical and a dogmatic approach, (2) between regulative and constitutive principles, (3) between
reflective and determinative judgments, and (4) between physics and
metaphysics.⁴⁸ Each of these distinctions is designed to keep us within the
limits of reason, and Kant's tale often implies that they comprise a mighty

wall between reason and the enchanted world of someone like Paracelsus. But, as I have emphasized, Kant's story also includes intimations that this wall, like the one Kafka describes in "The Great Wall of China," has multiple, incompatible functions. Its most highly touted function is to keep out the dogmatic teleologists and their alchemic admixtures, but it is not so impermeable that nature cannot occasionally provide a peephole onto the supersensible. Scattered throughout the *Third Critique* are instances of the enchanting power of sensuous nature. These instances mark the gaps in the wall between reflective and determinative judgments, gaps which, as Kafka puts it, "have never been filled in at all, an assertion, however . . . which cannot be verified, at least by any single man with his own eyes and judgment, on account of the extent of the structure."[49]

The marvelous quality of Kant's philosophical tale is felt most powerfully by readers who are relatively new to Kant and have not yet learned the story by heart. For these novices or for anyone able to read Kant with new eyes, a nature that gives out hints and a mind whose faculties spontaneously harmonize provoke a wonder not unlike that inspired by the idea of a world of magical herbs.

Becoming-Animal, Becoming-Thinker

Despite some profound differences, Paracelsus and Kant both picture the world as a well-conceived order—and for both it is our experience of its harmony and purpose that has an enchanting effect upon us. In other words, enchantment is the somatic correlate of a view of nature as somehow linked to divinity; it is the mood that follows in the wake of the belief that the world is a cosmological whole. I turn now to another kind of enchanted world, which is not to say that the Paracelsian and Kantian versions do not continue to find expression today. This other world bears no relation to a telos, and its power to enchant is not dependent upon the existence or even necessary appearance of harmony. But, like the magical worlds of Paracelsus and Kant, this world too is alive and highly motile. In it, there are animate forces, dynamic trajectories, changing patterns, and dancing ideas that simultaneously fascinate and unsettle us.

Chapter 2 tells the tales of several admixtures of human and nonhuman, and it links their power to enchant to their capacity for mobility, for shape shifting, recrystallization, and metamorphosis. That such crossings make up a growing segment of the population of late modernity is a point made by a group of contemporary theorists, among them Deleuze, but also Thom Kuehls, Donna Haraway, Tim Luke, and Bruno Latour. Haraway examines how the presence of cyborgs influences the gender, scientific, and Hollywood stories that we are able to tell about ourselves; Kuehls develops the point in connection with a critical exploration of the possibility of a "cyborg ecopolitics" in a global world; Luke explores the complexities of a cyborg liberalism and a cyborg subjectivity; Latour calls modernity the age of biotechnological hybrids and defines humanity as the "weaver" of its morphisms:

> The human is not a constitutional pole to be opposed to that of the nonhuman. . . . The expression 'anthropomorphic' considerably underestimates our humanity. We should be talking about morphism. Morphism is the place where technomorphisms, zoomorphisms, phusimorphisms, ideomorphisms, theomorphisms, sociomorphisms, psychomorphisms, all come together. Their alliances and their exchanges, taken together, are what define the *anthropos*.[50]

The world envisioned here is a technologically engaged world, where things are moving fast and metamorphoses abound. Where, for example, a manuscript morphs from a heavy pile of paper that crawls through space into a weightless electronic file that zooms around with almost instantaneous speed. Where a man with a fondness for drink shifts from a weak-willed sinner to, in a quick succession of transformations, an alcoholic, a victim of disease, and a bearer of a distinctive genetic code. Where a sweet, red, and pock-marked summer fruit called a tomato crosses over into a mild pink sphere available in all seasons. Where a whale leaves its sea-creature body to become a mammal and then a rival intelligence to humans. And where no one expects any of these morphings to be a final state. One might say that such a world, where things cross back and forth over the nature/culture divide, is a monstrous world. Or that the unlimited scope and pace of such crossings has provoked a crisis in meaning. Such interpretations bear the trace of a world construed as an order with purpose, where nature is naturally distinct from culture, and where meaning depends on the ontological stability of the things to which it is (variably) attached. But outside of that story, crossings and metamorphoses, while remaining matters of concern and regulation, also could be sites of enchantment.

Of course, the enchanting potential of anything might dissipate with familiarity, and the commercial forces attached to each of the crossings named above are usually thought of as dis-enchanting. But I wonder about that and make a case for an enchantment that coexists alongside commodification in chapter 6. Here, I want only to suggest that both late modern morphings and Paracelsian interminglings are uneasy admixtures of organic, fantastic, commercial, scientific, and moralizing forces. By drawing parallels between these two sets, the enchantment effect of the contemporary morphings might be enhanced. Why it might be a good idea to cultivate a capacity for enchantment in contemporary life is a question that I address most explicitly in chapter 7. My point now is that enchantment is not simply an experience to be received but something to be made, a technical or cultured effect.

Such enchantment can be induced by fiction of the fairy-tale variety. Kafka's short story "The Crossbreed" is one interesting example. It tells of a creature with a highly mobile identity, and it might call to mind your own exhilarating/unnerving experience of having a body (and an identity) that changes shape over time. Kafka's crossbreed spends an inordinate amount of time in, to use Paracelsian language, the "limbus" or fold of becoming. We enter the story when the crossbreed is already half cat and half lamb, though "formerly it was far more lamb than kitten." By the middle of the story, the narrator tells us that it has morphed again: "Sometimes I cannot help laughing when it sniffs around me and winds itself between my legs and simply will not be parted from me. Not content with being lamb and cat, it almost insists on being a dog as well." Later, the crossbreed takes on "the ambition of a human being," as it weeps in sympathy with the narrator's financial worries. Then, the "restlessness" of cat and lamb come to the fore, and the crossbreed's skin again "feels too tight for it." At the end of the story, the crossbreed, "with a look of human understanding," asks the narrator to "release" it to those future forms possible only after it has been eaten.[51] Now that's a real commitment to shape-shifting!

Kafka's story describes the "event moment"[52] of magic, when the usual structure of a thing dissolves and the newly released bits reconfigure with each other and with other bits of matter in the vicinity. Such unexpected transmutations can induce a sense of wonder at the world. For Deleuze and Guattari, the childhood game of becoming-animal is, like Kafka's story, a lively experiment with becoming-otherwise. The game suggests to them that children have a sense of themselves as emerging out of an overrich field of protean forces and materials, only some of which are tapped by a child's current, human form. In playing their barking, mooing, chirping, growling games, children bear witness to the depth field of necessarily underutilized resources in the vicinity that is theirs. Human children, more than human adults, are in touch with the "inhuman contrivance with the animal" within them:

> It is as though, independent of the evolution carrying them toward adulthood, there were room in the child for other becomings, "other contemporaneous possibilities" that are not regressions but creative involutions bearing witness to "*an inhumanity immediately experienced in the body as such. . . .*"[53]

Deleuze and Guattari often use the vocabulary of particles and molecules to describe these "creative involutions." They also invoke Spinoza's idea that what makes one thing different from another is a different relation to "movement and rest" among its particles. What is involved, for example, in the game of "becoming-dog" is to try to make

> your organism enter into composition with *something else* in such a way that the particles emitted from the aggregate thus composed will be canine as a function of the relation of movement and rest, or of molecular proximity, into which they enter. Clearly, this something else can be quite varied, and be more or less directly related to the animal in question: it can be the animals' natural food (dirt and worms), or its exterior relations with other animals . . . , or an apparatus . . . to which a person subjects the animal (muzzle . . .).[54]

For me, the significance of such talk about dogs, canine molecules, and our contrivances with nonhuman forms is that it exaggerates and thus makes visible the enchanting effect of human-animal encounters. There is a kind of pleasure-danger, fun-reluctance involved in playing at the edge of one's species-configuration—a kind of magic to it. To dip into the virtual field that pokes through various spots in actual life is, I think, to experience some more of the enchantment available in an undesigned world.

So might be the encounter with our own thinking. Deleuze figures thinking as a novelty machine, an arcanely complex, idiosyncratic machine out of which sometimes emerges a surprising idea, a weird alternative, an unsettling association. Thinking as a kind of bubbling limbus soup internal to human bodies. Out of thinking, enchanting novelties and strange becomings are always being born. But, then, most of these are transformed into useful "thoughts," which designate actualities and can be traded around with other people. Thoughts take the form of ordinary but indispensable representations and recognitions, such as: "This is a finger, this is a table, Good morning John." Thinking, as a producer of that which could not be anticipated, is a marvel.[55] But even the existence of thoughts is pretty wondrous: How *do* these communicable nodules persist in a world that is not itself made by thought, or invested with it, or designed for it? How *do* schools of thought—or other such coordinated assemblages as ecosystems, political coalitions, and life partners—rise up despite the non-harmonious, nondesigned, and unnecessary ground of their being?

Kant was inattentive to this site of enchantment, for he pictured thinking as having a natural talent for order and a natural affinity for what is true. In short, for Kant, thinking had what Deleuze describes as an "upright" nature.[56] To really get beyond a teleological imaginary, however, would be to explore the opposite set of assumptions. Why not suppose that thinking is not in alignment with the world and not upright in character, that it can be contrary toward things outside of itself and can be play-

ful and ill-mannered as well as upright? Under this set of contestable assumptions, thinking becomes a conglomeration of intentions, leaps,
intensities, trace elements, and accidents, out of which emerge the surprises that temporarily jar humans out of the stupor of their duly sequen-
tial representing and recognizing.

Kant wanted to clarify thoughts, refine representations, and strengthen
recognition of the moral law; Deleuze wants to encourage the unruly creativity of thinking. Both are, in my judgment, noble aspirations. Deleuze,
enchanted by thinking, also inquires into its conditions of possibility. And
here he follows Kant's method, if not his image, of thought. "Thinking is
not innate, but must be engendered," says Deleuze.[57] What can engender
thinking? "Sense" is the catalyst or midwife:

> Something in the world forces us to think. This something is an object not of
> recognition but of a fundamental *encounter*. What is encountered may be Socra-
> tes, a temple or a demon. It may be grasped in a range of affective tones: wonder,
> love, hatred, suffering. In whichever tone, its primary characteristic is that it can
> be *only* sensed.[58]

So it is "sense" that forces us to think. To sense something, for Deleuze,
is to discern a "difference in intensity" from amidst an indeterminate,
buzzing field of morphing.[59] Sense is the impetus or ground of thinking,
and the impetus or ground of sense is this virtual field of "difference-in-
itself." This virtual field is, Deleuze insists, a material and immanent one—
it is all around us. It nevertheless functions as a kind of structural analog
to Kant's supersensible and to Paracelsus's Iliaster.

Like Kant, Deleuze finds it difficult to describe this ultimate ground.
Kant, in spite of his claim that the noumenal realm is beyond experience,
describes a tiny window onto it opened up by "hints" and "prospects" of
reason and nature. Deleuze, too, says that access to the virtual field is
almost completely blocked—by the thousands of actualities (concrete
things with extension in space) with which we must engage. There are
still some ways, however, to get a sense of the ontological field of difference, some possibility of grasping "intensity independently of extensity or
prior to the qualities in which it is developed." Deleuze names three ways:
(1) you can pick up the sound of the virtual field through the "sensory
distortion" produced by psychotropic drugs; (2) you might be able to get
to it without drugs through "a pedagogy of the senses" like that entailed
in yoga or in the aesthetic disciplines of the American transcendentalists;
or (3) you can go to the top of a skyscraper and look down and up too
fast and experience vertigo, another window onto the overwhelming plenitude of the virtual. All three techniques "reveal to us that difference in
itself, that depth in itself or that intensity in itself at the original moment
at which it is neither qualified nor extended . . ."[60]

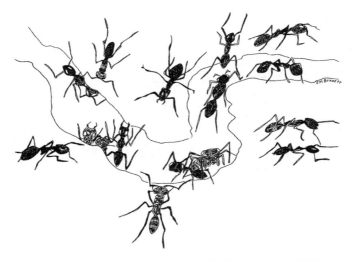

Figure 6. The Virtual Field. Drawing by Sue Bennett, 1997.

Kant began with the idea that the ground of thought is the categories of the mind and then, when he inquired into the ground of that ground, he referred to the infinite, the inscrutable, the noumena, the supersensible realm. Deleuze begins with the idea that the force behind thinking is sense and then, when he inquires into the force behind that force, he refers to an indeterminate immanent field of differences-in-intensity. Deleuze thinks Kant was right to try to conceive of the ground of thinking; Deleuze does not reject "metaphysics." What he does reject is Kant's picture of the transcendental field as "a completely undifferentiated abyss, a universal lack of difference, an indifferent black nothingness."[61] Deleuze imagines the virtual field not as a black hole but as a vibrant and crowded "swarm" of differences in intensity. It's a veritable army of "ants which enter and leave through the fracture in the I."[62] It's a place where "the reign of birds seems to have been replaced by the age of insects," where bird melodies compete with the more persistent "vibrations, chirring, rustling, buzzing, clicking, scratching, and scraping" of bugs.[63]

Imagine a place, then, where reason engenders, where faculties play, where nature gives hints, where molecules mutate, where tomatoes morph, where files zoom, where curves spiral and fields buzz, where ants swarm and vertigo reveals, and where thinking unexpectedly shouts out from the dutiful litany of thought. *That* world is not disenchanted.

My story of contemporary enchantment can proceed no further without listening carefully to the tale it shadows. In the last years of the eighteenth century, Friedrich Schiller lamented the fact that a science of clockworks had hounded the Godhead out of Nature; as Daston and Park note, "this accusation has been endlessly repeated and elaborated ever since."[64] I turn next to three different renditions of the story of the world's disenchantment.

4

Disenchantment Tales

IF YOU read popular magazines, you are familiar with the quiz format. Please give yourself one point for each "yes" response:

1. Do you long to be released from "the cold skeletal hands of rational orders, just as completely as from the banality of everyday routine"[1]

2. Do you lament the fact that it's a dog-eat-dog world, where the more "the modern capitalist economy follows its own immanent laws, the less accessible it is to any imaginable relationship with a religious ethic of brotherliness"?[2]

3. Is it hard for you to believe in "the primitive image of the world, in which everything was concrete magic"[3] even though you sometimes ache for communal life, for the enlivening "pneuma, which in former times swept through the great communities like a firebrand, welding them together"?[4]

4. Do you see nature and society as complex but systematic orders that are, at least in principle, susceptible to rational decoding?

5. Do you (privately) believe that we are better off than nonmodern peoples precisely because we approach the world with the confidence that "one can, in principle, master all things by calculation"?[5]

6. But does this picture of the world as a "causal mechanism"[6] also leave you wondering about the purpose of it all? In other words, has science stamped "the imprint of meaninglessness" on your life and death?[7]

7. Do you take comfort in the idea of progress, in the possibility of the continual advancement of humankind through reason and science, and yet still experience a nagging sense of futility because anything you achieve "asks to be 'surpassed' and outdated" by new and improved ideas, inventions, and institutions?[8]

8. Are mystical experiences and erotic adventures appealing to you because they seem to be gates "into the most irrational and thereby real kernel of life, as compared with the [lifeless] mechanism of rationalization"?[9]

The higher your score, the more you are living out the story of the disenchantment of the world. That is to say, the more your life—your experience—has been occupied by the images of nature, culture, and history sketched by Max Weber. As flexible and promiscuous as the story of Eden, the disenchantment tale, which purports to describe the existential and historical conditions in which we find ourselves, cannot be reduced to any one telling. But Weber's version is perhaps the most influential. One key process at work in the world that he describes is *Entzauberung*, or demagification, usually translated into English as "disenchantment."[10]

The quiz questions traverse the major contentions of the disenchantment tale: (1) our modern, highly rationalized world, characterized by calculation, stands in stark contrast to a magical or holistic cosmos, a cosmos toward which we have a double orientation of superiority and nostalgia; (2) although this world opens up a domain of freedom and mastery, we pay a psychic or emotional toll for demagification in the form of a lack of community and a deficit of meaning; (3) the idea of progress through science inspires both hope and despair; (4) even in societies in which rationalization has advanced the furthest, recalcitrant fugitives from rationalization persist, and these errant forces are understood through the categories of the mystical and the erotic.

In the next section, I elaborate these Weberian claims by presenting them as a story called "It's a Calculable World." I then tell two other versions of the disenchantment tale, Hans Blumenberg's account of what I call "Disenchantment without Regret" and Simon Critchley's narrative of an "Ethics of Finitude." I present each of the three stories in the first-person voice of its author. Thus better informed of the subtleties of the disenchantment story, I return to my alter-tale and, this time, focus on the picture of matter or the physics it employs.

"It's a Calculable World," by Max Weber

The Magical Cosmos

Once upon a time, magic was the favored way to get what you wanted from the powers that be. The specific rituals and techniques for the performance of magic depended on the specific object of one's desire—perhaps wealth? long life? honor? progeny? the improvement of one's fate in the hereafter?[11] But all magical arts worked best in the hands of a charismatic individual skilled in the theatrical use of color, sound, pattern, repetition, movement, scent, and texture. For magic was both performance and performative: it transformed one thing into another, in the flash of an eye, the very nature of a thing was altered; in a puff of smoke, new molecular alliances were formed. Magic sought less to beseech, worship, or pursue a quid pro quo with the gods than to gain a human share in their extraordinary powers of metamorphosis.

As a technology for the enactment of desire, magic contrasts with the less dramatic practice of rational calculation. Indeed, disenchantment names that gradual displacement of magic by calculation as the favored means "to master or implore the spirits."[12] Demagification is itself a manifestation of a more general process operative in history called *rationalization*. The "tion" form is important, for it emphasizes the extent to which these transformations are ever ongoing and never complete.

Rationalization encompasses a variety of related processes, each of which opts for the precise, regular, constant, and reliable over the wild, spectacular, idiosyncratic, and surprising. In addition to eschewing magic as a strategy of will (i.e., "scientizing" desire), rationalization also systematizes knowledge (i.e., pursues "increasing theoretical mastery of reality by means of increasingly precise and abstract concepts"); instrumentalizes thinking (i.e., methodically attains a "practical end by means of an increasingly precise calculation of adequate means"); secularizes metaphysical concerns (i.e., rejects "all non-utilitarian yardsticks"); and, finally, replaces traditional bonds as the basis of social order with those founded on the natural reason of men.[13]

The process of rationalization is not new, lately arrived, or unique to modern bureaucratic orders. Attempts to displace magic were made, for example, by the ancient Hebrew prophets, who, "in conjunction with Hellenistic scientific thought, . . . repudiated all magical means to salvation as superstition and sin."[14] This urge to demystify, pursued in fits and starts throughout history, did, however, reach its "logical conclusion" in Puritanism, an orientation that has had a profound impact on Euro-American culture—its ascetic ethic and idea of a "calling" eventually morphed into the entrepreneurship and acquisitiveness of modern capitalism. Still, it is important to emphasize the ongoing nature of the rationalization process—the enchanted world is always in the process of being superseded by a calculable world; the defeated world always returns; there is always new raw material for a rationalization whose work is never done. To put the point succinctly, rationalization never "come[s] out even with nothing left over."[15]

The Problem of Meaninglessness

A rationalizing culture encourages a particular style of thinking—the kind used in mathematics and scientific experimentation (that, unlike magic, is a "means of *reliably* controlling experience"[16]). One interesting implication of this habit of mind is the emergence, or at least enhanced salience, of an "in principle" realm of existence. One learns to relate to things by seizing upon their structure or logic, upon the principle of their organization, rather than, say, by discerning their inherent meaning as parts of a cosmos or by engaging their sensuous appeal in a world alive with animate bodies large and small. To residents of a disenchanted world, there is a significant difference between what a thing is in experience and what can be done to it or with it in principle.

> Does . . . everyone sitting in this hall . . . have a greater knowledge of the conditions of life under which we exist than has an American Indian or a Hottentot? Hardly. Unless he is a physicist, one who rides on the streetcar has no idea how the car happened to get into motion. . . . The increasing intellectualization and rationalization do *not*, therefore, indicate an increased and general knowledge of the conditions under which one lives. It means something else, namely, the knowledge or belief that if one but wished one *could* learn it at any time. Hence, it means that principally there are no mysterious incalculable forces that come into play, but rather that one can, in principle, master all things by calculation. This means that the world is disenchanted.[17]

Disenchantment does not mean that we live in a world that has been completely counted up and figured out but rather that the world has become calculable in principle. Although it is true that "the 'rational calculation' of business, societal rationalization, and the diminution of 'tradition' all combined to destroy *formal* magical practices and beliefs," the disenchanting world nevertheless retains "fragmented but still powerful magical elements."[18] It is quite possible for one to experience aspects of nature that currently defy understanding and still affirm the principle of the scientific calculability of the world. In a disenchanting world, the principle of calculability tends to overrule, even if it does not always overpower, experience. One might say, following Kant, that the calculable world functions as a "regulative ideal."[19]

Alongside confidence in the world's calculability, however, sits the uneasy feeling that the world has become meaningless. In other words, "The unity of the primitive image of the world, in which everything was concrete magic," gives way to "the mechanism of a world robbed of gods."[20] Or, as Charles Taylor will put it:

> People used to see themselves as part of a larger order. In some cases, this was a cosmic order, a "great chain of Being," in which humans figured in their proper place along with angels, heavenly bodies, and our fellow earthly creatures. This hierarchical order in the universe was reflected in the hierarchies of human society. . . . But at the same time as they restricted us, these orders gave meaning to the world and to the activities of social life. . . . The discrediting of these orders has been called the "disenchantment" of the world. With it, things lost some of their magic.[21]

The process of disenchantment, then, has more than one moral valence; it is both worthy of celebration and cause for complaint. In relation to the "basic historical antithesis of an intellectualized, progressive modernity vs. a primitively religious, cyclical peasant culture,"[22] it is a good thing. But the very same process that refines human intellect, stamps out superstition, establishes "modes of authority whose motives would in principle be transparent to all," expands "opportunities for self-legitimation in politics" and holds out the promise of increased "economic fairness"[23] is also the one that produces a cold and uninspiring world. This is the dark side of our disenchantment; we are "driven by purposive-rational or instrumental orientations, divided into opposed life-orders and value-spheres, without genuinely new prophetic truths, yet racked by endless searches for absolute experience and spiritual wholeness."[24]

We ought not to resent this fact too much, however, for an intrinsically meaningless world also brings new opportunities for freedom. One is now called upon to make one's own valuations, to decide for oneself what is significant, to choose for oneself among competing meanings:

> So long as life remains immanent and is interpreted in its own terms, . . . the ultimately possible attitudes toward life are irreconcilable, and hence their struggle can never be brought to a final conclusion. Thus it is necessary to make a decisive choice.[25]

Because demagification, though never complete, is not reversible or stoppable, it is most profitably met by the heroic will to choose rather than the cowardly slide into resentment.

Scientific Robbers, Religious Accomplices

But just how was the world robbed of gods and rendered meaningless? Modern science is the main culprit.[26] It strips meaning from the world by reducing it to pure immanence or materiality,[27] and matter is the antithesis of spirit and meaning. The logic of progress is a second way that science denudes the world. "In science, each of us knows that what he has accomplished will be antiquated in ten, twenty years. . . . In principle, this progress goes on *ad infinitum*."[28] As this logic of the perpetually receding goal is generalized throughout the culture, extending beyond the lab and the confines of experimental science, time itself comes to be figured as a moving line, a vector approaching but never reaching a vanishing point. This line plots not only the course of history or nature but also the existence of each individual, rendering it, too, tentative, contingent, provisional— and meaningless:

[T]here is always a further step ahead of one who stands in the march of progress. . . . [C]ivilized man, placed in the midst of the continuous enrichment of
culture by ideas, knowledge and problems, . . . catches only the most minute
part of what . . . life . . . brings forth ever anew, and what he seizes is always
something provisional and not definitive, and therefore death for him is a meaningless occurrence. And because death is meaningless, civilized life as such is
meaningless: by its very "progressiveness" it gives death the imprint of meaninglessness.[29]

Modern scientific practices first induce the expectation of a telos and
then flatly refuse to fulfill it; science first whets our appetite for completion
of purpose and then insists that no final satisfaction is attainable. And that
is why a disenchanted materialism carries with it a psychology of disappointment and an affect of meaninglessness. Disenchantment names both
this subjective state and the impersonal historical condition of the flight
of the gods. This disappointment can issue in a cynical resentment of the
world, but it also provides the occasion for a brave and responsible acceptance of the world.

Science is not, however, the sole agent of disenchantment. Religion is,
oddly enough, an accomplice. In general, modern religions have been
moving away from magic and toward ethical strategies of salvation—in
other words, away from erratic gestures and theatrical performances that
seek to "coerce spirits" and toward practices "systematically and unambig-
uously oriented to fixed goals of salvation."[30] Such ethical religions view
the world as an order responsive to rational attempts to alter and control
it, an order that is itself rational. Reality becomes a structure "governed
by impersonal rules" and inhabited by humans with "the desire as well as
the capacity" for its rational mastery.[31]

Confining our discussion of religion to the Christian sects of modern
Europe and America, there are two important ways in which demagification operates within the religious sphere. The first concerns the focus on
post-earthly Christian life, on a not-yet world where divinity, spirit, and
enchantment have their true home. This move to a transcendent realm
with monopoly rights to spirit not only concedes but advances the belief
that the immanent world here is indeed a calculable one.[32]

But an other-worldly focus was just one of the ways in which Christianity had a rationalizing effect. Another way was practiced not by theologians
but by artisans, traders, and enterprisers engaged in cottage industries.
Among this civic class, the displacement of magic proceeded not by way
of a "flight from this world" but via a stance of "active ascetic 'work in
this world.' "[33] For these pragmatic folk, "no matter how much the 'world'
. . . is religiously devalued . . . as . . . a vessel of sin, yet psychologically the
world is all the more affirmed as the theatre of God-willed activity in one's

worldly 'calling.' " This inner-worldly asceticism despised the secular values of dignity, beauty, power, and heroic pride as

> competitors of the kingdom of God. Yet precisely because of this refection, as-
> ceticism did not fly from the world . . . [but] wished to rationalize the world
> ethically in accordance with God's commandments. . . . In inner-worldly asceti-
> cism, the grace and chosen state of the religiously qualified man prove them-
> selves in everyday life. To be sure, . . . not in the everyday life as it is given, but
> in methodical and rationalized routine-activities of workaday life . . . rationally
> raised into a vocation. . . .[34]

To summarize: modern science and "ethically" oriented religions col-
laborated in disenchanting the world; they were sources of, even while
they proffered solutions for, the problem of the meaninglessness that
haunts us. Science progressively takes the spirit out of things and reduces
them to uninspiring matter; otherworldly religions desanctify earthly life;
and the vocationalism of the ascetic hard worker reinforces the sense that
all worlds, in this life and in the hereafter, are rationally calculable.

Fugitives from Rationalization

As already mentioned, rationalization and disenchantment are ever-ongo-
ing, asymptotic processes. "The calculation of consistent rationalism has
not easily come out even with nothing left over"[35]; even where rationalization has achieved its widest scope, there remain aspects of experience that
elude it, incalculable bits that float in and out of the iron cage, and inexplicable compulsions and convictions that make camp in the rationalized self.
Nevertheless, in a disenchanting world, such bits are not let be but are
treated as fugitives; they become targets of attempts to enclose them in a
rational scheme. Perplexing phenomena are, for example, defined as temporal mysteries that will be resolved as science evolves—they are calculable
even if we cannot yet do the math. Or, the fugitives can be referred to a
divine order of which they are surely a meaningful part. Finally, those
pesky irrationalities can be relegated to the private realm of mysticism or
personal "values."[36]

A masterful science not yet fully realized, a rational but inscrutable divine will, and an interiorized spiritual life all become official homes for
the incalculable. "The unity of the primitive image of the world, in which
everything was concrete magic, has tended to split into rational cognition
and mastery of nature, on the one hand, and into 'mystical' experiences,
on the other."[37] Eroticism, itself experienced as a kind of mysticism, also
functions as a container for enchanted fugitives.

The extraordinary quality of eroticism has consisted precisely in a gradual turning away from the naive naturalism of sex. The reason and significance of this
evolution . . . involve the universal rationalization and intellectualization of culture. . . . The total being of man has now been alienated from the organic cycle
of peasant life; life has been increasingly enriched in cultural content . . . . All
this has worked, through the estrangement of life-value from that which is
merely naturally given, toward a further enhancement of the special position of
eroticism. . . .[38]

In contrast to a magically whole cosmos, a demagifying world includes
an increasingly complex cultural value-sphere. But the values within a philosophy of life, or psychological theory, or set of therapeutic techniques
again only end up fostering meaninglessness. For they, too, participate in
the law of the diminishing returns of progress: the more cultural values
"differentiated and multiplied themselves, so much smaller did the frac-
tion become which the individual . . . could embrace in the course of a
finite life. So much the less therefore [was] . . . the probability that an
individual could absorb . . . the 'essential' [parts of culture.]"[39] Ultimately, those who live amidst rationalization will develop a craving for the
real; disenchanted selves will long for that which is not artifice or the
product of human minds or hands. That is why, for example, they turn to
eroticism as a "gate into the most irrational and thereby real kernel of life,
as compared with the mechanisms of rationalization."[40]

Weber's narrative of disenchantment includes six elements shared by many
versions of the tale. First, it positions itself against a bygone (golden or
dark) age when magic comingled with science, God lived in nature, agency
was distributed more widely (to include nonhuman animals, natural
forces, plants, and rocks), and human existence was meaningful by virtue
of its location within a larger cosmological order. This prequel describes
the particular model of enchantment that the story of disenchantment
presents.

Second, the lost cosmos conjured up by the tale is positioned as an
object of desire. Because the enchanted world is figured as the necessary
alter ego to the modern, disenchanted one, it takes on a clarity and defini-
tiveness that otherwise it could not have. One rhetorical effect of this is
to produce an attraction for this ever receding, but nobly resilient cosmos.
Under the haze of nostalgia (or the sway of sympathy for a besieged way
of life), the enchanted world becomes an object of longing. In Weber's
tale, this desire is encouraged by means of such phrases as the "cold skeletal
hands" of rationalization that form an "iron cage" blocking the "*pneuma*,
which in former times swept through the great communities like a fire-

brand."[41] Such formulations libidinally bind us to the story as they orient our attention toward that which we can no longer have—the mysterious, irrational, unifying cosmos.

Third, the disenchantment story describes the material world as consisting of lifeless stuff. We see evidence of this view in Weber's claim that, because science materializes (turns into pure matter) the world, it renders nature meaningless. But of course the problem of meaninglessness arises only if "matter" is conceived as inert, only as long as science deploys a materialism whose physics is basically Newtonian. For Weber, as for other disenchantment theorists, matter is the complete opposite of "spirit"— and only spirit can resist calculation and inspire us morally. For them, there are but two options: either an enchanting cosmology or a disenchanted materialism. There is no mention, as there is in my alter-story, of a materialism wherein matter has a liveliness, resilience, unpredictability, or recalcitrance that is itself a source of wonder for us. More on this enchanted materialism, which finds its ancient counterpart in the atomism of Epicurus and Lucretius, later in this chapter.

Fourth, Weber's story is set at a time in history when the ongoing series of transformations—of demagification, rationalization, secularization, materialization, scientization, mathematization, bureaucratization, alienation—are said to have speeded up, intensified, or reached some kind of logical conclusion. These movements—which, in Weber's version, are to be both embraced and lamented—constitute the central action or plot of the story.

Fifth, the protagonists, all humans, are depicted as suffering from this recent acceleration of change, in that they feel the existential pain of the loss of meaning, spirit, or sense of purpose. We are told that disenchantment is necessary and progressive—the magical cosmos belongs to "savage" cultures[42]—but we are not allowed to forget the price we pay in a tragic sense of emptiness. One can see how such a story could foster not only nostalgia for a lost cosmos but resentment against the rational order that blocks our experience of fullness. In Weber's version, we are both to regret and to embrace the cultural effects of disenchantment, which include an increase in the critical power of human intellect, a reduction in superstition, and a rise in skepticism. Whether these achievements are worth the price of meaninglessness, whether the self-improvement and scientific progress that we enjoy are worth the disorientation, is, says Weber, up to the thinking individual to decide. Though Weber attempts to diffuse resentment by focusing on the new possibilities for freedom here, among the many effects of the disenchantment tale is this sense that to be modern world is to be cheated out of something or, at the very least, to be deprived of an important psychic or existential resource.

Finally, there is a twist in the plot, in that fugitive experiences of magic are said to persist within the calculable world. This results in an increased interest among rational, calculating selves in mysticism, eroticism, and other curiosities of the "cultural" field.

In its emphasis on the inevitability of the disenchantment process, Weber's tale distinguishes itself from romantic attempts to re-enchant the world and to restore what Gilbert Germain describes as "man's ontological embeddedness in the world."[43] It also diverges from Marx's story of emancipation from capitalist and bureaucratic rationalization. More could be said about the economic subplot of Weber's tale—which claims that "the technical and economic conditions of machine production . . . today determine the lives of all the individuals who are born into this mechanism . . . with irresistible force."[44] In chapter 6, I look at how critical theory has taken up this theme; how, in particular, Horkheimer and Adorno combine Weber's image of an iron cage of rationalization with Marx's picture of a world of fetishized commodities. Weber's tale, as well, contrasts with less ambivalent orientations toward disenchantment like that of the twentieth-century historian of ideas, Hans Blumenberg.

Blumenberg is a pivotal figure to engage at this point. For, like Weber, he finds no basis for enchantment in the modern scientific world. But, more than Weber, he affirms disenchantment and the "incomparable energy" of the human "self-assertion" over nature that it engenders (148).[45] Blumenberg more or less accepts Weber's description of our condition, but he overcomes Weber's moral ambivalence toward it, perhaps because such ambivalence still harbors nostalgia for a cosmos that, as Blumenberg insists, was *self*-defeating. Weber recognized that there were religious modalities of rationalization; Blumenberg picks up and intensifies this theme.

"Disenchantment without Regret," by Hans Blumenberg

The Antimoderns

The specific targets of my tale are those so nostalgic for a purposeful world over which the Christian God presides that they view modernity as "illegitimate." These twentieth-century antimoderns decry disenchantment as the aggressive secularization of a formerly intact teleological world view; as they see it, "religious ties, attitudes to transcendence, expectations of an afterlife, ritual performances" (3) were expelled from public life by antireligious forces. A worldly bearing is thus seen as an "inauthentic manifestation" of an originally purposeful reality (18). This ethical "substance," they say, can be acknowledged or denied—but in either case, a sense of longing or alienation will persist, for the substance is too real to vanish completely (10).

Because the antisecularists identify a teleological Christianity (i.e., the cosmos of Scholasticism) as an authentic origin, the key notions and institutions of modernity figure as plagiarisms of this original source (137).[46] The antisecularists claim, for example, that the capitalist valuation of success in business is merely the secularization of the Calvinist's need to know if he has been saved; that the modern work ethic is but a secularization of saintliness; that the modern literary penchant for self-disclosure derives from the self-examination required by pietism; that the ideal of political equality only secularizes the concept of the equality of men before God. (These are claims that Weber too affirms, albeit without the qualifiers "merely," "but," and "only." Weber understood that the relationship between Christianity and modern forms of economy and society was too complex to fit the model of authentic source versus derivative imitation.)

The antisecularists do not object entirely to modern revisions of religious forms. What outrages them, they say, is modernity's denial of its debts and its audacious self-definition as a radically new epoch. Secularists owe their "uncanny success" to a Christian background, and yet these ingrates forget or deny their own, true preconditions (116)! Their claim of "epochal conformity to reason is nothing but an aggression (which fails to understand itself as such) against theology, from which in fact it has in a hidden manner derived everything that belongs to it" (97)! From the perspective of those who long to restore recognition of the divinized universe, secularism has cramped human horizons to the "things of this world."[47]

The antisecularists are right in that some important source of meaning indeed has been lost with modernity. Call it an ancient cosmos of cyclical events and natural hierarchies, or a world alive with wonders and hints from God, or a teleological substance at work in history and nature—we do indeed live amidst "the disappearance of inherent purposes" (147).[48] But this disenchantment is a fact toward which we have adjusted quite well! After all, a sense of insecurity and the spectre of meaninglessness are not specific to modernity; experiences of undeserved suffering and inexplicable evil have regularly called into question the safety and viability of the universe for humans. But the modern response to the "radical insecurity of man's relation to reality" (155)—that is, the "self-assertion" of reason and the organization of large areas of nature for human purposes—is an especially effective response and a particularly successful coping strategy.

On Nominalism or Christianity's Contribution to Disenchantment

The world of Scholasticism was not first and foremost the victim of such outside forces as reason, capitalism, science, and secular rejection; rather,

Christendom "worldified" itself during the late Middle Ages. Disenchantment is a process integral to Christianity. If the old teleological universe were somehow to be reinstated today, tensions within that unstable metaphysics would eventually manifest themselves again. There is no coherent (but now forgotten or disparaged) ethical substance to which to return. Modernity is a response to an internal failure of medieval Christianity, rather than a betrayal of its stable essence, and this is what the critics of secularism conceal. What is inaccurately described as the secularization of Christendom is instead the result of a theological response to a theologically induced problem of evil. The "driving onward" of interest in the transcendental realm and in salvation, like the waning of the belief in God's active presence in the world and the decline in the moral authority of theology, is not the effect of an alienation of religious truths but of a debate internal to Christianity.

In broadest terms, that debate concerned how best to conceive of a salvational God—that is, a God capable of providing an afterlife and thus overriding, in the case of humans, the seemingly inexorable forces of decay and death. Such a God would need to be very powerful, even omnipotent. The problem of evil, of the troubling coexistence of God and the suffering of innocents, had, early on in Christianity, posed a problem here. How could the God of Christ tolerate evil? There was a Gnostic solution to the problem, wherein evil was explained as the product of a vengeful creator god who shares power with a second, good god who "brings redemption without in the last owing it to man, whom he did not create" (129)—but this response failed to preserve monotheism because it undermined divine omnipotence. That is why, for example, Augustine condemned it as heresy. Gnosticism restricted the power of God and rendered Him inadequate to our salvation. Augustine, as is well known, countered the Gnostics with the claim that evil was integral to the design of the one God's creation— integral and yet inexplicable, as it must be given the puniness of human understanding. Humans must confess to their radical insufficiency, to their inability to comprehend even the slightest of God's attributes.

But this first "overcoming of Gnosticism" eventually proved insufficient to the task. Modern disenchantment is the unintended consequence of a *second* attempt to protect the doctrine of divine omnipotence, this time from the threat posed to it by the Scholastic idea of a teleological world. Medieval nominalism upped the Augustinian ante by arguing that the Scholastic notion of a purposeful world was itself a heretical restriction of divine omnipotence; an intrinsic purpose in the world, even one with which God was identified, restrained His absolute freedom to create and recreate as He willed. To save the picture of God's omnipotence, all remnants of teleology had to be drained from the human experience of the universe. Nominalism, by focusing so intensely on divine omnipotence, compelled man to "seek salvation outside the world" and drive him "to the unconditional capitulation of the act of faith" (151). But, overplaying its hand, nominalism backfired. It ended up destroying "trust in an ordered structure of the world oriented to man" (139). It became translated by those who could not accept its austere dictates into the experience of a disenchanted world over which man could assume control. A nominalist God unrecognizable in nature turned out to be the psychological equivalent of a nature devoid of God—and thus fair game for human mastery.

William of Ockham is a good example of how a nominalist commitment, against its intentions, ends up encouraging a stance of calculating self-assertion. Ockham argues that if God has complete, utter power, then matter surely cannot precede the Creation; it must be admitted that every single thing that exists is created *ex nihilo*, for only then "can the possibility be excluded . . . that God might restrict His own power by creating a particular entity, because any aspect of other concrete creation that happened to be identical . . . with the first could only be imitation and repetition, not creation" (153). This austere doctrine, which asserts the absolute inability of matter to limit God's will, also implies that any discernible connection between things—any theoretical order among natural objects—is merely something that humans have imputed to them or imposed upon them. Once again, Ockham's concern to sharpen our sense of God's omnipotence unintentionally led to the view that "divine spirit and human spirit, creative and cognitive principles, operate as though without taking each other into account" (154). This view, in turn, created incentives *within* Christianity to pursue modern instrumentalizing strategies that break with the theology of enchantment.

Self-assertion was further encouraged by the fact that the escape route into transcendence, like the road into nature, was also blocked by nominalism. For the decision about who would be saved had to be as inscrutable as the reason why God would allow evil. (Enter, later in history, the Calvinism that Weber describes in *The Protestant Ethic and the Spirit of Capitalism*.) Secular philosophy and science thus arose as instruments by which to overcome this insecurity generated by nominalism. And nominalism, again, arose as an attempt to give pure power to the divinity worthy of the purest devotion. The crucial achievement of modernity was the idea that man can attain his goals (be they paradise or a just society) "by the exertion of his own powers" without having to "rely . . . on the grace, which he cannot earn, of an event breaking in upon him" (86). This account parallels Weber's somber decisionism, that is, the idea that it is up to the individual to make choices in a world devoid of intrinsic purpose.

A later example of the theological obsession with "God's sovereign freedom to do what he pleases" is Samuel Clark's view, espoused in his letters to Leibniz in 1715–16. Clark said that the "act of creation was . . . the original fact, which could not be further inquired into and rationally grounded." Clark's theological absolutism here "denied man any insight into the rationality of the Creation. Leibniz, a teleologist on the defensive, countered that, except for the initial act of the creation of matter as such (which *was* an inexplicable act of sheer power), the material world as a whole had a structure recognizable to the systematically inquiring human mind:

> The rational dependability of the world, the condition of possibility of all theory, is the remnant of teleological order that Leibniz defends. On the other hand, absolute will, as a metaphysical principle, is the equivalent of the assertion that the dependability of the world cannot be proved and is therefore a mere fact, . . . subject to revocation at any time (149).

Now, Clark's insistence on the primacy of divine will was *meant* "to increase the binding force of the given over men." But it could be readily taken to render superfluous the idea of an intentional God and make the world seem rather chancy. That is just what bothered Leibniz about Clark's theological absolutism: the inscrutable creation moved perilously close to a world governed only by chance. If, as Clark asserted, the structure of creation was indeed completely inaccessible to human reason, then, from the perspective of humans, creation would feel no different than an accidental universe, as the godless Epicureans claimed it to be!

Leibniz was right: Clark's nominalist piety perversely enlarged the conceptual space for a materialism wherein the physical world was "something meaningless in itself, and consequently . . . a potentiality open to man's . . . disposition" (151). In other words, an attitude of self-assertion over a cosmos-turned-nature was eventually able to "occupy" the space opened up by nominalism, even if it was at odds with the nominalist intention. Self-assertion does not refer to "the naked biological and economic preservation of the human organism by the means naturally available to it," but rather to "an existential program, according to which man posits his existence in a historical situation and indicates to himself how he is going to deal with the reality surrounding him and what use he will make of the possibilities that are open to him" (138).

One last example of how nominalism undermined confidence in a teleological world and inadvertently called forth the response of self-assertion concerns the repudiation of cognitive universals. Nominalism claimed that there can be no such things—for even if the universal is defined as a divine concept that God Himself substantiates through His creation, it would still represent a limitation on His freedom to will. There can be no universals precisely because it is unthinkable that an omnipotent God and His boundless creativity could be constrained, even by His own divine thought. Many actual nominalists qualified this thesis, but when carried to its extreme form, the claim was that "absolute power is original in every one of its creations."[49] As a result of this position, the status of human concepts, theories, and knowledge changed. Science and philosophy now became both necessary (for making one's way in the natural world) and arbitrary (because one could never know if they represented nature's actual structure or design). Science could offer more or less useful constructs, but it could not represent nature. The very richness of God's "creative *abundance* put human reason in the . . . position of having . . . its . . . classificatory concepts [appear as a] . . . construct that is . . . as indispensable as it is inappropriate—in the position, that is, of being unable from the very beginning to interpret its theoretical mastery of reality as anything but self-assertion." In other words, we cannot "reconstruct an order given in nature," but only "reduce nature forcibly to an order *imputed* to it by man" (153–54).[50]

As the preceding accounts of nominalism suggest, while it is true that the "Middle Ages came to an end when 'providence' ceased to be credible to man," it is not true that providence was "secularized" into a notion of progress. Rather, "the burden of self-assertion" was laid upon man by developments within Christian theology itself (138). Modern science and self-assertion do not forget or occlude a unity that otherwise would be intact. Rather, they wrest a degree of control and use-value from a world that, for the sake of piety, had already been constituted as unaligned with human reason or purpose. This unhuman world is in principle unknowable in itself. Self-assertion is not a logically necessary response to this condition. But it does become the most credible response to those who seek to make something of their time on earth in a world now drained of any intrinsic purpose.

The Return of Atomism

Nominalist ideas, from the medieval to the early modern period in Europe, provoked a teleological meltdown and, eventually, against their intentions, gave rise to a self-assertive reason in the service of mastering a materialized world. But we have not yet reached the end of the story. For nominalism did not accomplish modernity all by itself: it was aided by the reappearance, at the end of the middle ages, of the Greek atomism of Epicurus. (The *De Rerum Natura* of Lucretius, Epicurus's Roman follower, was rediscovered in Europe in 1417.) It is the contingent historical coincidence of nominalism and Epicureanism that gave birth to modern self-assertion.

Lucretian physics described a universe of atoms forever falling in a void of space; these primordia, at unpredictable times and in unpredictable directions, swerve slightly from their downward paths, bump into each other, and so form the organisms and entities of the natural world. The first cause of this universe is not a god but rather the inscrutable chance of the swerve, also called the *clinamen* or the declination of atoms from the straight line of their fall. As a result of Lucretius's poem *De Rerum Natura*, there emerged, during the late Middle Ages, the idea that while the universe was in itself an impenetrable kind of order, there was a material subrealm of regular entities that was indeed "a potentiality open to man's rational disposition" (151).

What is intriguing about this is the fact that the idea of a material arena liable to human mastery had *not* emerged during the original time of Epicureanism, circa 300 b.c.e. (Before Common Era) Why? Why had not ancient atomism, with its explicit rejection of any providence or cosmic telos, unleashed the "incomparable energy" of modern technology and science? Why hadn't atomism produced, in ancient Greece, an immanent and mathematizable nature, as it would in the late medieval world? Because ancient Epicureanism did not engender the level of existential anxiety necessary to propel humans into developing their rational and technical wills to the fullest extent. Without the co-presence of nominalism and its nerve-wracking fixation on divine omnipotence, Epicurus's picture of the regular matings of atoms could compensate for the absence of divine providence. Sure, the gods are indifferent to human well-being, but no worries! Matter is reliable and predictable enough and, as chance would have it, quite in tune with our basic needs.

Ancient Epicureanism managed to convey this sense of ontological security through its idea that there was a finite set of combinations for atomic mixing, among which always would be human beings. Epicurus falls back "on a reserve of teleology," which is not at first apparent in his philosophy.

> Just as for Epicurus it is not really accidental *that* there are any worlds at all, so it is no accident *what* comes into being when worlds emerge from atomic vortices. . . . Epicurus [assumes] a definite, finite number of forms by which atoms are distinguished from one another. As though it were a matter of course, then, the products of Epicurean accident resemble one another, including the unquestioned matter . . . that . . . there [will be] . . . men (158).

The Epicurean notion that nature "made what is necessary easily accessible, and what is difficult of access unnecessary" also has this comforting effect. Be at peace, counsels Epicurus, for nature, by chance, provides all that we really need. The "groundlessness of nature permits the groundlessness of concern because the 'cosmos' is sufficiently powerful even in chance events to let needs and givens intermesh with one another just as the forms of the atoms themselves allow the formation of meaningful, organized configurations" (165).

As "a therapy meant to lessen the human uneasiness caused by natural phenomena," (151) ancient Epicureanism entailed a series of thought-experiments and bodily regimes designed to overcome fear of death and eventually achieve the ethical goal of *ataraxy* (blessedness or tranquility). *Ataraxy* was promoted by the notion of "a chance that nevertheless contains its own guarantees" (152). But the built-in reliability of matter, the "presupposition of the finite and hence completely describable possibilities of natural processes," and the fortuitous coincidence of human needs and natural givens would become *untenable* postulates once the world was experienced through the lens of a theology that emphasized not the benign neglect of the gods but the absolute, infinite potency of God. "Absolute will, as a metaphysical principle, is the equivalent of the assertion that the dependability of the world cannot be proved and is therefore a mere fact, always subject to revocation at any time" (149). If Epicureanism sought to put its followers at ease, nominalism "meant to make man extremely uneasy about the world—with the intention, of course, of making him seek salvation outside the world. . . ." (151) When Epicureanism reappeared in Europe in 1417, it had to share conceptual space with nominalism. And it was this co-presence that rendered atomism into a picture of the world as devoid of enchantment, as purely contingent, as a place where nothing stood between humans and suffering but their own "practical energy" (165).

Blumenberg's is a rich and fascinating story of the rise of modern self-assertion as the child of a historically contingent encounter between atomism and nominalism. The picture of modernity that he draws is a disenchanted place because for him both nominalism and the new atomism discouraged wonder at the world—both worked to expel any sense of marvel or fascination with material existence. And, though Blumenberg does not mention it, neither was the Scholastic cosmos a place of wonder or wonders. As Daston and Park show, although the Scholastics did indeed endorse the idea of a purposive world, a teleological order, their philosophical program was to minimize the role of wonder. Theoretical curiosity, yes; wonder, no. "In the medieval scholastic analysis, wonder become a taboo passion: the mark of the ignorant, the non-philosopher, the old woman, the empiric. . . ."[51] Nominalism, then, shared something with its Scholastic opponent.

As Blumenberg does show, nominalism rejected wonder at the world because God's unfathomable power was so great that it would be presumptuous, even blasphemous, to claim to be able to discern any trace of it in the everyday, sensuous world. In the case of Epicureanism, experience had to be purged of wonder because even such a positive affect was an impediment to the state of restful and carefree peace that was the ethical goal. No wonder, no worries. Epicureanism, says Blumenberg, preaches avoidance of hope and fascination as much as of fear and loathing, for "happiness is what is left over when nature no longer presses upon man, when it concerns him no more than it concerns the gods in the spaces between the worlds. . . ."[52]

But it is in Blumenberg's reading of Epicureanism that more work is needed. At least that is how it appears to me as a teller of an alter-tale of contemporary enchantments. I am particularly interested in the role that Blumenberg assigns to Epicurean atomism because I, too, draw selectively upon that imaginative physics. But I do so in order to articulate a conception of nature/culture that is neither the dull matter of a disenchanted world nor the lively stuff of divine creation. Blumenberg argues that Epicureanism, like nominalism, fosters an attitude of affective indifference toward matter; I find in pagan atomism the resources for a view of matter as wondrous, for a materialism that is enchanting without being teleological or purposive. Blumenberg, it seems to me, fails to discern in Epicurus the makings of a third way between a teleological cosmos and a self-assertive rationalism.

Blumenberg presents Epicureanism as a series of techniques for becoming *indifferent* toward the natural world, remaining unmoved by any of its diverse forms or by the sheer fact of their existence. For Blumenberg's Epicurus, "that there is a world is not at all a remarkable fact. 'Non est mirabile'; it is the least surprising—indeed, the 'natural'—state of affairs. . . ."[53] Epicureanism, including its picture of matter, is described as a therapy to "neutralize emotional states" and replace them with a cool nonchalance toward matter (psychologically affordable because the undesigned mechanism of nature, it just so happens, works to our advantage.) From my point of view, however, Blumenberg exaggerates the passivity engendered by an Epicurean (meta)physics, which seems to me to be a fabulous and poetic depiction of the energetic goings-on of the microscopic world. *Ataraxy* need not be interpreted as a kind of indifferent passivity; neither does it require a universe that is tranquil. On my reading, it entails the active affirmation of a world that swerves; it calls for us to work diligently to cultivate a cheerful, chagrined, or stoic (as the particulars require) acceptance of a world unsusceptible to human mastery. It makes sense that Blumenberg should underplay this energetic or activist dimension, given his interest in differentiating the modern cultural response to atomism from the ancient one: Epicureanism is introduced into his story to explain the emergence of active self-assertion as a peculiarly modern stance.

My contentions are, first, that Blumenberg replaces the Epicureans' marveling acceptance of nature with a bland indifference toward it, and, second, that this orientation of wonder-at-matter, of an enchanted materialism, persists as a fugitive element within the modern, scientific stance toward nature. What would happen if a modernized Epicureanism, participating in the new insights of modern science, were folded into the modern world of self-assertion? Perhaps it would be a place with dangerous modes of self-assertion, but also a place with various sites of wonder at a material world neither divinized nor dull. At the end of this chapter, I return to Epicurus to explore this issue, thus also returning to the enchantment tale begun in chapters 2 and 3.

Blumenberg does offers a compelling account of how theological speculations (nominalism and its critics), accidents of history (the rediscovery of Lucretius), and the quest for ontological comfort as a bulwark against existential anxiety (presented as inherent in human nature) have come to form a distinctly modern assemblage. He also helps to reveal why the disenchantment tale continues to hold such appeal. The antisecular version, by naming a source to blame for all that is unjust, evil, or painful in the current sociotechnical order, offers the (morally problematic) satisfactions of a moral reproach. But all versions of the tale, because a loss of some kind is their founding premise, also give witness to—in the sense of collectively acknowledging and thus helping to process or properly to mourn—the violent traumas inside contemporary life.[54]

Finally, Blumenberg's rejoinder to the charge that modernity is an ingrate and an aggressor, that is, his defense of modern self-assertion as the best and, really, the only viable response to the worldliness of our world (as what is left once we face up to the self-defeat of teleological perspective), opens the door to a story of modernity that is *not* founded on a fundamental loss. For one can resist, with Blumenberg, the idea of secularism as parasitic upon a religious substance that it denies, while still challenging the idea that the demise of teleology must spell the demise of enchantment. It might be that Blumenberg is more haunted by a sense of the loss of the old enchanted world than he realizes, enough to disable him from engaging other sites and modes of enchantment. In short, why present self-assertion as the only alternative to teleology? Unlike Weber, Blumenberg, and the Christian or romantic antimodernists, I tell of a world both worldly *and* enchanted.

Weber and Blumenberg together reveal the disenchantment tale to be a complex and flexible set of claims, all of which share the sense that modernity has significantly altered the shape of nature, culture, and the self, and all of which strive to identify the images and practices distinguishing the modern now from the premodern past. In addition, all versions proceed from the intuition that there is some kind of loss entailed in that shift. Antisecularists lament the loss as a betrayal of what the world really is and are pulled by the idea of a return to premodern forms; Blumenberg celebrates it for the technical superiority and rational self-assertion that it makes possible; and Weber braves the loss and calls on himself and others to make one's own order and meaning. Weber's story opposes both nostalgic and purely instrumentalist responses to disenchantment. I turn next to a more recent version, one that focuses more exclusively than Weber's did, on the need for an ethics of disenchantment. The "ethics of finitude" advocated by contemporary British philosopher Simon Critchley provides my example, not only because it reveals the kinds of ethical concerns framed by the story of our disenchantment but because it throws into sharper relief the picture of nature most consonant with that tale.

The issues identified by the disenchantment tale as most in need of ethical worry and redress typically include the excessive growth of instrumental rationality and the demise of a public sphere, a science and technology insufficiently regulated by democratic politics, the replacement of face-to-face relations with impersonal commercial and bureaucratic forms, and the disintegration of shared norms and meanings that is due to an overwhelming sense of social and informational complexity.[55] The picture of nature that infuses these themes is a dull, lifeless, and existentially unsatisfying place. But how might this list of ethical dangers[56] change if its imagined landscape were to be inflected by a different, say, more enchanted, (meta)-physics? The goal of my encounter with Critchley is to explore the relationship between the nature-imaginary of disenchantment and the range of ethical concerns made available by it.

Critchley designs his ethic as a response to the nihilism that the cultural self-understanding of disenchantment tends to foster. He eschews the romantic solution to nihilism but shares the diagnosis of disenchantment that prompts them both. After exploring how the image of an inert material world influences that diagnosis, I sketch an alternative picture of animate but not divinized matter—which selects out a different set of ethical dangers and advocates a different focus for ethical concern. I locate this alternative in the ancient writings of Epicurus and Lucretius, as well as in the hypercontemporary realm of nanotechnology.

"An Ethics of Finitude," by Simon Critchley

Accepting Death

The disenchantment of the world entailed the death of God. This event, which Blumenberg presented as the unintended consequence of medieval nominalism, in turn launched the problem of meaninglessness, aptly described by Weber. But what then "might count as a meaningful life . . . after one has rejected the founding certainties of religion" (134)?[57] In response to the spectre of nihilism, Weber pointed to the necessity of human acts of value-creation and called for us to rise to the challenge of this freedom. Such freedom, however, also provokes human arrogance, or what Blumenberg described in more positive terms as the self-assertion of reason. The ethical task before us, then, is how to "live with(in) the disappointment of religion" without succumbing to either nihilism or arrogance.

What is needed is a stance that consists, above all, in the acknowledgment of human finitude. This acknowledgment entails the paradoxical acceptance of one's own death as ungraspable and meaningless, as happening for no reason. It requires, in other words, that one accede to what one cannot understand. Such untranquil acceptance contributes to a positive ethical result (i.e., the "unworking of human arrogance")." This is the arrogance that purports to know the Other when, in fact, it is merely referring the Other back to some knowable version of the Same. To unwork such arrogance is to confess to the element of ineradicable difference that is the Other. Only then will the possibility of "compassion, . . . tenderness and generosity" toward him be possible (138). The potential for ethical respect lies within acceptance of finitude because "the first experience of an alterity that cannot be reduced to the self occurs in the relation to death." Owning up to death, then, raises the chances that the radical alterity of the Other will make a "claim on me" and change and challenge "my self-conception" (82).

An ethic for a disenchanted world requires humility but also the exercise of imagination. Though not quite an imperative, imagination is an interior "injunction," a "weakly messianic" urge to exercise one's capacity to see things as otherwise than they are. Imagination energizes us with alternatives, with the power of the new and startling and wonderful. The burden of this task falls to imagination now that, unfortunately, the outside, everyday world—disenchanted of spirit—is utterly unable to inspire and enliven us. Imagination is a counter to "the pressure of reality," (28) a reality that is not only meaningless but banal, dull, and dreary. The "violence of the imagination" combats the "disenchantment of the everyday," a process which has "tranquillized" ordinary experience and given it an "anaemic pallor" (99). The power of imagination has propelled certain writers to devise literary strategies to combat the everyday: Wallace Stevens' "paring down of language . . . transfigures things and draws them into a queer poverty, an eerie plainness, so that we might stand transfixed by them and see them anew, renewed" (102); Henry Thoreau, Ralph Waldo Emerson, and Stanley Cavell also use words to fend off the "tragic drone" of a disenchanted existence.

The Valuable Failure of Romanticism

Ethical life in a disenchanted world requires a difficult combination of attitudes and affects: One must accept finitude but refuse to acquiesce to everydayness; one must maintain a somber sensibility but a lively imagination. Romanticism, specifically the Jena variety of Friedrich von Schlegel and the journal *Athenaum* (1798–1800), provides resources for such a subtle and precarious stance. True, this romanticism was "recklessly" naive, overflowing with hymns to art and the desire to reconcile philosophy and poetry via the great work (of literature but also of politics conceived on analogy to art). Its grandiose aspiration was to harmonize aspects of experience and make the world again whole. But, it is precisely the *failure* of the Jena project that can be put to the service of an ethics of finitude.

Romanticism can be recuperated for a disenchanted world, for it provides the best response to the problem of nihilism even as it fails to solve that problem. Naive romanticism fails; there is no reconciliation; there is no wholeness; art is not up to the task. But insofar as romanticism is self-conscious of its own naivete—and its preference for the form of the fragment is evidence of this self-consciousness—it is worthy of endorsement and supportive of the ethics of finitude. The fragment, the literary form proper to romanticism, is an ambiguous form. On the one hand, it "aims at completion: it should be an entirely autonomous artistic droplet"; on the other hand, its very form suggests its failure to achieve wholeness or self-sufficiency—it is, after all, just a fragment, always breaking off before the end (109). The literary fragment is a synecdoche of the self in a disenchanted world; it exhibits "the restless futural movement of worklessness" (125).

Such exhibitions are morally valuable because they render the self "perpetually dissatisfied, perpetually craving more and perpetually frustrated by their seeming superficiality and evanescence" (124). The superficiality is seeming because, rather than marking anything trivial, the frustrating fragment calls to mind the deep finitude of all things, including oneself. The fragment "perpetually postpones the possibility of finding a meaning to finitude" and thus "provokes us into an acceptance of finitude" (138). It exhibits and reinforces the romantic's self-conception as a being who is alone, cut, adrift from any whole and from others. Skepticism turns out to be the epistemological stance most appropriate to this condition, for the "tragic teaching" of skepticism is the same as the dark truth of the romantic fragment: "I cannot know the other" (135).

The ethic of finitude shares with unrecuperated romanticism the diagnosis of modernity as having meaning-deficit disorder, as " 'a leaden time,' " or " 'a time of dearth' " (98–99), as disenchanted:

the problem to which romanticism attempts to find a solution is that of how to reconcile the values of the Enlightenment—secularization, humanism, the libertarian and egalitarian values of republicanism, the primacy of reason, and the ubiquity of science—with the disenchantment of the world that those values seem to bring about. . . ."[58]

The Death of Nature

The death of God spelled the end of nature as the earthly residence of the divine. The animated creation gave way to a field of lifeless matter. Although such corpses can serve as objects of scientific interest, the laboratory reports, no matter how extensive or detailed, can offer nothing in the way of *ethical* guidance. Nature was once enchanted by the word of God and inscribed with hints of His divine purpose, but it is now disenchanted, stripped of spirit and vitality and no longer wholesome. And neither are we, socially and existentially speaking. Like the fragments the romantic writes, the modern, disenchanted subject is both definitionally incomplete and aware of this lack.[59] Yearning, yearning, and suffused with nostalgia for a lost cosmos, the modern self is a being with a hole in her center. And how could she be otherwise, inhabiting as she does a physical world that shares the same constitution (though not the same degree of self-consciousness of loss)?

The incomplete self living in a ransacked nature will, throughout her life, long for something she cannot be or have or know. We long intensely for more time—time to become whole, to recover the theft of meaning, to locate our coordinates in the world—but everywhere we look we find only the heartless fact of finitude. As the disenchantment of nature progresses, as more and more habitats and gardens and landscapes and bodies are rendered devoid of spirit, there are fewer and fewer places where one might find comforting hints of the possibility of everlasting life. The disenchantment of nature ultimately reveals one's own death to be a final, meaningless end—a complete break, the bitter end.

The existential injustice of this fact is, as Weber recognized, all too likely to produce resentment, and a deep resentment of life does not conduce to respect for the Other. And so the moral task confronting us is to devise ways to combat this resentment. An ethic centered around finitude pursues this task: it invents philosophical exercises to force confrontation with—and thus eventual acceptance of—the fact of one's own final demise. And it supports this difficult acknowledgement with exercises of the imagination, with the bleak hopefulness of an "imagination that goes on imagining in the knowledge that imagination has come to an end" (28). Acceptance of the finality of death induces humility—humility in the face

of the Other and humility with regard to the possibility of knowing anything with certainty. That is why, in a disenchanted world, skepticism as-
cends to the level of a cardinal virtue. Only a perpetually vigilant skepticism can overcome the presumption that one can know the Other; only
an unrelenting skepticism can compete with the intense nostalgia for
wholeness that otherwise leads to a life of illusion, to "the deepest naivete
of romanticism, namely its aestheticization of politics"(131). To "aesthet-
icize" the world is to succumb to the arrogant presumption that it is an
intelligible whole. It is " 'to fall in love with the world' " (133). And, in
a disenchanted world, such love can be only a kind of necrophilia.

Critchley's story emphasizes the existential dangers provoked by the
eclipse of God and the reign of disenchantment—not simply meaninglessness but nihilism, and the arrogant failure to acknowledge the radical
alterity of each self. His tale counsels humility as the best way to ward off
these dangers, a humility fostered by keeping one's attention trained on
the inevitability and finality of one's own death. Temporality is very difficult for humans to bear without resentment, so difficult that nihilism—
the refusal to take up the Weberian burden of meaning-making—looms
large. Kafka's story, "Give it Up!" can be read as symbolizing this refusal,
which emerges from an acute anxiety about time:

> It was very early in the morning, the streets clean and deserted, I was on my
> way to the station. As I compared the tower clock with my watch I realized it
> was much later than I had thought and that I had to hurry; the shock of this
> discovery made me feel uncertain of the way, I wasn't very well acquainted with
> the town yet; fortunately, there was a policeman at hand, I ran to him and
> breathlessly asked him the way. He smiled and said: "You asking me the way?"
> "Yes," I said, "since I can't find it myself." "Give it up! Give it up!" said he,
> and turned with a sudden jerk, like someone who wants to be alone with his
> laughter.[60]

Critchley's faith is that humility will issue in generosity. This link is, of
course, a contingent and unstable one. One could, for example, point to
situations where humility does not foster generosity or where generosity
emerges from joyful self-affirmation rather than from a self-consciousness
of mortality. Nevertheless, every ethic relies on some such tenuous, contingent linkage; no ethical theory can guarantee its desired outcome, not
even one like Kant's that purports to include a moral imperative.

Critchley sees a need to supplement humility with acts of imagination
and draws on the Jena romantics to do so. Why is there need for a supplement? He doesn't quite say, but perhaps he senses that humility—with its
sobering, depressing-of-affect effect—is unable to generate the motiva-

tional force necessary to induce generous concern for others. Indeed, a
large quantity of energy would have to be present in order to make finite
selves spend some of their limited resources, to make them give away
something of themselves to other beings. Generosity is the *active dispens-
ing of oneself*. To think this way about ethics, that is, to focus on its aesthetic-affective dimensions, is thus to ask: Under what circumstances can
such magnanimous sentiment or fullness of will arise? From what internal
and external sources can such energy be generated, borrowed, captured,
or redeployed? I pursue these questions actively in chapter 7.

Finally, Critchley shows how the narrative of disenchantment figures
the everyday world as banal. Ordinary experience labors under the burden
of passivity, enervation, and dullness. This is because, though humans still
have imagination, the nonhuman world has had all life stolen from under
it. Special effort, a whole literary-ethical regimen, is needed to infuse everyday objects artificially with energy or force. The startling austerity of
Stevens's poetry, the intricate puns of Thoreau, the paradoxical play of
Emerson's essays, the dense circularity of Cavell's prose are all needed to
animate or vitalize ordinary things. Only then is it possible for nonhuman
things to appear as active, as acting upon us. And even then, it is just a
useful appearance. In short, in a world experienced as disenchanted, humanity figures as the primary, if not the sole, locus of agency and vitality.

That this is itself an arrogant conceit is not acknowledged by Critchley.
But other griots of disenchantment do take note of it. Martin Heidegger
and his deep ecology heirs, for example, offer trenchant criticisms of the
"subjectivism" of modernity, of its failure to give nonhuman things their
due respect. They do this even as their disenchantment tales assign to those
things the status of victims of grand theft who have been stripped of their
capacities and powers.

"Toward an Enchanted Materialism"

But what if, despite what Weber, Blumenberg, and Critchley say, the world
is not disenchanted, that is, not populated by dead matter and fragmented
selves? What kind of ethical dangers, themes, and projects might then
come to the fore? What if nature consisted, as Epicurus and Lucretius told
that it did, of tiny but active, alert, and highly mobile particles called
"primordia," which combine and recombine with each other as their
shapes and textures allowed? Primordia (atoms) from which barbed hooks
protruded would regularly link up with primordia with irregularly shaped
and soft surfaces; primordia with smoother and harder surfaces would
enter into affiliations less often and for shorter durations. According to
this materialism, things "endure with body unharmed, until there meets

them a force proved strong enough to overcome the texture of each" (I, 225).[61]

For the Epicureans, all varieties of primordia are too fine and subtle to see, and yet everything that exists is made up of them and them alone— there is only matter (primordia and its permutations) and void (utterly empty space). With unfathomable minuteness and speed, the indivisible matter-bits travel "downwards straight through the void by their own weight," and yet "*at times quite undetermined and at undetermined spots they push a little from their path:* yet only just so much as you could call a change of trend. [For if they did not] . . . swerve, all things would fall downwards through the deep void like drops of rain, nor could collision come to be, nor a blow brought to pass for the primordia: so nature would never have brought anything into existence" (II, 216).

A certain willfulness or at least quirkiness and mobility—the "swerve"—is located at the very heart of matter, and thus is dispersed throughout the universe as an attribute of all things, human or otherwise. This swerve does not appear as a moral flaw or a sign of the sinful rebelliousness of humans. For the nature in which primordia move about and form alliances is not a divinely inspired nature. As Lucretius puts it:

> [N]ot by design did the primordia of things place themselves each in their order with foreseeing mind, nor indeed did they make compact what movements each should start. But because many of them, shifting in many ways throughout the world, are harried and buffeted by blows from limitless time, by trying movements and unions of every kind, at last they fall into such dispositions as those, whereby our world of things is created and holds together (I, 1021).

Primordia are not animate with divine spirit, and yet they are quite animated—this matter is not dead at all. The Epicureans described an enchanting world in which there was no divine purpose, meaning, or command.

What do thinking entities, particularly humans, look like within this (meta)physics? They appear as composite entities composed of a particularly wide and rich variety of primordia. They too are nothing but matter, but matter is, remember, quite an amazing and vibrant thing. The set of capacities and experiences generally referred to as mind too is material. Again, Lucretius: "For when it is seen to push on the limbs, to pluck the body from sleep, to change the countenance, and to guide and turn the whole man—none of which things we see can come to pass without touch, nor touch in its turn without body—must we not allow that mind . . . [too is] formed of bodily nature" (III, 161)? Mind is a collection of particles that are small, even by the minuscule standards of primordia, and hence exceedingly light. So fragile are these particles that if they are "robbed" of their "shelter" in the larger human body, that is, driven from the primordia-set that constitutes that body, they "would not only be unable to last on through all time, but could not hold together even for a moment" (III, 603).

Because of the ceaseless movement of the primordia and because of their swerving, the universe consists of one big interactive hubbub. The hubbub is not chaotic, however, for, as Blumenberg noted, the texture and shape of the primordia put limits on how they can join with each other. But join up and interact they do, as is to be expected when complementary particles bump into each other. Anything large enough to be sensed by ears, eyes, nose, skin, tongue is thus a composite entity, a hybrid, a mingling of many different kinds of primordia. Moreover, the fact that human beings exhibit, relative to other entities, a high degree of capacities and powers, suggests that they are constituted by a particularly diverse mix of primordia. And within Epicurean physics, the more diverse the better:

> It is right to have this truth . . . surely sealed and to keep it stored in your remembering mind, that there is not one of all the things, whose nature is seen before our face, which is built of one kind of primordia, nor anything which is not created of well-mingled seed. And whatever possesses within it more forces and powers, it thus shows that there are in it most kinds of primordia and diverse shapes (II, 581).

If the primordia themselves, apart from the conglomerations they form, are too small and too fast to be perceived by the senses, how does one know they are there?[62] The Epicureans offer, first, a kind of transcendental argument for their existence. It is an obvious, observable fact that there are changes in quality in a composite entity; this means that "when the composite bodies are dissolved, there must needs be a permanent something . . . left behind, which makes change possible."[63] In addition, the Epicureans offer an argument by analogy to the macro-perceptible world. Just as "the ring on the finger becomes thin beneath by wearing, the fall of dripping water hollows the stone," so too "what particles leave them at each moment, the envious nature of our sight has shut us out from seeing . . . (I, 311)."[64] We clearly have different sensual responses to different objects of taste, touch, etc., and the existence of differently shaped primordia can account for these different affects: "those things which can touch the senses pleasantly are made of smooth and round bodies, but . . . things which seem to be bitter and harsh, . . . are held bound together with particles more hooked, and for this cause are wont to tear a way into our senses . . . (II, 398).

Within a world of animate primordia continually entering into particleular proximity with each other, within a world where objects are macrolevel assemblages of billions of invisible primordia, within a world where mind is a form of body, but a form made up of particles so fine and fragile that their survival requires the larger composite body as a protective shell—in *this* world, thinking, like sensing, is a matter of perception. Some of the assemblages too minute and fleeting for our nose, eyes, and ears to sense are nevertheless "perceptible" by the more delicate and subtle receptors of the mind's matter. Note, however, that the mind perceives according to exactly the same mechanism as do smell, sight, and hearing. In order to understand this, it is necessary to introduce the concept of "simulacra."

Simulacra are the "films" that emanate from all composites; they are made up of the primordia that swerve off from the assemblage that they had formed. At any given moment, many primordia, of course, remain behind, and the object appears to remain intact. What we are seeing, however, is not the object itself but rather the image of it as expressed by the fleeing primordia, who retain a semblance of their space coordinates vis-à-vis each other:

> There are what we call simulacra of things, which, like films stripped from the outermost body of things, fly forward and backward through the air. . . . [We name these] films or even rind, because the image bears an appearance and form like to that, whatever it be, from whose body it appears to be shed, ere it wanders abroad (IV, 45).

If these simulacra are made up of sufficiently large particles, they form films whose smooth surfaces we receive with pleasure or whose hooked-and-barbed texture we receive with pain. But some simulacra contain particles that are "too fine" to touch our senses, though not so fine that they can't be received by the more delicately woven mind. When the mind receives these hyperfine films, thoughts are produced. Thoughts are the kind of sensations that happens in the (matter that is) mind. Here is how Lucretius describes the operation of these superfine thought-films: They

> wander about in many ways in all directions on every side, fine images, which easily become linked with one another in the air, when they come across one another's path, like spider's web and gold leaf. For indeed these simulacra are far finer in their texture than those which fill the eyes and arouse sight, since they pierce through the pores of the body and awake the fine nature of the mind within, and arouse its sensation (IV, 724).

Anything we know, then, is the result of perception. Perception consists in the crash-mixing of (1) bits of free-floating primordia and (2) the primordia (temporarily) congealing as our body, including our brain and mind. The crash issues in a new assemblage of primordia on the surface of our skin or our mind (which, for Lucretius, is located in the center of the chest or heart) and we receive the news of this new alliance as a pleasant or unpleasant texture, sight, sound, taste—or thought.

In this story of animate, swerving nature, death gets figured as neither meaningless nor total but rather as the corollary of the abundance of new primordia-affiliates coming into being. Death is not devoid of meaning—for the Epicureans work hard not to project the hope or expectation of meaning into it in the first place. Death is the condition of life, and it is life that can be filled with meaning. "Not utterly then perish all things that are seen, since nature renews one thing from out of another, nor suffers anything to be begotten, unless she be requited by another's death" (I, 262). The "sum of things is ever being replenished, and mortals live one and all by give and take. Some races wax and others wane, and in a short space the tribes of living things are changed, and like runners hand on the torch of life" (II, 77). One's own death is something to delay until the time has come; but it does not "destroy things as to put an end to the bodies of matter, but only scatters their union" (II, 1,002).

Nanotechnology

One way to call into question the diagnosis of disenchantment is to recall alternative stories about the nature of things. The Epicurean (meta)physics, for example, reminds that there are ways of picturing the world that do not presuppose an originary loss or expulsion from a beautiful cosmos. Indeed, acquaintance with this pagan imaginary reveals just how much the story of Eden stands in the background of the disenchantment tale. I do not, of course, recommend taking Epicureanism just as it was in ancient times, but it can be adjusted to contemporary circumstances, just as Christianity and secularism have been. It is atomism's potential relationship to modern enchantment that moves me.

Another way to loosen the hold of the disenchantment tale, perhaps opened by the first strategy, is to keep an eye out for contemporary practices and experiences that are anomalous within a world understood to be wonder-disabled. In other words, to foreground cultural sites that ought not to exist, or ought not to exist in the way that they do, within a disenchanted world. In chapters 2 and 3, I identify several such sites of enchantment—animals who display powers previously thought to be reserved for humans alone; the captivating dimension of human-electronic interfaces; the emergence of surprising and beautiful ideas and eventually social movements amidst the enormity of human stupidity, conformity, and cruelty. Now, I point to what might constitute another site of enchantment: nanotechnology.

The *rerum natura* of the Epicureans is a picture that shares some remarkable resemblances to the world envisioned by late twentieth-century practitioners of nanotechnology. *Nano* means one-billionth; a nanometer is the scale of measurement appropriate to molecules; a molecule is a collection of atoms "bound together by their mutual interactions for long enough to be observed as an entity."[65] The DNA molecule, for example, is about 2.3 nanometers wide. (The smallest thing that it is possible to observe with a light microscope measures about 120 nanometers.) Until recently, then, nano-things went about their business below the purview of the senses.

Nanotechnology is, according to B. C. Crandall, the "art and science of building complex, practical devices with atomic precision. [It applies] . . . the techniques of engineering to the knowledge generated by the sciences that study molecular structures."[66] Nanotechnology seeks to "learn to manipulate matter as finely as the DNA and RNA molecules that encode our own material structures." Nanotechnologists, for example, are working to replicate the minuscule molecule-assemblers in the human body called *ribosomes*. Ribosomes, themselves molecular assemblages, "assemble proteins, which make up almost all living tissue" from other, free-floating molecules called *amino acids*. Nanotechnology is more ambitious than genetic engineering: "While ribosomes and other naturally evolved mechanisms of protein formation are today exploited by recombinate DNA technology and genetic engineering, the goal of molecular nanotechnology is the construction of *general purpose assemblers* able to build molecular structures with any conceivable configuration."[67]

If they pulled that one off, it would be possible to design new, self-generating, and evolving forms of matter. It would also mean that humans would be able to arrange existing forms of matter *all the way down* (i.e., to engage in fabrication at the atomic level). A variety of lucrative applications of nanotechnology, for example, permanently blond hair, are anticipated to emerge within the next three decades. Here is how the hair color change would work:

> [a] nanomachine—little more than a carefully designed molecule—[would be injected into the bloodstream and] circulate . . . until it finds itself in a hair follicle in the scalp. Then it inserts itself into one of the follicles' melanocytes, the cells . . . that color the hair, where it benignly but persistently regulates the production or delivery of the pigment melanin. . . . [In short,] a brunette could . . . become a blond from the inside out.[68]

Other applications include temperature-sensitive cloth that changes the tightness of the weave, depending on the ambient temperature; new techniques for terrorism and assassination, such as food that, once swallowed, turns into razor blades; and self-cleaning bathtubs that are smooth at a molecular scale so that dirt cannot stick. There already exists an "in-vivo nanoscope," a submicroscopic threadlike sensor small enough to enter the immune system T cell of a pregnant mouse's embryo. The tip of this thread "left no wound when it withdrew, for its surface carried the same phospholipid pattern as the membrane of the cell. . . . [T]he thread is accepted by the membrane in the same way that the membrane accepts large proteins that also cross it in their role as molecular pumps."[69] In July 1999, a research team from Hewlett-Packard Company announced that it had "fashioned simple computing components no thicker than a single molecule," in which chemical processes rather than light were used to make the on-off switch of a computer circuit. Ultimately, such technology "could create a new class of 'Fantastic Voyage'–style machines, like sensors traveling within a person's bloodstream, issuing alerts if health problems are encountered."[70]

Nanotechnology, like ancient atomism, invokes a particular image of how the world is structured at the most fundamental (i.e., atomic or primordial) level. Nanotechnologists have a nature-picture or (meta)physics, one that shares much with the Epicureans. Here's how nanoscientist Crandall describes it:

> In watery solutions, such as those found in the interior of most plants and animals, the general jostling caused by thermal excitation bumps protein-sized molecules into each other from all angles very rapidly. This bumbling, stumbling dance allows molecules to explore all possible "mating" configurations with the other molecules in their local environment. By variously constraining and controlling the chaos of such wild interactions, biological systems generate the event we call life. And it is exactly this mechanism of molecular *self-assembly* that may lead to the construction of complex structures designed by human engineers.[71]

Crandall's image of awkward dancers (teen molecules at their first rave?) resonates with Epicurus's vision of

> primary particles . . . in continual motion through all eternity. Some of them rebound at a considerable distance from each other, while others merely oscillate in one place when they chance to have got entangled or to be enclosed by a mass of other particles shaped for entangling.[72]

Crandall and Epicurus together call to mind the Deleuzean claim that if one is to become otherwise than one is, one must place oneself in "molecular proximity" to alien bodies. One might, for example, try to explore one's nonhuman animality by experimenting with dogginess. Recall that, for Deleuze and Guattari, becoming a dog is not merely a matter of imitation, but rather of making "your organism enter into composition with *something else* in such a way that the particles emitted from the aggregate thus composed will be canine as a function of the relation of movement and rest, or of molecular proximity, into which they enter."[73]

Ethics and Animate Matter

At various points in their stories, Weber, Blumenberg, and Critchley express concern over what each identifies as an ethical danger intrinsic to the disenchanted world. Weber worried about the emergence of a debilitating sense of meaninglessness, Blumenberg about nostalgia for religious forms that would oppress selves and impede reason, and Critchley about the nihilism that Weber glimpsed and the arrogance that Blumenberg encouraged. So what kind of ethical project emerges from a (meta)physical imaginary of animate matter, as distilled from the writings of Epicurus, Lucretius, nanotechnology, and Deleuze? That is a difficult question, both because there are important differences among Epicurean, nanotechnological, and Deleuzean atomisms and because the relationship between a (meta)physics and an ethics is unavoidably somewhat diffuse. As Stephen White notes, an ontological imaginary does not "determine categorically" a specific set of ethical judgments, but rather "helps engender certain dispositions toward ethical-political life that alter the affective and cognitive direction one takes into specific issues."[74] The comments about the content and sensibility of an ethics of enchanted materialism that follow should be read with these caveats in mind.

The Epicureans are explicit about the link between their atomism and their ethical project, and so I begin by drawing on them. A life of *ataxary* (blessedness, contentment, tranquility) entails for them the following: (1) the prudent pursuit of pleasant experiences ("every pleasure, because it is naturally akin to us, is good, but not every pleasure is fit to be chosen"[75]); (2) a simple lifestyle, for minimal reliance upon possessions allows one "to be unafraid of fortune"[76]; (3) a cultivated capacity to wonder at the invisible complexity of the most ordinary, everyday things, for such wonder is part of a life of contentment even as it helps compensate for life's difficulties; (4) the exercise of one's (circumscribed) freedom, for while one does possess "power in determining events," this power always competes with the forces of natural law, chance, and the swerves of all other primordia-assemblages; (5) the refusal to dread death, in part through an understanding of it as a transition to other matter-formations.[77]

For the Epicureans, there is not much ethical need to reinvigorate ordinary experience, for all material things, natural and artifactual, already engage in a fascinating array of lively and motile morphings. Neither is it necessary to place finitude at the center of ethical reflection, for not dearth but abundance is painted into the material world. Likewise, there is no emphasis on the need to acknowledge the necessary failure of attempts to know an Other, for to insist upon the primordially hybridized nature of every thing, in particular the human thing, is to emphasize the interconnectedness of all things across large and notable differences. In Epicurean materialism, everything is, more or less, made of the same stuff, and although the arrangement of that stuff counts a lot, there really is no such thing as "radical alterity." Rather, there are real differences that can take the form of painful disparities, but these do not have the character of an abyss. The negotiation of significant differences between human beings is more likely when all the parties involved have overcome, in one way or another, their resentment against the contingency of being. And so, more than confronting the bitter end that is death and the unbridgeable chasm that is the Other, the ethical task is to en-joy life with discipline, to receive it with wonder and to add, by one's actions, to its stock of joy. This might sometimes include moments in which one "falls in love" with the world, for here enchantment is more ethically valuable than skepticism.

I draw more selectively from nanotechnology for ethical inspiration, for it has at its disposal the technical means to do widespread harm, means that ancient atomism lacked. Nanotechnology arouses enthusiasm for both the wondrous complexity of molecular goings-on and for the wonderful (and potentially deadly) power of science. Both molecules and laboratories are indeed marvels. Both capture attention and engage affect, but they do not provoke the same level of ethical concern. The first marvel is morally untroubling—to attend to molecular complexity may have little effect on ethical sensibility or, if I am right, it may provoke the joyful affect from which ethical generosity might emerge. The second marvel contains many dangers, including the emergence of nanowarfare and edible razor blades; intensification of the injustices of class, gender, or global inequalities (some people get nanomedicine and some do not, some control the direction of nanoresearch and others bear the brunt of its side effects), and the inadvertent creation or unleashing of viral compounds deadly to humanity or other life forms. In short, the enthusiasm generated by nanotechnology can foster the quest to master nature and the idea that human life is the only one that counts.

I endorse nanotechnology for the wonder at matter that it provokes, as well as for the new opportunities for creative human intervention into matter it creates. I find nothing, in principle, objectionable about attempts to alter the micromaterial world to render human life healthier or less burdensome or even more beautiful. But, caution and reservation are needed here because of the complex interdependence of all things. I draw a distinction, then, between the necessary and valuable project of creative intervention and the quest to master a world conceived as raw material for human use. Nanotechnology requires collectively organized vigilance to identify and contest instances where the former slips into the latter. This critical stance is rare in reports about nanotechnology that, too often, are unreservedly enthusiastic; it is as if the joyful affect generated by wonderful matter works to conceal the dangers of wonderful science. During their foray into molecular wonder, Deleuze and Guattari are more alert to its ethical dangers. As noted in chapter 2, they warn those who would pursue BwO to be cautious, to go slow, to check to see what effects are being produced, to think about them, to respond to them, and then to redesign the experiment. Refuse the temptation to de-organ-ize with abandon; remember the "rule immanent to experimentation: injections of caution."[78]

Perhaps what distinguishes Lucretius and Deleuze and Guattari here from contemporary nanotechnologists is the fact that they understand their atomism as a (meta)physics more than a physics, as an imaginative picture more than an empirical claim or even an ontological position. As I am using the term, a *(meta)physics* is a set of aesthetic images depicting the stuff of which all things are made and speculating about how that matter is arranged or is liable to arrangement. Different (meta)physics vary in their explicitness, their artfulness, and their wildness or degree of divergence from culturally dominant icons, graphics, and banners. But they are generally displayed for an expressly ethical purpose, presented in the hope that we will invest our own imaginations in them and thus be more susceptible to the ethical project of the artist. My alter-tale of enchantment pays special attention to (meta)physics for this reason.

Why put the "meta" in parentheses rather than speak simply of a physics? Because I am ambivalent about the "over" or "above and beyond" connotations of meta, as in a Kantian metaphysics of the supersensible. Etymology does seem to warrant the thesis that meta can also mean "that which bridges" or "the relational transition point"—in which case, (meta-)physics could describe a system of relations between (rather than beyond) molecular bodies. There is, however, also a bit of Kant's meta that I wish to retain. I like its utopian gesture, aura, or scent, that is, its willingness to venture above and beyond, onto the plain of virtual things and not-yet-realized possibilities. Such a willingness is, I think, necessary to the development of a sense of wonder, to the project of cultivating what Brian Massumi describes as "side-perception."[79]

Chapter 5 examines more carefully the role of complexity in an enchanted materialism, and chapter 7 returns to the question of ethics and develops the tentative claims made above. For now, I shall let Crandall, in a rather reserved mood, offer this closing thought:

Are molecules sacred? If not, what is? . . . Perhaps life. But what is life other than temporarily existing molecular configurations with a . . . capacity to carry certain self-reproducing patterns of information. . . . All life . . . consists of an intricate molecular dance. . . . That these festivities give rise to ant colonies and peacocks, computers and geodes, . . . is both bizarre and wonderful. Perhaps molecules deserve our reverence and deep gratitude.[80]

5

Complexity and Enchantment

THERE IS A genre of environmentalist writing called *ecospirituality*, which tells of the waning of nature-as-sacred and the emergence of nature-as-resource-for-exploitation, and of how this shift in moral outlook issued in the ecologically disastrous practices and technologies of modernity.[1] As ecospiritualist Matthew Fox puts it, "[H]umankind has been involved in a gross desacralization of this planet, of the universe, and of our own souls for the last three hundred years. Here lies the origin of our ecological violence."[2] Ecospirituality links environmental pollution to moral decline, or the de-souling of ourselves, and seeks to recover a sense of the sacred. Its goal is to reenchant nature.

How does the ecospiritual project relate to my attempt to highlight the enchanting sites in contemporary culture? I have learned from ecospiritualism and from the mystical traditions it draws upon—about the contemplative life and other disciplines of the self; about the power of aesthetic experience; about the value of tacit knowledges, simplicity, and small acts of respect;[3] and about how the experience of enchantment can motor ethical and political change.[4] But I also think that ecospiritual discourse tends to overstate the flatness of a technologized nature—in order to show just how serious the ecological problem has become. And so a strange equivalence gets set up between environmentalist conviction and narrativistic despair: the more alarmed an author is about ecodecline, the more thoroughly nature is depicted as a disenchanted set of defeated and exhausted objects. How could such sickly objects inspire the kind of careful attentiveness that ecological living requires? There is, then, a self-defeating element within ecospiritual tales: they risk undermining the very sensitivity toward nature that they seek to revive. They imply that nature *is* dull and lifeless unless we experience it as infused by the love, will, or design of God.

My contention is that enchantment never really left the world but only changed its forms. I do not join the ranks of the reenchanters, not only because I fear that another story of a world in crisis might do more to undermine ecological concern than to raise awareness of ecological destruction, but also because I don't assume that only a sacralized nature is capable of inspiring wonder and concern. For that matter, why must nature be the exclusive source of enchantment? Can't—don't—numerous human artifacts also fascinate and inspire?

In this chapter, I pursue these questions by listening to three minority accounts of the physical world, none of which depicts it as devoid of or even low on enchantment, and all of which tame the urge to read telos into the world. Together, they support a way of life that is technologically engaged but not disenchanted, Green but not "arboreal."[5] Together, they evoke a nature that is neither the alienating place described by Critchley nor the purposive order of Paracelsus, the antisecularist, or the ecospiritualist. I draw upon these minor tales to develop my enchanted materialism, an onto-story of matter that is lively and wondrous but not necessarily part of a divine creation. Like the ecospiritualist, however, I too object to the treatment of nature as (what Heidegger termed) *standing reserve*, that is, an inert set of resources awaiting human deployment. The minor tales also introduce the idea that complexity—the intricacies and convolutions in nature and culture—today functions as a site of enchantment.

The first minor tale comes from Henry Thoreau. Thoreau can be read as an ecospiritualist, and indeed he does treat nature as a kind of spiritual tonic. But more interesting perhaps is the way that he includes artifacts within "the Wild" that enchants him. Indeed, on my reading, Thoreau is a master of the nature/culture finesse; the world he describes is full of admixtures of the raw and the cooked. Thus Thoreau anticipates our world, where such crossings proliferate, charm, and disturb. This is the modern world as described by Bruno Latour, author of the second minor tale. For Latour, the very categories "nature" and "culture" are becoming anachronistic, and he proposes instead the more textured image of a network. A network is an assemblage of all sorts of entities, including natural beings, man-made tools, derived theorems, protean urges, background climates, intentional designs, and geological accidents.[6] The third minor tale is a neo-Lucretian one, and it appears in the writings of one of the founders of chaos theory, Ilya Prigogine. Prigogine's kind of science does not disenchant the world but rather affirms the fabulous "diversity and natural becomings" of nonhuman things.[7] I use his account of physical systems at far-from-equilibrium states as another example of how the complexity of the material world can enchant. At the end of the chapter, I consider, via Kafka, the possibility that social forms of complexity—like bureaucracy—share this enchantment-power with their chemical and molecular counterparts.

Thoreau's Nature

Nature, as it appears in Thoreau's writings, is a tricky devil. Sometimes it is pastoral, lovely, and inspiring like Walden Pond; sometimes it is hostile, even horrifying, like Mount Ktaadn. But it is not only nature in the sense of an external force or object of experience that is tricky, nature as a concept or a Thoreauian term of art is also mobile, deceptive, and complex. Thoreau often invokes nature as the conceptual opposite of society, but he just as often finesses that distinction. He invokes the nature/culture dichotomy when he wants to appeal to a transcendental moral source—a "pure Nature"—that houses unfamiliar and thus countercultural moods, ideas, and practices. He finesses the divide when he wants to acknowledge the agency and creativity—the cultural activities—of animals and when he wants to emphasize the power of poetic idealizations to spur political and ethical reform.

Thoreau's invocations of the dichotomy are more overt, of course, than his finesse. He regularly asserts, for example, that society dulls, rusts, and domesticates while Nature provokes and invigorates. Take the following lines from "Walking":

> I wish to speak a word for Nature, for absolute freedom and wildness, as contrasted with a freedom and culture merely civil,—to regard man as an inhabitant, or a part and parcel of nature, rather than a member of society. I wish to make an extreme statement, if so I may make an emphatic one . . . [8]

To listen with manly ears is to hear of two radically separate spheres—a liberating nature and an enslaving culture. But to listen with small ears attuned to the complexity of syntax is to hear an admission that pure Nature is a poetic creation in a world where admixtures of the given and the made are, empirically speaking, the rule. "I *wish* to speak a word for Nature," that is, Thoreau dreams of a place absolutely untainted by convention, and so he inflects the outdoors as just such a source of inspiration. "I wish to *speak a word* for Nature," that is, Thoreau translates the complex world (with which we and our affects, projects, and effects are inextricably mixed) into the idea of pure nature, itself a hybrid of artistic imagination and lived experience. Thoreau says both that pure nature is morally superior to culture and that nature is not purely natural. He states the first claim loudly and insinuates the second quietly by employing the rhetorical equivalent of a card-game finesse.

Alongside Thoreau's "extreme statement" of the purity of nature, then, is a more subtle claim that Nature is no thing-in-itself but is his inflection of the outdoors, the result of his intensive engagements with a world that extends beyond his comprehension. Inflection is Stanley Cavell's term: The writer lets words "come to him from their own region, and then tak[es] that occasion for inflecting them one way instead of another then and there, or for refraining from them then and there; as one may inflect the earth toward beans instead of grass, or let it alone . . . "[9] Thoreau does not advertise his act of inflection, for, as a poet, he tries to "hit the nail on the head" without letting us "know the shape of his hammer."[10]

Thoreau gently acknowledges—he hints—that the nature from which he draws moral sustenance is at the same time an effect of a literary culture he employs.

Both Thoreau's invocation and his finesse are parts of an ethical strategy. And here he offers insight into the affective and sensory dimensions of moral conduct. Thoreau's double orientation is integral to his quest to cultivate a kind of sensibility, one subtle enough to discern the fascinating specificity of a thing. This sensibility, crafted by means of a special relationship to the wild and surprising elements in experience is, Thoreau believes, indispensable to *activate* his will to resist the lure of social conformity.[11] He will use the Wild to educate his sense-perception, and he will use the bodily excitement generated by sense to propel a life lived deliberately.

The Wild is one of Thoreau's key notions, but it is the exclusive property of neither natural nor cultural entities. It is lodged in a refined experience of all sorts of things. The Wild refers to the surprise element that lurks in every object of experience, however apparently familiar. Take, for example, his encounter with a flock of birds:

> My acquaintances, angels from the north. I had a vision thus prospectively of these birds as I stood in the swamps. I saw this familiar—too familiar fact at a different angle, and I was charmed and haunted by it. But I could only attain to be thrilled and enchanted, as by the sound of a strain of music dying away. I had seen into paradisaic regions, with their air and sky, and I was no longer wholly or merely a denizen of the vulgar earth. Yet had I hardly a foothold there. I was only sure that I was charmed, and no mistake.[12]

The pine grosbeaks of which Thoreau speaks stop him in his tracks and throw him into the virtual world that ordinarily hovers below the surface of the actual and thus below the threshold of routine perception.

Thoreau also stumbles into the virtual whirl at Ktaadn, a mountain that he describes as "vast, and drear, and inhuman, . . . something savage and awful, though beautiful. . . . Here was no man's garden, but the unhandselled globe. . . . Man was not to be associated with it."[13] Thoreau is disturbed and disoriented by the Wild of Ktaadn even as he is fascinated by it, and the effect is heightened by his writing about it. The Wild, as his experience of the mountain, compels him to question his identification of Earth with home and, by extension, his treatment of the body as the automatic or secure home of the self. Ordinary matter now appears marvelous to him, something whose very existence is inexplicable. Enchanted, he can now discern the awesome infra/intra/extra-human world of matter:

> I stand in awe of my body, this matter to which I am bound has become so strange to me. . . . What is this Titan that has possession of me? Talk of mysteries!—Think of our life in nature,—daily to be shown matter, to come into con-

tact with it,—rocks, trees, wind on our cheeks! the *solid* earth! the *actual* world! the *common sense! Contact! Contact!?*[14]

But, as I said, the Wild is not solely a property of natural or nonhuman matter. Thoreau fronts it as well in the railroad ("Though straight is wild in its accompaniments—all is raw edges"[15]); in the Greek language of the *Iliad* ("It is worth the expense of youthful days and costly hours if you learn only some words of an ancient language, which are raised out of the trivialness or the street, to be perpetual suggestions and provocations"[16]); in his own prose ("the volatile truth of our words should continually betray the inadequacy of the residual statement"[17]); and in his brain ("Nothing was ever so unfamiliar and startling to a man" as his "winged thoughts" that "are like birds, and will not be handled."[18]) Thoreau, you see, is as taken as Epicurus and Lucretius were with the fugitive thoughts that pass through our brains with extraordinary speed, sometimes reappearing to be saved in language and sometimes not.

Thoreau courts the Wild so that he might experience the charm/disruption that I call enchantment.[19] What is also interesting about Thoreau is the role that this wild enchantment plays in his project of self-fashioning. A particular conception of nature/culture is part of Thoreau's attempt to refine in himself a deliberate and vivid way of seeing, hearing, touching, smelling, and moving. Thoreau cultivates this sensibility via a series of techniques of the self or daily exercises and disciplines performed in conjunction with the Wild in nature/culture. He uses this hybrid creature-notion to induce in himself an aesthetic and libidinal attachment to the ethical principles of nonconformity, material simplicity, and ecological living. Enchantment is a state conducive to the formation of a discerning sensibility, and Thoreau believes sensibility to be an indispensable part of ethics. He shares in advance Michel Foucault's conviction that "there is . . . no moral conduct that does not [also] call for the forming of oneself as an ethical subject."[20]

Latour's Network

According to Latour, Thoreau's strategy of invoking the purity of Nature even as he deploys hybrids like the Wild is a typically modern strategy. Latour argues that to be modern is to define oneself as a purifier who, in contradistinction to confused premodern thinkers, is skilled in separating the natural from the cultural. And yet, says Latour, this very proficiency in purification has had the effect of accelerating the production of hybrids that refuse to fit either category. Thus, the very same people who excel at purification are also those most fluent in "translation," or the mixing of the natural and the cultural in such a way as to produce creatures and concepts that are neither. These mixtures abound in contemporary experience, says Latour, and they constitute the realm of the given, a realm that used to be occupied by a nature defined in contrast to an artifactual realm of culture.

Translation and purification are the twin procedures of modernity; but purified categories go hand and hand with the proliferation of admixtures. Indeed, the very demand for sharp distinctions between nature and culture relegates more and more things to the status of hybrid. Sometimes Latour speaks as if purification and translation are mutually constitutive, each producing raw material to be processed by the other,[21] but, more often, he suggests that purification is the cause and translation the effect. Here he endorses something like a theory of the productive power of prohibition: "[T]he more we forbid ourselves to conceive of hybrids, the more possible their interbreeding becomes."[22] To apply the pure categories of nature and culture is to find that pretty much everything contains elements of both; pretty much everything has a degree of "transcendence" or resistance to human design, as well as a degree of "immanence" or susceptibility to human design. The very practice of purification reveals that allegedly fixed objects—atoms, birds, trees, operas, nature, identities, culture, turbines, God—are strange and mobile complexes of the given and the made. Such hybrids, or what I call *crossings*, are products not amenable to the established categorical distinctions—as, for example, an animal that speaks a language or a machine with a mind of its own or a thinking born of what Deleuze and Guattari call "sense." The human immune system—with its internal swarm of cells who were once illegal micro-aliens but are now productive citizens regulating the flow of new immigration—is a good example of a crossing between human and nonhuman.[23] Such, then, is the world as induced or inflected by the moderns. By imagining the pure concepts of nature and culture, we actually produce a large number of objects, processes, experiences, and energies that are neither.

To be modern, continues Latour, is not only to purify and to create hybrids but also to celebrate the first activity and officially deny the second.[24] Indeed, the power of modernity as a political and conceptual regime relies on the relegation of hybridization to the status of an open secret. Moderns are smart enough to see that their categories are reductionist, but they are also instinctive enough to see the advantage in suppressing this knowledge. (Like Thoreau, the moderns try to hit the nail on the head without revealing the shape of the hammer.) There's cultural profit to be had in keeping translation in the shadow of purification, for then it is possible to trade on the hybridity of things, on their double character of immanence-transcendence.

For example, moderns can appeal to pure Nature in order to challenge oppressive political practices, but they can also invoke the historical specificity of conceptions of nature to contest intrusions upon individual, ethnic, or national autonomy. The same have-it-both-ways tactic is used with regard to the category of society. Say, you want to criticize the heteronuclear family—here you appeal to the immanence of ideals (i.e., their status as historical constructions). But, on another occasion, you might want to chasten excessive expectations for political reform or revolutionary change, and here you emphasize not the immanence of the cultural but its transcendent or iron-cage quality. The device of the "open secret" offers the moderns a very wide range of argumentative tactics. One can see how this has enabled the "critical spirit" or enthusiasm for unmasking, debunking, and denouncing.[25]

Latour shows how the practical and conceptual successes of modernity are linked to the way that it sanctions a kind of principled inconsistency. On some occasions, moderns foreground the autonomy of the moral self and revel in their dignity as free beings, but, on others, they foreground the fixity of nature and culture and take fatalistic comfort in that. To be modern, Latour says, is to deploy both kinds of arguments despite their mutual incompatibility:

> Solidly grounded in the transcendental certainty of nature's laws, the modern . . . can criticize and unveil . . . [but] the exclusive transcendence of a Nature that is not our doing, and the exclusive immanence of a Society that we create through and through, would nevertheless paralyze the moderns, who would appear too impotent in the face of things and too powerful within society. What an enormous advantage to be able to reverse the principles without even the appearance of contradiction! In spite of its transcendence, Nature remains mobilizable. . . . [And] . . . even though we construct Society . . . , it lasts, it surpasses us, it dominates us . . . [26]

In Latour's terms, it is Thoreau's very insistence on the radical difference between nature and culture that produces the Wildness that, as a crossing, fits neither. And this insistence is shared by all of us who are pulled by the image of ourselves as intellectually and practically superior to nonmodern peoples. Indeed, says Latour, the price we pay for the extraordinary flexibility of modern thinking is that we are unable to conceptualize ourselves in continuity with the premoderns.[27] Thus it is that modernity, an inconsistent and paradoxical combination of claims about nature and culture, passes itself off as the clean, enlightened alternative to a messy, primitivistic cosmology that confuses the natural with the cultural, mixes the animal with the human, mistakes the inanimate for the animate, and contaminates the moral with the prudential. Latour reminds us that modernity too is a kind of cosmology, even though its sense of itself as a radically new event and its recurrent suppression of this or that side of its own vision prevent it from acknowledging this fact. Hybridization must be kept secret and the hybrid life-forms that it produces must be left unregulated because, otherwise, they would draw modernity too close to a premodern animism that confused the dead with the live. To acknowledge modern hybridizing would call into question modernity's standing as the progressive triumph over an enchanted world.

Rejecting this modern conceit, Latour argues that the difference between modern and other collectives is only a matter of "lengthened networks." If modern critiques are more global, if modern self-consciousness is more explicit, if modern weapons are more destructive, if modern technology is more complex, it is only because of a quantitative difference in the "scope of mobilization." This bigger scope "is important, but it is hardly a reason to make such a great fuss."[28] Moreover, the idea of modernity as a radical break is a function not only of conceit but also of guilt. We are proud of our power but also dimly aware of the extraordinary crimes against nature and other cultures that it makes possible. This vague sense of guilt makes us long for punishment, *a punishment we self-inflict by means of the disenchantment tale*. We picture ourselves," according to Latour, as "thrust into a cold soulless cosmos, wandering on an inert planet in a world devoid of meaning . . . [and] subject to the absolute domination of a mechanized capitalism and a Kafkaesque bureaucracy."[29]

Latour rejects the disenchantment tale as a masochistic fantasy. For do not the magical and the fabulous positively abound in modernity? "How could we be capable of disenchanting the world, when every day our laboratories and our factories populate the world with hundreds of hybrids stranger than those of the day before?"[30] My stories of crossings in chapter 2 are riffs on the theme introduced here by Latour. For Paracelsus, magic was a means by which the elements of the world could be made to form new alliances. Magic broke down the usual structure of a thing and then reconfigured the newly released bits with each other or with the disaggregated fragments of other (former) wholes. The essence of such magic was mobility or the morphing transformations from one state, space, or form to another. Such transits are precisely what modern hybridization is about (i.e., the experimental mixing of elements that, in the current order of things, it is important not to conjoin). Latour helps me to identify hybridization as a modern form of magic and a potential site of enchantment.

Latour himself responds to this potential with some trepidation. He identifies a thriving underground population of crossings—that is, frozen embryos, sensor-equipped robots, gene synthesizers—and suggests that they can inspire the kind of life-affirming wonder that we officially reserve for pure nature. But, he also fears that they are proliferating haphazardly and without enough thought given to their moral and political implications. It is time, says Latour, to replace the Thoreauian finesse with open acknowledgment in order to accept responsibility for our creations and for a world that exceeds the boundaries of nature/culture.[31]

One of the first steps here is to develop a better vocabulary for talking about the multispecied residents of nonmodernity, a language comparable in sophistication to that developed to express the modern ideal of the self (e.g., "the free agent, the citizen builder of the Leviathan, the . . . human person, the other of a relationship, consciousness, the cogito, the hermeneut, the inner self, the thee and thou of dialogue, presence to oneself, intersubjectivity."). Like Donna Haraway's cyborg[32] or Gilles Deleuze's assemblages, Latour attempts to develop a language for those things, among them humans, that are more social and fabricated than the hard data of nature, but more independent and resistant than social constructions:

> The human is not a constitutional pole to be opposed to that of the nonhuman. . . . The expression "anthropomorphic" considerably underestimates our humanity. We should be talking about morphism. Morphism is the place where technomorphisms, zoomorphisms, phusimorphisms, ideomorphisms, theomorphisms, sociomorphisms, psychomorphisms, all come together. Their alliances and their exchanges, taken together, are what define the anthropos. A weaver of morphisms—isn't that enough of a definition?[33]

I agree with Latour that there are good reasons to subject the production of biotechnological and other hybrids to more deliberation and to make more explicit the ethical ramifications of these new entities and becomings. It also makes sense to develop a vocabulary for thinking about the internal and external crossings that we encounter and join, as long, that is, as these projects take care not to dampen the capacity to discern the incredible and unpredictable morphings happening around us. For these complex transits harbor, as did Thoreau's pine grosbeaks, the power to inspire and enchant the humans who engage them. The experience of enchantment is, Thoreau and I agree, an essential component of an ethical, ecologically aware life. In the mood of enchantment, we sense that "we" are always mixed up with "it," and "it" shares in some of the agency we officially ascribe only to ourselves. For a fuller picture of this nonhuman kind of agency, I turn to the third minor tale, a neo-Lucretian physics.

The Return of the Swerve

According to the Epicureans, matter falls endlessly through the void, but every now and then, without warning, at no regular interval of time or space, these bits swerve from their downward path, bump into others, and so form the assemblages that make up the physical world as we know it. These assemblages are us and the things around us. Michel Serres describes the *clinamen*, or swerve, as a declination from the plane of a surface or lamina: "In nature, living beings are born from flows. And these flows are laminar, their laminae parallel to one another; the declination is the tiniest angle necessary and sufficient to produce turbulence."[34] The declination: as in declining an invitation. This declining is accompanied by no explanation or reason; it is, put on another register, the decline of Herman Melville's Bartleby the Scrivener who simply "prefers not to." The primordia simply, arbitrarily, but politely—they take the minimum angle necessary to veer away—prefer not to go with the flow.

Lucretius's idea of a primordial declination speaks to our intuitive sense that the world is open-ended, that the future is not determined until the moment of its arrival, that chance is in the nature of things. Our equally intuitive sense that things are ordered, that they repeat more or less familiar patterns, that matter arranges itself and lends itself to arrangement, is also given expression by Lucretian physics in the idea that the shape and texture of the different primordia limit the kinds of associations likely to occur and stabilize many that do occur. (This is what Blumenberg described as the "reserve of teleology" within Epicureanism.) The collisions of primordia result in a more or less reliable set of natural entities because, for example, S-shaped primordia will most readily combine with those having curvilinear surfaces, primordia with left-handed hooks tend to join those with right-handed ones, and so forth. So there are wood, cats, toenails, and blades of grass but not unicorns, flying toes, hairy rocks, and chunks of smoke. I say a more or less reliable, rather than a fixed set, because the swerve means that it is possible, under just the right conditions and just the right combination of angles of declination, that some collisions will result in unlikely associations and novel alliances—out of which is born something new under the sun.

What are we to make of this ancient atomism? Does its charming, even fanciful, quality disqualify it as a picture of nature worthy of modern consideration? Many natural scientists seem to think so. But Prigogine, who won the Nobel prize in chemistry in 1977, does not agree. According to him, Epicurean atomism continues to be worthy of attention. In particular, the notion of a swerve in matter is an idea to which, today, scientific inquiry into nonequilibrium systems has returned. Prigogine figures molecular systems as having an irreducible element of unpredictability—a capacity to surprise that no increase in knowledge and no improvement in measurement is likely to overcome. His aim is to examine experimentally, and describe systematically, the swerve in action: "We began with Epicurus and Lucretius, and their invention of the clinamen to permit the appearance of novelty. After twenty-five hundred years, we can at last give a precise physical meaning to this concept, which originates in instabilities identified by the modern theory of dynamical systems."[35]

Prigogine and his collaborator, Isabelle Stengers, focus on physical systems that are unstable or "far from equilibrium."[36] A system in equilibrium is such that its dynamics are maintained despite environmental fluctuations.[37] Far from equilibrium states, however, things get weird. Fluctuations stop being background noise, and the law of large numbers, by which fluctuations become statistically unimportant the larger and more diverse the system, no longer applies. This is because the molecules in the system start acting as "singularities" who move in exquisitely specific response to the tiniest shift in the parameters of their existence, as well as to each other. In other words, they stop being "hypnons" and become lively, "socially" interactive beings: "At equilibrium molecules behave as essentially independent entities; they ignore one another. We [could] . . . call them 'hypnons,' 'sleepwalkers'. . . . However, nonequilibrium wakes them up . . . "[38]

Far from equilibrium, a fluctuation can become a bifurcation point or site of a swerve, where the system spontaneously chooses a path that no scientist—herself a molecular system—can predict. In some chemical solutions, for example, there comes a moment where one of two new stable solutions will result, but no mathematical equation can predict which path the system will take.[39] In such cases, we "have to abandon the deterministic description associated with (classical) dynamics. The system 'chooses' . . . (and this) introduces an irreducible probabilistic element."[40]

Prigogine and Stengers identify classical dynamics with the disenchantment of nature and their own explorations with its enchantment. Classical dynamics presented "a silent world . . . a dead, passive nature, a nature that behaves as an automaton which, once programmed, continues to follow the rules inscribed in the program."[41] Their work instead engages that sector of the physical world where creativity and novelty abound and "where the possible is richer than the real."[42] One could say that, whereas the matter of classical dynamics practices what Deleuze called bare repetition, matter in far-from-equilibrium states participates in spiral repetition. Here's how Prigogine puts it: "Matter near equilibrium behaves in a 'repetitive' way. On the other hand, . . . far from equilibrium we may witness the appearance of . . . a mechanism of 'communication' among molecules."[43] Far from equilibrium, successive repetitions are not identical to each other because each is the unique response to a unique set of spatio-temporal events.

Lawful Nature as a Regulative Ideal

Classical dynamics provides the image of nature that Prigogine and Stengers contest. Dynamics treats nature as a series of points, with each point locally expressing a global law, each singularity functioning as a particular case of a universal structure. In other words, nature is approached as an integrable system, that is, one in which any given state can be translated into a set of differential equations, and any dynamics problem can be resolved, ideally, by integrating these equations to obtain the set of trajectories taken by the points of the system.[44] This integrable world has two defining characteristics: its trajectories are reversible and they are determinist.[45] They are reversible or indifferent to time because any possible evolution within the system is defined as equivalent to any other one—each is a particular expression of the universal laws of dynamics. They are determinist in the sense that once one knows (1) the laws governing the forces of interaction inside the system and (2) the initial conditions of the system, then one can predict all movements within the system. Of course, it is only in the closed system of the laboratory that initial conditions can be known, and many natural systems can be described only probabilistically. Practitioners of classical dynamics readily acknowledge these points but retain as a regulative ideal the notion of an integrable world. Matter is in principle determinate.[46]

Prigogine and Stengers take issue with even the regulative ideal of deterministic matter. They suggest that, for much of nature (i.e., systems far from equilibrium), determining initial conditions is not only impossible in practice, it is "unthinkable."[47] Whereas in stable systems, as the precision of one's account of initial conditions increases, so also does the accuracy of predictions about the trajectories in the system; in unstable systems, prediction requires infinite precision and only that will do.[48] Unstable systems do more than raise an epistemological issue, according to Prigogine and Stengers. They create a new way of relating to nature through physics:

> [T]the impossibility of conquering the indeterminacy essential to unstable dynamic systems is not [a] . . . discovery which only concerns the relation of our knowledge to the world. . . . It is not a question of recognizing that we are incapable of calculating . . . trajectories; rather, it is a question of realizing that the trajectory is not an adequate physical concept for these systems.[49]

Prigogine and Stengers skate just short of making claims about nature in itself. They do not quite say that matter is intrinsically indeterminate, only that matter is indeterminate for reasons not entirely reducible to correctable human error or to specifiable limitations of experimental control.

They do not quite say that classical dynamics gets nature wrong, only that a trajectory is not an adequate concept for some kinds of systems. Although these two kinds of points are very close, they are not the same. To maintain this tiny space is to conceive of science not as an outsider's discovery of nature but as a "dialogue" between human and nonhuman forms of material groupings. Prigogine and Stengers are best described as advocating a change in the style of engaging nature rather than as claiming to represent nature the way it is outside of our engagement with it.[50]

The Bifurcation Point as a Swerve

One can think of a bifurcation point as a singular point of transition, a point of no return. Prigogine and Stengers note how the existence of such points in life are well-known: " 'For example, the rock loosed by frost and balanced on a singular point of the mountain-side, the little spark which kindles the great forest, the little word which sets the world a fighting. . . .' "[51] Crossing a bifurcation point is a "stochastic process, such as the tossing of a coin."[52]

Bifurcation points, although an example of the work of chance in nature, also mark the transition to a new state of order. The unpredictability of matter does not necessarily imply an unintelligible world. For Epicurus and Lucretius, the finite number of primordial textures and shapes is what ensures regularity of natural forms, a regularity that paradoxically emerges from the swerve in matter. For Prigogine and Stengers, too, unstable systems produce their own kind of order. Order can emerge from a series of random events, as when "a few 'decisions' in an unstable situation might channel a system . . . toward a global structure.[53] Prigogine and Stengers cite a termite mound as an example of this peculiar kind of order. The mound is initiated by a series of random droppings but then takes on a highly structured form as a result. Termites wander around, and the spots at which each drops its lump of earth is undetermined or stochastic; however,

> in doing so they impregnate the lumps with a hormone that attracts other termites. . . [T]he initial "fluctuation" would be the slightly larger concentration of lumps . . . , which inevitably occurs at one time or another at some point in the area. The amplification of this event is produced by the increased density of termites in the region, attracted by the . . . hormone.[54]

The result is the structure called a termite mound.

Prigogine and Stengers offer a very interesting kind of materialism, one that is neither reductive nor mechanistic. Its emphasis on the complexity, vitality, and even agency of matter repels accusations of biological reductionism; its picture of matter is anything but mechanistic, insofar as that word evokes the image of a loud, hulking machine in monotonous motion. The nature they study surprises, disturbs, charms, and swerves. Echoing the Spinozist claim that we do not yet know what a body can do, Stengers says that "we do not know a priori what a chemical population can do, and we can no longer tell once and for all the difference between what we must take into account and what we can ignore."[55] Yet Prigogine also contends that, even in its most complex and indeterminate state, a physical system continues to possess a kind of intelligibility.[56] The far-from-equilibrium world, then, is neither the static order of classical dynamics nor some random state that is unrecognizable as a world—"a new formulation of the laws of nature is now possible . . . , a more acceptable description in which there is room for both the laws of nature and novelty and creativity."[57]

Social Complexity and Kafkaesque Enchantment

The mood that I call enchantment is provoked by a surprise, by an encounter with something that one did not expect. Surprise itself includes both a pleasant, charming feeling and a slightly off-putting sense of having been disrupted or tripped (up). In enchantment, these two are present in just the right measures so as to combine, fortuitously, in a way that engenders an energizing feeling of fullness or plenitude—a momentary return to childhood joie de vivre. Enchantment begins with the step-back immobilization of surprise but ends with a mobilizing rush as if an electric charge had coursed through space to you. In enchantment, a new circuit of intensities forms between material bodies.

Enchantment, then, is a precarious concatenation, it requires a delicate balance of forces, a set of fortuitous circumstances, and some practice in order to develop the somatic habits conducive to it. It is such a complicated assemblage that one wonders how it ever occurs. Yet it sometimes does. A similar unlikeliness characterizes any sensory state, for example, the act of sight or the event of a thought. Even a cursory examination of the physiology of each reveals it to be an enormously complex process: So vast is the web of interconnections! So specific is the particular constellation of events that must be in place! To study the mechanism of sight or thought is to render marvelous the fact that one sees and thinks at all.

This chapter has suggested that enchantment, as an uneasy combination of charm and disturbance, can issue from encounters with the Wild of Thoreau, or the hybrids of Latour's nonmodernity, or the swerving molecules described by Lucretius, Prigogine, and Stengers. Face to face with the vastness of macro- and micro-material complexity, the charm of wonder comingles with the discomfiting frustration of dealing with nonlinear events and dissipative structures resistant to understanding and prediction. The complexity of physical events is, as Prigogine's work reveals, both attractive and repellent. Attractive because it places my body among other natural bodies possessing a kind of agency or swervy vitality, and because it portrays the physical universe as a marvelous place that uncannily repeats the material liveliness of me and you. Repellent because this nonhuman complexity reduces the prospect of rendering nature safe for humans and confounds claims to the radical uniqueness of humans.

It seems to me that something akin to this alluring confusion also characterizes modern bureaucracies. Is it possible that maligned structures are also powerfully attractive to us, that bureaucratic entanglements are also sometimes occasions for enchantment? When enchanted, one is intensively engaged, and dealing with a bureaucracy might very well require high levels of attentiveness. Does this affective engagement have anything to do with the ethically energizing mood that I call enchantment?

Such a possibility is unlikely, according to the Weberian account of bureaucracy as a necessary evil. Bureaucracy, says Weber, is an impersonal form of authority with the potential to administer social needs fairly and impartially, but this very impersonality also alienates—its machinic quality dehumanizes even as it is an expression of human rationality. As the other to magical or charismatic modes of authority, bureaucracy cannot function as a source of enchantment, that is, as a provocation of the joyful recognition of one's profound attachment to life. It is, rather, an iron cage.

How might bureaucracy appear if one loosened this Weberian frame and stretched complexity theory to include man-made, macroscopic systems? Perhaps as a cage with a seductive aura. Bureaucracy would enclose and suppress, and, like Rotpeter's locker, propel the urge to break out, but it would also sometimes fascinate and lure. Both sets of effects would have the same source, the complexity of the structure. This conception of bureaucracy—as provoking both painful and pleasurable affect—is one that I find explored in Kafka's stories.

His stories, especially those with ostensibly political themes, such as *The Trial*, *The Castle*, and "In the Penal Colony," are more typically read as expressing a Weberian critique of bureaucracy. Indeed, the term *Kafkaesque* refers to the irrationality of official institutions and the intense frustration engendered by encounters with them. Bureaucracies define themselves as complex and dynamic machines devoted to efficiency, but their clients often experience an immobile and idiotic labyrinth. A minor official in *The Castle* describes this paradox:

And now I come to a peculiar characteristic of our administrative apparatus. Along with its precision it's extremely sensitive as well. When an affair has been weighed for a very long time, it may happen, . . . that suddenly in a flash the decision comes in some unforeseen place, that moreover, can't be found any longer later on, a decision that settles the matter, if in most cases justly, yet all the same arbitrarily. . . . Now as I said, it's just these decisions that are generally excellent. The only annoying thing about them . . . is that one learns too late about them and so in the meantime keeps on still passionately canvassing things that were decided long ago.[58]

The Castle overflows with ambiguously incompetent and definitively inaccessible bureaucrats, characters whom one meets again in real life at the Motor Vehicle or Social Security Administration or at the Department of Public Works. Take, for example, the elite official Klamm, who has been rarely, perhaps never actually, glimpsed, or the ominously inept "assistants" to the land surveyor who, in one scene, are indistinguishable from a pile of rags in the corner but who nevertheless function as efficacious agents when it comes to impeding each of K.'s attempts to be recognized as the town's land surveyor.

But I don't think that Kafka's stories are simply Kafkaesque, if that term refers only to the negative or unnerving effect of interacting with official complexes. His stories reveal bureaucratic entanglement to be both maddening *and* attractive. The characters are oppressed by the obscurity of power, but there is also something about this officialdom—some magnetic force—to which they find themselves inexplicably drawn. Kafka's stories might not be only critiques of bureaucratic rationality but also experimental forays into the ambiguous charm of institutional complexity. Kafka is politically incorrect enough to explore, or temperamentally perverse enough to assert, or existentially sensitive enough to discern, the wonder of the labyrinth. His stories do perform the anxiety and vertigo of a bureaucratic encounter, but they also enact its strange pleasure. They allow an underground and even shameful attraction to poke through the surface.

Another way to put this point is to say that the stories reveal what is uncanny about the experience of institutional complexity. Freud defined the uncanny as an essentially double feeling, where a sense of strangeness emerges simultaneously with a sense of familiarity. One recognizes something even though one does not quite remember having experienced it before.[59] Kafka's characters return again and again to the vicinity of the bureaucratic entities that vex, perplex, and torment them. They appear to derive some kind of physical relief, even pleasure, from this proximity. What is it about bureaucracy that draws them near? Kafka points to, by exaggerating, the unpredictability of bureaucratic decisions and their perverse eschewal of any direct path of action. Note here that unpredictability and indirection are the very same attributes of the molecular

systems that Prigogine studies. Perhaps, then, bureaucracy attracts humans because it mimics the complexity that marks the material world that
we live in—and that we are. The macro-molecular assemblage (bureaucracy) repeats the microscopic assemblage (a chemical population far-
from-equilibrium), and both repeat the structure of our own bodies. We
uncannily recognize our material selves in the disturbing complexity of
the institutional form.

Such is a theme of Kafka's "Great Wall of China." In that tale, no matter
how ridiculous, cryptic, or irrational its actions and decrees, the Empire
fascinates the villagers and attracts their acute devotion.[60] The Empire,
says the narrator, is "one of the most obscure of our institutions," and yet
"except for the nature gods and their ritual, . . . we think only about the
Emperor. But not about the present one, or rather we would think about
the present one if we knew who he was or knew anything definite about
him."[61] The obscure, unpredictable complexity of power is also the theme
of the following parable inserted into the story.

On his death bed, the Emperor instructs his messenger to inform a
humble villager of his final dying words. Despite vigorous effort, however,
the messenger cannot get past even the first circle of the court's groupies
and hangers-on:

> [But even] if he succeeded in that nothing would be gained; he must fight his
> way next down the stair; and if he succeeded in that nothing would be gained;
> the courts would still have to be crossed; and after the courts the second outer
> palace; and once more stairs and courts; and once more another palace; and so
> on for thousands of years; and if at last he should burst through the outermost
> gate—but never, never can that happen—the imperial capital would lie before
> him, the centre of the world, crammed to bursting with its own refuse.[62]

Never, never can the trajectory of the political order be discerned, says
Kafka. Never, never can the trajectory of systems of far-from-equilibrium
states be predicted, says Prigogine. And the never-never dimension of both
systems—their fractal complexity—holds us in its uncanny sway.

"The Great Wall of China" is compatible with a Weberian critique of
bureaucratic power. Because the villagers seem unaware of their alienation, a Foucaultian reading is also warranted—the villagers are so riddled
with biopower that they fail even to discern their subjugation. Also plausible is the Derridean reading of Kafka as marking the indeterminacy of
language and noting how language-users always already know this, adjust
to it, and exploit it when they are in a position to do so. The reading I
emphasize, however, understands the story as a statement of the magical,
magnetic attraction between human bodies and other complex assemblages, an attraction that derives from material affinities between them.
We recognize institutional complexity, if it is sufficiently labyrinthine, as

kin, which might be why we villagers feel an urge to throw our own movements, voices, and bodies into its fray.[63]

This same kind if abstruse but alluring complexity marks the bureaucratic language within Kafka's stories. Kafka is a master at parodying such speech. Note, in the following excerpts, the surfeit of qualifying terms and second-thought phrases, and how the quest for excruciatingly complete accuracy results in a failure to say anything at all:

> The wall was to be a protection for centuries, accordingly the most scrupulous care in the building . . . [was] indispensable. . . True, for the more purely manual tasks ignorant day laborers . . . could be employed; but for the supervision of even every four . . . laborers an expert . . . was required. . . . And such men were actually to be had, if not indeed so abundantly as the work . . . could have absorbed, yet in great numbers."[64]

Or:

> I guard against large generalisations. . . . Yet perhaps I may venture to assert on the basis of the many writings . . . I have read, as well as from my own observation—the building of the wall in particular . . . provided a man of sensibility with the opportunity of traversing the souls of almost all the provinces—on the basis of all this, then, perhaps I may venture to assert that the prevailing attitude to the Emperor shows persistently and universally something fundamentally in common with that of our village. Now I have no wish whatever to represent this attitude as a virtue; on the contrary. True, ... On the other hand, however. . . .[65]

Kafka's characters seem to thrive on such convolutions and near-nonsense, perhaps because they take pleasure and amusement in the ridiculous complexity of such writing, a complexity that mirrors that of the natural world. One can laugh at both, a laughter expressive of one's perverse attachment to a maddeningly complex social and natural existence. According to Max Brod, Kafka's friend and literary executor, when Kafka read the first pages of *The Trial* to friends, he laughed so much that at times he could not read any further. Deleuze and Guattari claim that

> only one thing really bothers Kafka and angers him, makes him indignant: when people treat him as . . . an author of solitude, of guilt, of an intimate misfortune. However, that's really Kafka's fault, since he held out that interpretation in order to anticipate the trap through his humor. There is a Kafka laughter, a very joyous laughter, that people usually understand poorly. . . . He is an author who laughs with a profound joy a *joie de vivre*, in spite of, or because of, his clownish declarations that he offers like a trap or a circus.[66]

Perhaps the following bureaucratic encounter in *The Castle* will call up such laughter in you. K. is a conscientious citizen, who has responded promptly to a letter requesting his services as official Land Surveyor. When he arrives in the village, no one expects him and the mayor says they have no need of a land surveyor. "But I'm Land Surveyor already," K. desperately insists, "here is Klamm's letter."[67] Unfortunately, the signature is illegible. But K. persists in his quest for the post. In the passage below, K. is trying to milk young Hans for information about Hans's mother, who might be able to influence her husband Brunswick, who, in turn, might be enlisted as an ally against the superintendent, who might be the one keeping K. from making contact with the crucial castle official. Hans is wary of strangers, and so K. tries to question him gingerly and inquires first about Hans's mother's health:

> Now he, K., had some medical knowledge, and, what was of still more value, experience in treating sick people. Many a case which the doctors had given up he had been able to cure. At home they had called him "The Bitter Herb" on account of his healing powers. In any case he would be able to give her good advice, for if only for Hans's sake he would be delighted to do it. At first Hans's eyes lit up at this offer, exciting K. to greater urgency, but . . . Hans replied . . . that no stranger was allowed to visit his mother, she had to be guarded so carefully; although that day K. had scarcely spoken to her she had had to stay for several days in bed, a thing indeed that often happened. But his father had then been very angry with K. and he would certainly never allow K. to come to the house; he had actually wanted to seek K. out at the time to punish him for his impudence, only Hans's mother had held him back. But in any case his mother never wanted to talk with anybody whatever, and her inquiry about K. was no exception . . . ; on the contrary, seeing he had been mentioned, she could have expressed the wish to see him, but she hadn't done so, and that had clearly make known her will. She only wanted to hear about K. but she did not want to speak to him. Besides it wasn't any real illness that she was suffering from, she knew quite well the cause of her state and often had actually indicated it; apparently it was the climate here that she could not stand, but all the same she would not leave the place, on account of her husband and children, besides, she was already better in health than she used to be.[68]

Already better! The contradictions, implausibilities, childish mendacity, and sheer silliness of this account breaks out within the very heart of its involuted complexity. For here, Kafka's prose—word and sentence combinations that make a claim, then take it back, then grant it with qualifications, then qualify the qualifications, then specify the conditions under which the claim is unaffirmable, then assert the unlikeliness of such conditions, then reassert the claim, and so on—mimics the complexity of the castle, which mimics that of ourselves, which mimics that of the macro- and micro-material worlds.

My experimentation with the idea of institutional complexity as a contemporary site of enchantment has focused on bureaucratic encounters as they occur in fiction, where no harm accrues to real people. I draw analogies from Kafka's fiction to my own bureaucratic encounters, which occur within in a political system that, in principle and sometimes in practice, holds bureaucracies to a standard of democratic accountability. When I refer to the frustrations of such encounters, I refer to minor indignities and inconveniences. Bureaucracies are, to be sure, also responsible for violent and profoundly unjust effects. What is more, these unjust effects can themselves provoke a kind of enchantment. For some people or for all people under some circumstances, there can be pleasure and fascination in participating in or observing violence and cruelty. One way to respond ethically to this possibility is to repudiate the mood of enchantment altogether, to devote oneself to its demystification and to its replacement with less morally ambivalent or rational states of mind. But is this the only way or even the most effective way to oppose or ward off cruelty and violence?

Another strategy is to strengthen the will to resist the enchantment of violence by feeding that will with the food of another kind of enchantment, the enchantment of the wondrous complexity of life. The idea here is to fight enchantment with enchantment, to weaken the appeal of violence by infusing oneself with the affective energy of a more life-affirming mood. The project is to cultivate a more generous disposition in oneself by drawing sustenance from the rich abundance of nature/culture.

As I suggest in chapter 4, the disenchantment tale tends to miss or dismiss the enchanting potential of material complexity, especially in its manmade forms. This is so, even though the disenchantment tale is itself a marvel of complexity. It is a multifaceted and grand narrative that offers an account of the key intellectual and material processes of modernity; a diagnosis of the political, ethical, and psychological dangers these entail; and a characterization of the natural world and the human relationship to it. I hear the complex grandness of the tale as an echo and implicit recognition of the complex interconnectedness of all matters—of the personal with the political, the dispositional with the rational, the aesthetic with the ethical, the conceptual with the material. The alter-tale of enchantment that I tell by way of Thoreau, Latour, Lucretius, Prigogine, Stengers, and Kafka also aspires to the status of grand narrative. All such tales are slightly mad, for it is crazy to think that any story could capture the complexity of relations among the beings and becomings in life. This delusion of grandeur is one way to acknowledge the networked quality of existence and of our profound attachment to it.

6

Commodity Fetishism and Commodity Enchantment

> A study of commodity culture always turns out to
> be an exploration of a fantastic realm in which
> things act, speak, rise, fall, fly, evolve. . . .
>   (*T. Richards*)[1]

Swinging Khakis

Picture a world where wondrous events compete with acts of cruelty and violence, where magical gestures occasionally displace instrumental reason, where molecular activity is both surprising and responsive to scientific investigation, where governments and economies are neither as competent as many hope nor as overwhelming as some fear, and where the social fabric is continually reassembling rather than progressively fragmenting. There, wonder and fascination cohabit with realism and fear; there, enchantment is a real possibility. Enchantment is a mood of lively and intense engagement with the world, and I have been thinking about how it plays into an ethical comportment of generosity toward others. Enchantment consists of a mixed bodily state of joy and disturbance, a transitory sensuous condition dense and intense enough to stop you in your tracks and toss you onto new terrain and to move you from the actual world to its virtual possibilities.

For me, the 1998 GAP ad "Khakis Swing" both induces and expresses this state of enchantment. American swing music from the 1930s and 1940s is, as a GAP executive says, "very energetic. Its ebullience calls you in from the next room."[2] The ad is set in a large space where about twenty young people in beige pants are dancing to Louis Prima's "Jump, Jive and Wail." At several points in the video, as the music continues uninterrupted, the camera freezes the image of the foreground dancer in midflight. Although everyone has stopped in their tracks, the vitality of the scene continues, for now it is the room that—thanks to the "stop and pan" camera technique—spins and swings. Then, after that frozen yet mobile moment, the organic connection between music and dance resumes. The ad first turns the dancers into statues, as if victims of the wrath or whimsy of an Olympian god. As such, they can be panned around, as one would video a sculpture garden. But then, again as in Greek mythology, the frozen beings reanimate. The ad suggests some irony on the part of the videographers, as if to issue a challenge: "You say these are mere pants! I'll show you *pants*!"[3]

I position this GAP ad, wherein the room and the khakis dance along with the human bodies in them, in a tradition of works of art that explore the phenomenon of animation—of dead things coming alive, of objects revealing a secret capacity for self-propulsion. Several of Kafka's stories, for example, depict the crossing from an inert thing to a thing that can exert itself. In "The Bucket Rider," a pail transports a cold man in search of coal:

> Seated on the bucket, my hands on the handle, the simplest kind of bridle, I propel myself with difficulty down the stairs, but once downstairs, my bucket ascends, superbly, superbly; camels humbly squatting on the ground do not rise with more dignity. . . . Through the hard-frozen streets we go at a regular canter; often I am upraised as high as the first storey of a house; never do I sink as low as the house doors.[4]

And, in "The Cares of a Family Man," Kafka's star-shaped spool for thread reveals an inner capacity for playfulness, not to mention speech: "Of course, you put no difficult questions to him, you treat him—he is so diminutive that you cannot help it—rather like a child. 'Well, what's your name?' you ask him. 'Odradek,' he says. 'And where do you live?' 'No fixed abode,' he says and laughs. . . ."[5]

As Freud points out in "The Uncanny" about Hoffmann's tales and as Bruno Bettelheim notes in his study of fairy tales, such animations can disturb as well as delight.[6] They disturb perhaps because they explore the possibility of the animateness of humans, nonhumans, and nonanimals alike. If the power to self-move, to laugh, or to dance adheres, albeit differentially, in all material things, then humans must reckon with a much larger population of entities worthy of ethical concern, and humanity faces the difficult prospect of moderating its claim to uniqueness. At the same time, animations can delight, perhaps for the same sensory reasons that a kaleidoscope does—metamorphoses of shape, color, size, and pattern capture the imagination. If things that we had previously considered to be but the passive context for our activity are themselves mobile, vital matter, then the world becomes so much more interesting.

Perhaps you will grant that, under the right circumstances, a fable by Kafka or Hoffmann or Grimm can enchant. Perhaps you will also grant that the plenitude of feeling evoked by the morphings that they describe can be cultivated into a disposition of presumptive generosity toward others. But, even if you go that far, the question remains whether such laudable effects can also issue from animations designed to make you purchase something. Can the enchanting potential of animation survive commercialization? Can advertisements qualify as sites of an ethically useful kind of enchantment? Even if they can, should we not seek our enchantments elsewhere?

There is no doubt that some kind of enchantment is the goal of advertising and that many people in rich societies are caught up with consuming. Popular and academic critics agree that consumption structures much in everyday life, including identities, aspirations and imaginations. One influential interpretation of this social fact condemns it as "commodity fetishism," the idolatry of consumption goods. Commodity fetishism is a kind of perceptual disorder. Humans become blind to the pain and suffering embedded in the commodity by virtue of an unjust and exploitative system of production, even as commodities—mere things—appear as active agents capable of commanding attention and determining desire. The explanatory power of this notion of commodity fetishism has endured the many developments in capitalism since 1857, when Marx first elaborated it. But some recent work in cultural studies has argued, against it, that our commerce with bought things has a more politically ambivalent effect: commodity culture both expresses and exposes "a social disorder that would otherwise remain hidden"[7]; particular repertoires of consumption are also said to function as a "language of invention with which radical groups can think about, refine, and ultimately advertise their ideologies."[8] Such perspectives, which emphasize the liberatory possibilities internal to consumption, contest the idea that only revolutionary action can alter the economic terms of justice.

I, too, argue that the theme of commodity fetishism is not capacious enough to account for our fascination with commercial goods. This is not to deny the value of demystifying the commodification process or the commercial advertisements that support it. If one immediate effect of ads is the urge to possess this or that product, a long-term, cumulative effect might be described as normalization. Ads have tended, for example, to inculcate on the senses—to write into the body—an aesthetic image of the slim, beautiful (male or female) body. Demystification is indispensable as a counter to this normalizing power, but it is also valuable to appreciate the capacity of ads to work on us in unpredictable ways. For me, the issue is not whether to live with commodities but how to participate in commodity culture, for there is no vision of capitalist or noncapitalist economy today that does not include some role for the commodity form. The pertinent questions become how to reform commodity culture to render it more just and more ecologically sustainable and how to extract the ethical potential within commodity culture.

The phenomenology of consumption that I pursue focuses on the sense of vitality, the charged-up feeling often generated in human bodies by the presence or promise of commodity consumption; I see similarities between that affective state and the "moral sentiments" that, in the history of European thought, have been associated with the beauty or sublimity of nature. In short, I explore the possibility that enchantment, from multiple sources, can be used to feed or fuel an ethical will. I think about how commercial items—more specifically, how their artistic representations (in ads as well as in the potential consumer's imagination), can enchant. I locate the enchantment effect primarily in the aesthetic or theatrical dimension of commodities and in the way that commodities function as tangible and public elaborations of, and experimentations with, personal and collective identities. A *New York Times* article about the sequel to the "Khakis Swing" ad ("Khakis a Go-Go") was headlined "Style over Substance"[9]; my story, instead, explores the ethical substance internal to the style of the ads. That style can be described as an aesthetic of vibrant mobility, of the ever-present possibility of bursts of vitality that violate an order ranking humans incomparably higher than animals, vegetables, and minerals.

The Dangers of Commodity Culture

Consistent with Marx's critique of commodification is the environmentalist position that the level of consumption typical of middle-class Americans is both ecologically disastrous and integral to the economy as currently organized.[10] I endorse this environmentalist critique and support political efforts to reconstruct an economic infrastructure that demands increasing levels of consumption and waste and regularly overpowers individual efforts toward ecological living. Perhaps a symbol of this unequal relation is the "REDUCE, REUSE, RECYCLE" banner hanging above the Wal-Mart checkout aisles—what possible effect could it have alongside the thousands of low-priced and ultimately disposable goods for sale?

Such consumption practices are indeed part of a system that tolerates a deplorable level of economic inequality; they often entail the suffering of other cultures and species; they promote greed and, eventually, military adventurism among administrations; and they work to eclipse the project of deliberately considering which ends we want to pursue in common. But I believe that a modified organization of commodification and advertising could respond to structural injustices in existing patterns of consumption without seeking to eliminate the enchanting effects of commodities. It is the form of commodification, not the fact of it, that is problematic. The existing political economy is built too much around what Michael Best and William E. Connolly call exclusionary goods, and it needs to build more inclusive goods into the order. As it is extended to more and more people, an exclusive good (1) decreases the private value of the good to those who already had it, (2) increases the private costs of its use, (3) accentuates the adverse common or social costs of its use, and (4) increases, directly or indirectly, the per-capita costs borne by the state in subsidizing its use and rectifying its adverse effects. Inclusive goods reverse these tendencies. Few goods fit either model perfectly, but the car, private medical care, private education, and private security arrangements move in the first direction, whereas public transport, universal health care, public education, and jobs and education to prevent crime move in the second direction. The point is that moving toward inclusive goods can reduce inequality and protect the environment. It need not, however, seek a world without GAP ads, or moralize against the commodity form or technologized art, or disqualify minor displays of consumption as a source of pleasure, creativity, self-expression, and enchantment.[11]

It makes sense to use whatever ethical resource might be derived from commercial culture and to pursue an ecology that draws positive sustenance from the moods and energies engendered by some modes of advertisement. We ought to work toward what E. F. Schumacher described as a "Buddhist" or sustainable economics[12] and, through micro- and macro-politics, invent ways to delimit the sensory assault of advertisements. Again, I would hope that creative advertisements and the aesthetic pleasure of minor luxuries would persist in the new order.[13] Even today, the electricity generated by running on the treadmill of consumption is not a closed circuit, and those charges are also powering other, noncommercial phenomena. John Jervis makes a similar point about advertisements: "If ads are about selling things, they are not *only* about selling things; their images can carry symbolic meanings, transmit messages, and create moods in ways that cannot be reduced to the conscious intentions of their creators and cannot be wholly controllable and predictable in their effects."[14] Like most social formations, the effects of commodity fascination include some strange bedfellows, and it might very well be that lodged within it is a kind of exhilarating energy akin to magnanimity. After all, those khakis do *swing*.

A story like mine, which highlights the noncommercial effects of commercial commodities, runs the risk of what Wendy Brown describes as the "renaturalization of capitalism." I work to avoid that effect. I aim instead to deny capitalism quite the degree of efficacy and totalizing power that its critics (and defenders) sometimes attribute to it and to exploit the positive ethical potential secreted within some of its elements.[15] What image of power do I invoke in my story? One that shares Deleuze and Guattari's conviction that "there is always something that flows or flees, that escapes

. . . the overcoding machine," one that affirms the view that though "capitalists may be the master of surplus value and its distribution, . . . they do not dominate the flows from which surplus value derives."[16]

My tale of commodity culture proceeds by critically engaging Marx's notion of commodity fetishism and then Horkheimer and Adorno's adaptation of it in their famous essay, "The Culture Industry." I pay particular attention to Marx's claim that, when commodification "animates" mere artifacts, it also enervates their producers and consumers, and also to Horkheimer and Adorno's picture of power as a hypercompetent and impermeable fortress. This image is born of their outrage at a system that seeks to dominate every aspect of life, and they emphasize the pervasive power of the system in the hopes of inflaming a comparably strong degree of opposition to it. While this image of power can indeed provoke political resistance to commodity culture and promote a more self-conscious relationship to it, there is also a way in which it works against that goal—why should one bother to criticize what is inevitable or challenge what is omnipotent? And so, I emphasize the openings, ambiguities, and lines of flight within systems of power, doing so to work positive effects within and upon the system.

The phenomenology of consumption that I pursue emerges, then, through a dialogue with Marx, Horkheimer and Adorno, and Deleuze and Guattari around these questions: What does it mean for ethics and politics when objects appear as animate or as capable of making claims upon us? Is this best described as "fetishization?" What is the relationship between animated objects and dulled (human) subjects? What are the theatrical techniques by which commodities exert power over human bodies? What is the role of repetition in commodification? What dimensions of the consuming self does such repetition act upon? What is the relationship between the pleasure afforded by mass-produced entertainment and ethico-political complacency? How does a zest for commodified art coexist with critical awareness of its manipulative intent?

The Commodity as Fetish

Inaugurating the distinction between use-value and exchange-value, Marx defined a commodity as an article produced from the start for large-scale market exchange rather than "for its own immediate consumption."[17] In commodity form, "the product becomes increasingly one-sided. . . . [I]ts immediate use-value for the gratification of the needs of its producer appears wholly adventitious . . . and inessential. . . ."[18] Commodification homogenizes objects; it destroys their "sensuously varied objectivity as articles of utility"[19] by defining them in terms of equivalent units of exchange. Anthropologist Michael Taussig puts it this way:

> In its exchange-value the shoe is qualitatively identical with any other commodity, no matter how much they may differ in terms of their use-value properties—their physical features, symbolic attributes, and so on. By virtue of this abstraction, which is based on market exchange and the universal equivalence of money, a palace is equal to a certain number of shoes. . . .[20]

Marx presents the alchemy of exchange-value, through which unequal things are made equal, as a sinister process.[21] It is not sinister because commodification does violence to artifacts (by stripping them of their specificity and reducing them to transactional goods), for such a defense of objects would give too much life to mere things. Instead, Marx makes it clear that the harm of commodification accrues to humans—they are the ones deprived of the "sensuously varied objectivity" of "articles of utility." As commodities, labor and the laborer are "objectified," an objectification that enables the swindle that is profit, for although a portion of the labor "is exchanged for the equivalent of the worker's wages; another portion is appropriated by the capitalist without any equivalent being paid."[22] The masking of power relations is the most pernicious effect of commodification. But second to that is its unnatural animation of artifacts. It is this second effect that I examine further.

Commodity fetishism bestows a "phantom objectivity,"[23] it animates artifacts and then obscures the source of that animation. Marx compares this trickery to the mystification that is religion:

> The mysterious character of the commodity-form consists . . . in the fact that the commodity reflects the social characteristics of men's own labour as objective characteristics of the products of labour themselves. . . . [T]he definite social relation between men . . . assumes here . . . the fantastic form of a relation between things. In order, therefore, to find an analogy we must take flight into the misty realm of religion. There the products of the human brain appear as autonomous figures endowed with a life of their own, which enter into relations both with each other and with the human race. So it is in the world of commodities. . . .[24]

In capitalism as in theism, things are empowered and persons are deadened. Mere things, the self-expression of living, laboring human beings, come to exercise power over those beings as if they too had "a life of their own." I think Marx is too dismissive of animism. Within his frame, it is reduced to the atavistic practice of fetishization.

Marx describes fetishism as a "religion of sensuous desire" that debases men. "Fantasy arising from desire deceives the fetish-worshipper into believing that an 'inanimate object' will give up its natural character in order to comply with his desires. Hence the crude desire of the fetish-worshipper *smashes* the fetish when it ceases to be its most obedient servant."[25] We might inquire further into Marx's choice of the term *fetish* by looking at its dictionary definition:

> Fetish: 1.a. Originally, any of the objects used by the negroes of the Guinea coast and the neighboring regions as amulets or means of enchantment; b. By writers in anthropology . . . used in wider sense: An inanimate object worshipped by savages on account of its supposed inherent magical powers, or as being animated by a spirit.[26]

If one places this definition alongside Marx's likening of animated artifacts to religious mystifications and his account of the "fetish-worshipper;" and his "crude" and childish form of desire, some of the worrisome features of the theory of fetishization come to the fore. The phrase "commodity fetishism" now seems to draw some of its power from an image of the masses in Western Europe as creatures who bear the repulsive trace of the African savage. Its drama aligns the primitive with the negro, the negro with pagan animism, animism with delusion and passivity, passivity with commodity culture. And this line of equivalences is contrasted with another consisting of the modern, the light, the demystified, the debunking critical theorist.[27] This strain in Marx's thinking does, however, coexist with others that run counter to it.[28]

More central to my own interest is the tendency of Marx's critique of commodity fetishism to picture a matter whose "natural character" is dead or inert: for him nature is disenchanted. That is to say, it is drawn against the background of a superceded pagan world wherein all things were enlivened with divine spirit. In doing so, it supports an onto-story in which agency is concentrated in humans, either in the capitalist mode of apparent individuality and market rationality or in the socialist mode of true collective agency and mastery.

I see the GAP ad, for example, as expressive of a different ontology; in it, the liveliness of matter itself is once again apparent, this time by the grace of cinematic technology rather than God or the Spirits. You can call those pants "commodified" and you can call fascination with the advertisement a "fetish," but the swinging khakis also emerge from an underground cultural sense of nature as alive, as never having been disenchanted. Out of the commercialized dance erupts a kind of neopagan or Epicurean materialism—an enchanted materialism. The term *mechanistic* does not describe *this* materialism, for the khakis display a playful and surprising will not unlike the swerve of which Epicurus speaks. Perhaps it is true, then, that the "facts of commodity culture always [turn] . . . out to be . . . a fantastic realm in which things act, speak, rise, fall, fly, evolve."[29]

Marx and the Swerve

Marx himself wrote his doctoral dissertation on Epicurus. Could it be that his thinking contains more resources for an enchanted materialism than I have credited? Let us take a look, then, at Marx's treatment of Epicurean philosophy and ask: What is the matter inside Marx's materialism? What picture of nature, what physics, is entangled with the political economy that he comes to endorse? In particular, might Marx's interest in Epicurus suggest that he, too, had a sense of the vitality of matter?

Marx turned to ancient atomism because he was intrigued by the possibility of a materialism that was not deterministic, that is to say, a philosophy that gave primacy to the sensuous, natural world but did not picture that world as a mechanistic realm of necessity. After reading the French Enlightenment philosophers Holbach, Condorcet, and Diderot, each of whom endorsed a "concept of the *internal* movement of material elements,"[30] Marx was drawn to Epicurus's idea that the atom occasionally swerved from its straight, downward path through the void. In his dissertation, "The Difference between the Democritean and Epicurean Philosophy of Nature," Marx argued that Epicurus rejected the deterministic universe of Democritus. For Democritus, chance was an illusion created by humans to explain their own "perplexity" about the order of things. But for Epicurus, " 'necessity . . . does not exist, . . . some things are *accidental*, others depend on our *arbitrary will*. . . . It is a misfortune to live in necessity, but to live in necessity is not a necessity. On all sides many short and easy paths to freedom are open.' "[31]

Epicurus's emphasis on freedom—exemplified by his notion of the swerve—was what made Marx rank him above Democritus. The straight line formed by the downward fall of the atoms represented the fateful "materiality" of the atom, while the swerve expressed the atom's "formal determination" or freedom:

> The atoms are purely self-sufficient bodies or rather bodies conceived in absolute self-sufficiency, like the heavenly bodies. Hence, again like the heavenly bodies, they move not in straight but in oblique lines.[32]

According to C. J. McFadden, the young Marx thought of matter as too recalcitrant or unruly to be part of an order of natural necessity: "all the existing forms of materialism were unacceptable to Marx because they lacked a vitalizing principle. They regarded matter as inert, and Marx did not believe that it was such."[33] Marx's statement that the declination of the atom is "that something in its breast that can fight back and resist"[34] supports this interpretation of him as a kind of vital materialist.

More often, however, Marx reads the swerve in a more Hegelian manner, as Epicurus's way of expressing the moment of "pure individuality" within self-consciousness's struggle to realize itself in the larger world. Under the sway of Hegel's philosophy of self-consciousness, Marx translates the swerve of the atom into an assertion of self-consciousness; the activity of declination is reduced to "a symbol of the active self"[35]; the vitality of matter serves only as an analogy for the intrinsic human quest for freedom. The swerve is thus presented as belonging to human self-consciousness rather than to both nonhuman and human matter. By the time Marx gets done with it, the fighting spirit of matter has settled down into the bodies of men.

Marx describes the swerve as the atom's "abstracting" of itself from "its relative existence, the straight line."[36] This act of abstraction is the cornerstone, says Marx, not only of Epicurus's physics but of his ethics of *ataraxy* or tranquillity. Just as "the atom frees itself from . . . the straight line . . . so . . . the purpose of [human] action is to be found . . . in abstracting, swerving away from pain and confusion. . . ."[37] Marx notes that Epicurus even makes the truth of nature dependent on the subjective effect it has upon the self, quoting Epicurus's claim that "since eternity of the heavenly bodies would disturb the ataraxy of self-consciousness, it is a necessary, a stringent consequence that they are not eternal."[38]

For Marx, this strange, subjective science was yet another indication of Epicurus's defense of "the absoluteness and freedom of self-consciousness."[39] Unfortunately, however, the dialectically unsophisticated Epicurus could only conceive self-consciousness as something that "arises in *opposition* to the material world, and not *through* it." Epicurus did recognize, says Marx, that in order for the atom to attain concrete "existence," it would have to take on determinate, material attributes—which would contradict its "essence" as abstract individuality. According to George F. McCarthy, Marx credits Epicurus as the first philosopher in history to "incorporate the notion of the contradiction between essence and reality into his thought."[40] This was for Marx a profound achievement even if Epicurus failed to resolve the contradiction.[41]

Finally, Epicurus's dialectical failure would become Marx's goad; McCarthy claims that Marx would make it his task to "move . . . from abstract self-consciousness and freedom to concrete self-consciousness in the political economy. In order to overcome the contradictions of existence and essence . . . implicit in Epicurean physics, the alienation of the objective and physical world must be overcome through social praxis."[42] As Marx himself says in his "Notebooks on Epicurean Philosophy," he will give "a quite different account of the matter from that of Epicurus."[43]

From my point of view, however, it is equally important to note the strange fact that, for Marx, Epicurus is an antinaturalist! Though Marx is, I think, justified in criticizing Epicurus's bracketing of those aspects of nature whose metaphysical implications would disturb human tranquillity, Marx overplays his hand. He loses touch with the remarkable appreciation of agency *within* nature that Epicurus actively affirms.

Marx did celebrate Epicurus's indifference toward the gods, or what George McCarthy calls his "critique of all forms of alien objectivity."[44] But, here again, it seems as though Marx was overzealous. So keen to debunk this "alien objectivity" was Marx that he lost touch with his own, original attraction to the quirky and resistant objectivity of micromatter. This willfulness within the very smallest speck as well as larger assemblages, this something in the breast of matter that "can fight back and resist," becomes merely a symbolic representation of a stage of self-consciousness. And Marx's too-quick translation of atoms into human beings might have had a profound effect on his future thought. Instead of a reminder of the lively resistance of material bodies, of their capacity to act on other bodies, including ours, the swerve becomes *man's* capacity to resist social forms. The physics of Epicurus transmogrifies into a Marxist philosophical anthropology. The swerve of matter becomes the persistent urge for freedom within human nature. The refusal of atoms to tow the line morphs into a revolutionary will to overthrow unjust social forms. These are themselves interesting and ethically laudable transformations, and they reveal a rarely discussed Epicurean influence on Marx. What they do not mark sufficiently, however, is the possibility that nonhuman matter also counts. Though he might have, Marx did not allow himself to draw upon Epicurus to develop a more enchantment-friendly materialism.

The Critical Potential of (Commercial) Art

Like Marx, Horkheimer and Adorno find nothing positive about the animation of objects, a liveliness that, given their onto-story of disenchantment, can be only a dangerous illusion. Commodified objects are implicated in an unnatural transference of energy from persons to things; commodification operates as a zero-sum game. To respond to things as if they were alive is to steal animus from the humans who own the monopoly rights to it. Horkheimer and Adorno's essay on "The Culture Industry" can be read as an extended effort to awaken man's critical faculties that have been deanimated in a world saturated by commercialism. In particular, it argues against the possibility of an affective response to commodities able to challenge the socioeconomic system that generates it. There is no aesthetic sphere independent of and, hence, a potential site of resistance to "the iron system" of capital (120).[45] So, it would be impossible for a GAP ad—no matter how technically interesting and aesthetically innovative—to fuel any sensibility other than consumerism.

"The culture industry can pride itself on having energetically executed the previously clumsy transposition of art into the sphere of consumption" (134–35). Every increase in the sharpness of video cuts or the peppiness of hit songs issues in a decrease in the critical faculties of its audience. Mass entertainment is replete with images of novelty and surprise, but the upbeat "tempo and dynamics" are carefully calibrated to preclude the exercise of mental effort and independent thinking. The result is a passive, consumptive audience (137).

If art provided the Romantics with a line of flight from banality into creative self-expression and if art offered Nietzsche a theater in which to redeem the world through beauty, (capitalist) art for Horkheimer and Adorno has become ideology. They acknowledge that artists have good intentions: the "promise held out by the work of art that it will create truth by lending new shape to the conventional social forms is as necessary as it is hypocritical," for it is in the very nature of art to aspire to transcend the status quo. But, this aspiration always fails. Art ends up tracking and recapitulating the social hierarchy, it is "derivative" of "the real forms of life as it is" (130). The history of art does include feeble instances of criticism and protest, but the reign of the culture industry now prevents even these fleeting moments:

> When the [stylistic] detail won its freedom, it became rebellious and, in the period from Romanticism to Expressionism, asserted itself as free expression, as a vehicle of protest against the organization. . . . The totality of the culture industry has put an end to this. Though concerned exclusively with effects, it crushes their insubordination and makes them subserve the formula, which replaces the work.[46]

Part of what propels Horkheimer and Adorno to tell their story is their moral outrage at the culture industry's colonization of human creativity.[47] Culture products, they say, are designed with extraordinary care and expertise, such that "no medieval theologian could have determined the degree of torment to be suffered by the damned . . . more meticulously than the producers of shoddy epics calculate . . . the exact point to which the leading lady's hemline shall be raised" (128).[48] In lieu of authentic, spontaneous creativity, we get a sophisticated science of entertainment in the service of squeezing out more consumption. This science "demands an astounding productive power," but only "absorbs and squanders" it (129). Creativity, presented as a kind of primary drive whose authentic aim is self-expression, is said to be now fully in the service of system-legitimation. It becomes "entertainment," which diverts us from dehumanizing forms of work even as it mirrors its monotonous structure (137).

This colonization of creativity occurs by means of the technologization of art qua television, radio, and film. Precapitalist art, at least, had the potential to challenge injustice; technologized art has no such promise. This is because, according to Horkheimer and Adorno, technology does not issue from the drive to create but from another fundamental drive, to dominate: "The basis on which technology acquires power over society is the power of those whose economic hold over society is greatest. A technological rationale is the rationale of domination itself" (121). And so every rise in the technical sophistication of entertainment is accompanied by a decline in the political will to justice: "The idea of 'fully exploiting' available technical resources and the facilities for aesthetic mass consumption is part of the economic system which refuses to exploit resources to abolish hunger" (139).

It is by means of this image of human drives that Horkheimer and Adorno are able to transform the truism that technically sophisticated forms of entertainment operate within an unjust economic system into the morally powerful claim that such entertainment *keeps people hungry* and that improvements in the science of entertainment *proceed only at the expense of* advances in human welfare. In particular, their image of technology as inherently oppressive is what allows them to suggest a causal link between high-quality commercials and low-quality antipoverty efforts and between the impressive special effects in the GAP ad and the expanding gap between the rich and the poor.[49]

To sum up their critique—the culture industry squanders artistic energy, shores up a dehumanizing work structure, and enervates the will to social justice. But, and this is the rub, its consumers fail to object to these connected effects. Instead, they lap up the entertainment slop. That is to say, they fetishize the art-commodity and enter its thrall as if it was alive. Everyone is well aware that art has become commodity—indeed, art "deliberately admits it is one; art renounces its own autonomy and proudly takes its place among consumption goods" (157)[50]—but no one seems to mind. Horkheimer and Adorno devote considerable energy to explaining the psychological mechanism of this failure to contest the march of commodification, and, in doing so, they make an original contribution toward a phenomenology of consumption. And yet, as I argue in the next section, they prematurely abort a promising line of inquiry, the line connecting commodity consumption to a somatic energetics. In so doing, they fail to discern a moment of affinity between commodity fascination and wonder at the world.

Affect and Thought

How is it possible that we accept the unholy admixture of art and commodity? How has an enlightened society returned to the fetish? The crux of Horkheimer and Adorno's response is this: by means of repeated exposure to a form of entertainment that activates and stimulates the senses *in order to* dull them. The creature who walks out of the cinema leaves with the pleasant, refreshed feeling that he has just been exercising his creative imagination. And he has indeed been exerting himself. But, this self-exertion has been working in exquisite, intimate cooperation with techniques of slumber exercised upon him by the culture industry. He has been put through his paces pleasantly and rendered stupid and sleepy through the effort. The same, of course, can be said about the experience of advertisement. Advertising and the culture industry are both instances of "psychotechnology," a "procedure for manipulating men" (163). I might feel exhilarated and enchanted by "Khakis Swing," say Horkheimer and Adorno, but this effect is purchased at the price of stupification:

> The stunting of the mass–media consumer's powers of imagination and spontaneity [can be] . . . traced back to . . . the objective nature of the products themselves, especially to the most characteristic of them, the sound film. They are so designed that quickness, powers of observation, and experience are undeniably needed to apprehend them at all; yet sustained thought is out of the question if the spectator is not to miss the relentless rush of facts. Even though the effort required for his response is [only] semi–automatic, no scope is left for the imagination (126–27).

Horkheimer and Adorno here offer a good account of the subtle relationship often forged today between personal, authentic-feeling experiences and external manipulative forces. At the movies, one's own mental acuity ("quickness"), one's own sensory perception ("powers of observation"), and one's own bodily affect ("experience") comingle with the calculated design of an industry devoted to exchange-value. As a result, we are enlisted in our own commercialization; we voluntarily exercise our imagination in ways that stunt it while enjoying pleasurable feelings of activeness or vitality. We get what we ask for: culture commodities are artificially induced needs but felt needs nonetheless.[51]

In this analysis, Horkheimer and Adorno begin to explore the active side of what they typically depict as consumer passivity, and they draw our attention to what might be called the affective energetics of consumption. But, they do not pursue this dimension long or hard enough. Instead, they allow their insight into the way commodities manipulate/activate our bodies to drown in a vocabulary of mind. In the end, they reduce the mechanism of commodification to thought control. Their nuanced reading of the self's pleasurable investment in consumption thus gives way to a cruder picture of a high-tech industry that imposes a series of mind-numbing techniques on a population already rendered mentally deficient by its work. Perhaps the best example of their slide into intellectualism is the summary statement that follows the quotation cited above about "quickness, powers of observation, and experience": "The might of industrial society," Horkheimer and Adorno conclude, "is lodged in men's minds."[52]

Yet, they have just shown that at least some of this might is lodged not in minds (home to self-conscious thought) but also in bodily sites of potentially critical (albeit not originally self-conscious) thought: the eyes that widen, the stomach that roils, the skin that galvanizes and registers "the relentless rush of facts." Here, one can detect the influence of the model of materialism inherited from Marx—once matter is figured as "naturally" inert, it will be difficult to sustain the idea of the matter of human bodies as an active, and potentially disruptive, force in commodity culture. Horkheimer and Adorno do not ignore the role of affect, as is evidenced by their focus on aesthetic commodities and by their acknowledgment of the role played by moods like love.[53] But, they underestimate and then, too quickly, lose sight of the spunk or swerve of bodies.

Another source of this tendency, alongside the disenchanted materialism of Marx, might be their indebtedness to a Kantian model of self organized into "faculties," including the faculty of aesthetic judgement. Horkheimer and Adorno affirm the need to update that model, but, at base, endorse its idea that only self-conscious thought is thought and only thought can have critical force. This assumption is operative even in their criticism of Kant: Whereas Kant saw the individual as the one who would "relate the varied experiences of the senses to fundamental concepts," today the culture industry does the individual's schematizing for him.[54] It seems to me, however, that if Horkheimer and Adorno had allowed their insight into the role of affect in commodification to stand, they might not have had to bestow such omnipotence upon the culture industry or present the consumer as so thoroughly stripped of agency.[55] They might not, in other words, have had to foreclose all lines of flight save that opened up by the self-conscious and relentlessly skeptical demystification of the sort displayed in their essay. For, if the industry operates upon us by means of our affective participation in it, this means that its control over us is simultaneously deep and unpredictable. And that is because affect itself is both deep and never entirely predictable in its movements. This element of unpredictability also opens up the possibility that commodities operate not only with mind-dulling (bare) repetition but also with an ethic-enabling (spiral) repetition of the sort described in chapter 3. It opens up the possibility that commercial items can enchant and not just mystify. Let me return briefly to the matter of repetition.

Repetition

Consistent with Marx's idea that commodification is homogenization is Horkheimer and Adorno's analysis of mass-produced art as monotonously uniform and deadly to the new. Despite its constant invocation of novelty, the culture industry serves up only formulaic amusements.[56] Moreover, commercial culture not only repeats, it repeats perfectly. It is portrayed as having the ability to reproduce things exactly. One could even say that Horkheimer and Adorno fetishize the culture industry by animating it with a supernatural degree of efficacy.[57] This power of perfect duplication is predicated upon the prior process of leveling enacted within exchange-value. Use-value, you will recall, is a realm of sensuous variety, whereas exchange-value operates on a dull and flat plane.[58] In this latter space, "all are free to dance and enjoy themselves, just as they have been free, since the historical neutralization of religion, to join any of the innumerable sects. But freedom to choose an ideology—since ideology always reflects economic coercion—everywhere proves to be freedom to choose what is always the same."[59] Or, put in Deleuzean terms, the culture industry practices bare repetition.

Recall that bare repetition is what happens to the absolutely unique material specificity of any assemblage (its "haeccity") once it is placed within a Kantian framework—wherein it becomes "particularity." According to Kant, thought proceeds by means of the subsumption of "particulars" to "universals." Horkheimer and Adorno still work with that image of thought. But, outside of it, difference itself can persist within repetition; each rotation is recognizably close but not identical to the one before. In this spiral repetition, the "same" repeats but with a twist.[60]

From within a Deleuzean imaginary, then, Horkheimer and Adorno overstate their case about the dulling effect of the repetition of the commercial realm. For why assume that even a system of "mechanical reproduction" is able to produce flawlessly identical copies? At the very least, each copy is put to slightly differential use, thus allowing a bit of the new to take hold. Why assume that matter is such that differences can take only the form of "particularities"? If there is difference within repetition, then fetishization is not the only way to describe what is going on. And demystification is not the only response to commodification. Moreover, the animation of artifacts that Marx, Horkheimer, and Adorno lament might not be all bad. It might embody several dissonant possibilities; it might have all of the following incompatible effects—pressing people to submit to the call to consume, distracting them from attending to the unjust social relations embodied in the product, reminding them that they share the world with nonhuman modes of agency, drawing them to the wonders of material existence, and opening them to unlikely ecological connections and political alliances. If so, then the encounter with animated objects would call sometimes for demystification, sometimes for appreciation of the ability of nonhuman things to act upon us, and sometimes for both at once. That is, it might be part of our job to bring out the positive elements of advertisement that other forces leave in the shadows. This recognition opens the way for a deliberate receptiveness toward, even an active courting of, those "fetishes" among whose effects can be counted surprise, wonder, even enchantment.

Yea Saying

I am not saying that enchantment is the only effect issuing from encounters with commercial artifacts. Very often, one effect is what Horkheimer and Adorno call "amusement," a state of being without the unsettling, even dangerous, "swing" element of enchantment. Horkheimer and Adorno contrast amusement, which disables systemic thinking,[61] with the physical humor and "mindless artistry" of the circus, which "represents what is human as opposed to the social mechanism."[62] Such "nonsense," they say, is good art—it provokes a free play of imaginative possibilities that stands in stark contrast to the uniform monotony of capitalist culture. But, such artistry is "relentlessly hunted down by a schematic reason" and transformed into the "idiotic plots" of amusement. In this way, the culture industry colonizes "genuine personal emotion."[63]

Amusement is an affective state that shares a certain pleasurableness with enchantment but lacks its disturbing dimension. One of the ways that enchantment works is by slowing down or speeding up the usual tempo of something, as when the dancers' movements are temporarily frozen in "Khakis Swing." The differential in tempo delights but also unsettles. In contrast, amusement is too smooth a feeling to admit wonder and surprise, too contented for critical thinking to emerge as an aftereffect. Horkheimer and Adorno fail to distinguish between amusement and enchantment (and even amusement could contain rebel energies that might be mobilized in support of ethical concern), and so they equate pleasure per se with moral lassitude:

> The original affinity of business and amusement is shown in the latter's specific significance: to defend society. To be pleased means to say Yes. . . . Pleasure always means not to think about anything, to forget suffering even where it is

shown. Basically it is helplessness. It is flight. . . . from the last remaining thought of resistance.[64]

"To be pleased means to say Yes." It does seem that pleasure entails some kind of affirmation. But, is the subject to which this assent is addressed always the system hegemon? "Yes to GAP investors and a corporate system of worker exploitation!" "Yes to WW II and swing dancing!" "Yes to the creativity of the film technician!" "Yes to a human body that can fly with birds and fuse with sound!" "Yes to the exuberance of beige cotton molecules!" Which is it?[65]

And what is the ethical import of pleasurable affirmation? For Horkheimer and Adorno, to say "Yes" to pleasure is to say "No" to critical thinking. Although pleasure can entail stupidity, passivity, and, eventually, moral indifference, I contend that it can also enliven, energize, and, under the right circumstances, support ethical generosity. Enchantment and critical theory probably do entail different affective constellations. One cannot be enchanted and skeptical at the same time, and the unrealism of wonder could induce a sense of generosity but reduce insight into the mechanisms of power. On the other hand, part of the energy needed to challenge injustice comes from the reservoir of enchantment—including that derived from commodities. For without enchantment, you might lack the impetus to act against the very injustices that you critically discern.

The Limits of Refusal

Horkheimer and Adorno do not distinguish between amusement and enchantment. Neither do they cultivate generosity as a possible counter to the fascist mentality of the culture industry.[66] For them, the forces of stupor had recently proved so hideous, so easily reactivated in even liberal, democratic contexts, and so deadly to the large-scale transformations that they sought, that even an ethically useful kind of enchantment was not worth the risk. These forces include not only amusement but also the cynicism generated by the culture industry:

> In this age of universal publicity any invocation of an ideal appears suspect to us. We have learned how to identify abstract concepts as sales propaganda. Language based entirely on truth simply arouses impatience to get on with the business deal it is probably advancing.[67]

We have learned to equate idealism with con jobs by means of repeated exposure to commercials that invoke ideals for precisely this purpose.[68] Our two master demystifiers lament this cynicism and acknowledge that political change requires not only critical suspicion but a hefty dose of idealistic energy—energy, for example, on behalf of economic justice and Enlightenment freedom. They assert that the cynicism induced by commercial culture wields little political force. To develop this thought further, one can see how cynicism supports not only complacency but active, right-wing agendas. Cynicism reduces expectations of the state and thus diminishes the will to respond collectively to injustices; it is easily mobilized on behalf of antitax and get-tough policies that disdain liberal ideals about human rights, the power of education, and the legitimacy of a diverse array of social and personal identities.

Horkheimer and Adorno end their essay by noting that widespread cynicism about commodification fails to interfere with the commercialized consumption that generates it. We see through ads but keep on buying. Horkheimer and Adorno interpret this remarkable fact as the crowning glory of a culture industry bent on controlling the entire life-world. But, this is not the only reasonable interpretation of the coexistence of commodity culture and cynical self-consciousness. The consumption that continues alongside knowledge of its manipulative intent indeed could be a sign of just how deeply that manipulation has entered into us. But it might also betoken the presence of some noncommercial value that the consumer derives from consumption or from its aesthetic representation in advertisements, some pleasure whose force may be susceptible to ethical deployment.

Horkheimer and Adorno offer a phenomenology of consumption that resonates with much contemporary experience. The primary fear motivating their story is that we live in a system where the forces of domination have become resistant to all but the most relentless strains of critical reflection. That is why they are so adverse to any mood, including enchantment, that falls short of a Kantian standard of thinking. They tend to assimilate such moods to one of these negative forms—mystification, reification, or fetishization. In spite of their portrayal of the culture industry as a closed system, Horkheimer and Adorno still harbor hope for a way out by means of radical critique and demystification. Their essay, an enactment of these techniques, is designed to help us see through the mist, to expose the connections among commodification, human stupefaction, and economic injustice.

Built into Horkheimer and Adorno's project, then, is an Enlightenment faith in the efficacy of debunking, in the idea that clear sight into injustice carries with it its own impetus for undoing wrong and enacting right.[69] This faith sits uneasily with their depiction of a commodity cynicism that has little practical effect. If they had applied this insight into the limits of critique to their own strategy of debunking, they might have understood more profoundly how an ethical politics requires more than rational demystification. They might have pursued further the affective component of the will to social justice and ethical concern. They might have seen that, by discrediting so thoroughly the minor pleasures and inspirations currently available to people, they depress the ethical life and deaden the idealism and somatic will required for significant political and economic reform.[70] At issue is the moral and political efficacy of critical refusal. Are the effects of commodity culture sufficiently confronted and challenged by a Marxist critique? Or can other modes of engagement that figure the political field as more contingent and imagine the material world as more animate also make a difference?

Ethical Energetics

> Beauty quickens. It adrenalizes. It makes the heart
> beat faster. It makes life more vivid, animated, liv-
> ing, worth living.
>   (*Elaine Scarry*)[1]

The Aesthetic Disposition

Enchantment as a state of openness to the disturbing-captivating elements in everyday experience. Enchantment as a window onto the virtual secreted within the actual. Enchantment, in the model I am defending, as operative in a world without telos. I have been suggesting not only that an array of minor experiences in contemporary life enchants us but also that enchantment is a mood with ethical potential. More specifically, my contention is that enchantment can aid in the project of cultivating a stance of presumptive generosity (i.e., of rendering oneself more open to the surprise of other selves and bodies and more willing and able to enter into productive assemblages with them). This particular ethos emerges in conjunction with a picture of the world as a web of lively and mobile matter-forms of varying degrees of complexity. It is linked, as well, to a particular conception of how ethics works, of what it requires in order to function as such.

The key claim is that ethics requires both a moral code (which condenses moral ideals and metaphysical assumptions into principles and rules) and an embodied sensibility (which organizes affects into a style and generates the impetus to enact the code[2]). Moral codes, for example, the Ten Commandments, remain inert without a disposition hospitable to their injunctions, the perceptual refinement necessary to apply them to particular cases, and the affective energy needed to perform them. Regardless of whether the ethical code is conceived as divine command or pragmatic rule, if it is to be transformed into acts, affects must be engaged, orchestrated, and libidinally bound to it—codes alone seem unable to propel their own enactment, at least for many people under most circumstances.

This model of ethics puts the question of motivation, the "how" of ethics, at its center. The aim of this chapter is to articulate that perspective more closely and to confront some of the ethical dangers intrinsic to it. I consider three such dangers. The first has been described as the capture of ethics by aesthetics; to include the latter in the former is to license the unruly and selfish or, at best, morally indifferent forces of appetite and desire. How can one be sure that such forces will issue in presumptive generosity and concern for others? The second danger concerns the apolitical or at least noncollective character of this model, the way it presents ethics as an individualized exercise and so ignores the economic and social factors that condition ethical relations. An affective model of ethics is also seen sometimes to entail the reverse danger—it is too political. Its focus on building good character, even if framed in the more innocuous language of the cultivation of sensibility, draws perilously close to the project of sensuous manipulation and to media, state, cultural, or corporate forms of disciplinary power. I acknowledge the legitimacy of these fears. I also argue, in what follows, that as long as affect remains an indispensable part of human life, it makes more sense to discipline it into a magnanimous sensibility than to try to ban it from ethical life.

The idea that there is an energetics of ethics has been considered by a variety of thinkers, several of whom I engage. I begin with Kant. His official project disqualifies somatic energies from a morality conceived as a self-motivating "law within us," but the role he assigns to the moral sentiments suggests that even he saw a need to draw upon affective energies to supplement, or perhaps activate, morality as law.[3] I suggest that Kant's treatment of the moral sentiments of respect, awe, sublimity, and wonder allows affect to enter into morality through the backdoor.

I move next to Friedrich Schiller's romantic variation of Kant's project. Schiller assigns a central ethical role to the *aesthetic disposition,* a cultivated state that is neither brute feeling nor sublime Reason. In so doing, Schiller lets the body have a say in moral life in order to harness its energies, albeit in a modulated and disciplined form. The aesthetic disposition, says Schiller, is a particular inflection of an inherent human impulse to play. I endorse Schiller's idea that playfulness has ethical import, even while I do not share his faith that the aesthetic disposition can harmonize selves and social life. One of the interesting things about Schiller is his attempt to combine Kant's idea that the rational will is morally autonomous with his own sense that an aesthetic disposition must augment reasoned principle if the latter is to be ethically effective. Why does Schiller retain Kant's notion of moral autonomy? Because it serves as a bulwark against the dangerously amoral character of aesthetic pleasure. I do not think that Schiller thus solves the problem of how to harness aesthetic energy to ethical enactments. But, he does define clearly the issues for those who, like me, are moved by an onto-picture neither Kantian nor Romantic.

I turn for help here to Michel Foucault, whom I position as heir to Schiller's project of aestheticizing ethics. He pursues the common-sense conviction that ethical actions always entail both "code" and affective dimensions, and he does so in a world where, as Elaine Scarry put it, "the metaphysical referent" for truth is in doubt.[4] My treatment of Foucault in relation to contemporary critics of his aestheticization of ethics allows me to revisit the question of the moral indifference of the aesthetic and also to consider the charge that an affective model of ethics reduces ethics to a narcissistic practice of care of the self.

After focusing on the aesthetic-affective dimension of ethics, I end the chapter by considering its code dimension, or the principles and ideals consonant with the sensibility of generosity and enchantment I advocate. What ethical stance emerges from enchanted materialism? To address this question is also to think about the role of language and articulation in ethics. Here I invoke a model of language that acknowledges its somatic, as well as semantic, functions and rely on the work of Richard Flathman and Deleuze and Guattari. Flathman argues that language is such that there always will be a gap between articulated rules and actual conduct; linguistic indeterminacy ensures that ethical outcomes always will be somewhat unpredictable. I agree with Flathman here, but his orientation toward language, like Kant's approach to morality, is shy about addressing its somatic dimensions—in particular what Deleuze and Guattari call the "sonority" or sound-effects of language.

My encounters with Kant, Schiller, Foucault, Flathman, and Deleuze and Guattari are designed to provide a clearer picture of the model of ethics within which enchantment can function as a positive resource.

Moral Sentiments

What enables the jump from recognizing a moral code to living it out? How do moral injunctions become laudable acts? What are the means by which a categorical imperative, for instance, transmogrifies into the treatment of others as one wishes to be treated oneself? What role can perceptual moods, muscular habits, and bodily energies play in these transformations? One reads Kant somewhat against the grain if one approaches his texts, as I do, through these questions. For, although Kant is quite willing to discuss what the moral law says and to provide careful argumentation on behalf of its "subjective necessity," he is wary of saying too much, or too much explicitly, about how it is that the moral law comes to be taken up and acted upon. The experience of moral motivation is undertheorized in Kant. And perhaps it must be. The moral law is "recognized" as something one has a duty to obey, and Kant would prefer to leave it at that. To go further into the matter—to give a close account of how recognition and duty manage to enliven the will and how the will comes to move the body—would be to risk treating morality as a mechanism, a model only appropriate for physical entities. Likewise, to say too much about the how of recognition or duty might end up reducing them to mere affects and, again, confuse the moral with the sensible. In short, too much attention to the how of morality would violate Kant's fundamental distinction between the noumenal (supersensible) and the phenomenal (sensible) domains.[5]

I do suggest, however, that Kantian morality does not—cannot—avoid the phenomenal fray altogether. In what follows, I gather together the odd bits in Kant that form a subterranean theory of moral motivation, a Kantian picture of the affects of ethics. My aim is to trace the affective topography of his morality and to thematize more overtly than he does its somatic or energetic dimensions.

I begin with Kant's familiar, and quite fantastic, assertion in *Religion within the Limits of Reason Alone* that the experience of conscience (the voice of the ought) implies the ability to realize the ought: "We *ought* to conform to it; consequently we must be *able* to do so."[6] But how is it consequent? Well, it seems that the law has a correlate of "respect," and this "simple respect for the moral law within us . . . is the motivating force of the will."[7] The moral law, then, carries with it respect; respect motivates the will; and, though Kant leaves this next point unstated, the will eventually arranges face, arm, legs, and voice into the expressions, gestures, and sounds of ethical acts. I say that the law has a correlate or carries respect, but these might not be the best verbs, as Kant's own formulations leave the character of that relationship vague.[8]

For Kant, the workings of the moral law must remain somewhat mysterious to us, but what about the relationship between respect and the will? How does Kant characterize that? Respect, he says, motivates the will, and it does so as a "moral sentiment." Kant here invents the category of a moral sentiment distinct from a sensuous sentiment. Moral sentiments are hardly sentimental; there is nothing of the sensuous in them. The somatic motions that follow from respect—for example, the straightening of the back as one resists the urge to steal or the bending of the knees in the presence of the bishop—are of a wholly different nature than respect. Why not then describe respect as a moral spirit rather than a moral sentiment? That would have clearly distinguished it from bodies and senses. But the "spirit" designation would not be as good at denoting the motivating quality of respect, its function as the (active, lively, energizing) motor or fuel for the will, the back, and the knees. Moral "sentiment" better captures the idea of respect as will-*power*.

But, if respect has nothing of the sensible in its own nature, how is it, then, that it motivates? What kind of thing is this that is creaturely enough to be felt as a push or motivational urge but not material enough to qualify as within the sensible world? Kant is surely not saying, as Lucretius might have, that moral sentiments, while subsensible to us, remain material in nature and thus capable of impact; rather, he is claiming that moral sentiments are supra-sensible by nature. Now, here one can begin to lose sight of what respect *is*—isn't the feeling or experience of respect essential to it? Without the somatic gearing up, the tensing of muscles, the change in breath, the alteration in chemical-neural flows, what is left of "respect?"

Kant officially resists any such association between, on the one hand, the moral law and will (the realm of freedom) and, on the other, somatic affects and material effects (the world of sense). For him, the force of the moral law first derives from a supersensible source and then intervenes in the sensible world in a way that preserves the primacy of the supersensible. Chapter 3 indicates how that intervention sometimes consists in the "hints" or "prospects" provided by nature. Respect, along with a small army of other moral sentiments, also resides in that nebulous space between the noumenal law and the amoral body. In the following set of Kantian claims, we get a glimpse into that secret, unofficial realm: (1) the majesty of the moral law "instills *awe* (not dread, which repels, nor yet charm, which invites familiarity)"; (2) the "simple respect" that we note in ourselves while in the presence of majesty "awakens a sense of the *sublimity* of our own destiny which enraptures us more than any beauty"[9]; (3) "we cannot cease from regarding with the highest *wonder* . . . the original moral predisposition . . . in us."[10] In these formulations, we witness Kant's inventive attempt to describe the force of the moral law in terms that do not participate in somatic experience. We are to think of "awe," "respect," "sublimity," and "wonder," as categorically distinct from "dread" or "charm," in that the former rise somewhere above sense experience and the materiality of bodies, even while they possess the power to move bodies and impel action. These moral sentiments are both forceful and immaterial.

"Exaltation" is another middle-realm creature. As a "feeling of sublimity," it possesses the power to "awaken the moral sentiments," which, in turn, can prompt ethical acts of "sacrifice":

> . . . [T]he very incomprehensibility of this predisposition [within us for the moral law], which announces a divine origin, acts perforce upon the spirit even to the point of exaltation, and strengthens it for whatever sacrifice a man's respect for his duty may demand of him. . . . [T]o excite in man this feeling of the sublimity of his moral destiny is especially commendable as a method of awakening his moral sentiments.[11]

To review the chain of relations just described: The undeniable presence of the moral law, which is internal to oneself but not of oneself, is something that we cannot comprehend; we take our failure to understand as a sign of the divinity of the laws; this recognition of the close-at-hand divinity exalts the spiritual part of us, and this strengthens our ability to make sacrifices. In short, the law *excites* a *feeling of sublimity* that *awakens* moral *sentiments*. Once again, we find Kant asserting that nonsomatic feelings (perplexity, sublimity, exaltation) have the power to awaken nonsomatic (moral) sentiments. But, do these nether-creatures also participate in the somatic natures they are supposed to govern? Is Kant here darkly acknowledging the affective dimension of ethics?[12]

If the first element in this acknowledgment concerns the sentiments of respect, awe, wonder, and sublimity, the second concerns what I call the performativity of the voice of Reason. Kant says that certain demands (i.e., those spoken with the voice of Reason), produce or bring into being the very thing demanded. We've seen how this works in the case of the self-realizing power of the voice of conscience; this magical performativity is also at work in the internal call to courage. This is how: To become morally good is not simply a matter of letting the "seed of goodness implanted in our species . . . develop without hindrance," it also requires active "combat" against the innate propensity to evil.[13] So, moral goodness requires internal combat. What provides an incentive to this combat? Courage. What provides an incentive to courage? The very call to courage, which is made by Reason: "[F]or simply to make the demand for courage goes halfway towards infusing it."[14]

Like courage, hope is also a self-enacting mood. The very act of hoping that one has a pure disposition, for example, aids in the creation of such a disposition.[15] One can only "hope" that one's disposition is good because the actual character of that disposition forever remains opaque to the self: "[N]ot even does a man's inner experience with regard to himself enable him to fathom the depths of his own heart."[16] For Kant, self-doubt about one's disposition is inevitable and pervasive. I have a hunch that this fundamental doubt also plays a motivational role in the Kantian system, perhaps by making one fidgety (Kant calls it "apprehensive") and thus more interested in seeking the "peace" and (somatic) tranquility afforded by actions governed by traditional conceptions of duty. But, again, Kant is not forthcoming on this topic.

The third element in Kant's circumspect theory of moral motivation involves the power that he attributes to moral exemplars and archetypes. These ideal, pure forms have a kind of centripetal force that draws humans in their vicinity into their orbit; they infect free beings and induce conduct resembling that of the exemplar or archetype. Take, for example, the exemplar Jesus: "Now it is our universal duty as men," writes Kant, "to *ele-*

vate ourselves to this ideal of moral perfection, that is, to this archetype of the moral disposition in all its purity— . . . *for this the idea itself* . . . *can give us power.*"[17] The idea of pure goodness has great efficacy; it can transform will into effect. Jesus, or his exemplary life, or the very idea of Jesus (an archetype "already present in our reason"[18]) "opens the portals of freedom to all who, like him, choose to become dead to everything that holds them fettered to life on earth. . . ."[19] Jesus has "radiant" power; but Kant's rigoristic distinction between the sensuous and the moral prevents him from describing this power as operating upon the affective register of sense-experience.[20]

Do good exemplars exert the same kind of force as exemplars of evil— but in a different direction? Are embodied exemplars like Jesus more potent than pure archetypes like the idea of Jesus? Do all of these share the same modus operandi? And how exactly does that work? Kant insists that the answers to such questions are "inconceivable," beyond the limits of reason alone. But I think that we can get a general picture of the how of his morality by paying attention to the role played by nonsensuous sentiments, by a performative reason, and by infectious exemplars. To provide a fuller phenomenological account of the psychosomatic triggers or affective components of the power wielded by morality requires me to go beyond the limits of Kantian morality alone. I agree with Kant that no one has an exact account of how these things actually work. But, I also think that his two-world metaphysic, even if construed as what Romand Coles, following Robert Pippin, describes as a "methodological" distinction integral to Kant's "transcendental story,"[21] constrains him from pursuing the issue further and pushes him to distinctions in kind when differences in degree would be more credible.

Aesthetic Play and the Barbarism of Reason

I try to show above how Kant's official efforts to confine morality to the realm of reason and divinity and their lawful imperative voice run into difficulties of clarity and credibility at crucial points. My claims about the latent somaticism within his terms do not suffice to disprove the Kantian model of moral energetics, but they do create space for alternative readings. Moral sentiments are an uneasy combination of impelling force and ethereal intellectuality.[22] They have nothing of the sensuous about them, and yet somehow they possess the power to provoke human bodies into action. Their existence in Kantian philosophy suggests that Kant himself saw a need for some motivational supplement to the moral law. Kant's (perhaps strategic?) refusal to address more directly the ethical potential of somatic moods and sentiments, however, compels him to engage in conceptual acrobatics. It also prevents him from exploring deeply enough how such affective elements might be orchestrated into an ethical sensibility designed to shore up and support the law.

Schiller, however, takes up the task that Kant drops. One might say that he pulls Kant's underground theory of moral motivation into the light of day in a way that leads to an early modern version of the aestheticization of ethics. Kant, in his *Critique of Judgment*, had already made a place in his system for the aesthetic, but it is an aesthetic conceived as disinterested judgment rather than the heart-felt mood of which Schiller speaks. A judgment of taste, said Kant, is devoid of any interest in the particular object judged beautiful. "What matters is what I do with this presentation within myself," not what utility, value, of affective impact the object might have.[23] What one is doing during an aesthetic judgment is harmonizing one's faculties with each other in "a free and indeterminately purposive entertainment of the mental powers," a "free play" akin to the action of flames in a fireplace.[24]

Schiller treats the aesthetic not as a disinterested judgment but as the pleasing sensation that all's well with the world. Humans have a built-in desire for such a contentment; it is called the "play-drive." In addition to the (receptive) "sense-drive," which "wants to be determined, wants to receive its object" and the (take-charge) "form-drive," which "wants itself to determine, wants to bring forth its object,"[25] we are also graced with a play-drive that seeks peace between the two and works to interfere with the single-minded seriousness with which each pursues its goal. The play-drive wants the egoistic sense-drive to lighten up and the imperialistic form-drive to give it a rest. The play-drive is a protean force that can be cultivated into an aesthetic disposition, a state of being wherein both our active and passive natures are engaged without either one dominating.

The existence of some kind of play-drive is consistent within the enchanted materialism that I am developing. Less amenable to it, however, is Schiller's claim that the aesthetic disposition has the power to *harmonize* self and society by bringing our "selfish and violent" nature into alignment with the moral will. "Taste alone brings harmony into society, because it fosters harmony in the individual," says Schiller, and "we must continue to regard every attempt at political reform as untimely, and every hope based upon it as chimerical, as long as the split within man is not healed."[26] For Schiller, taste has this power by virtue of its status as the agent of a (transcendental) Reason (itself the ultimate source of the moral law).

In positing this transcendental Reason, Schiller follows Kant, but Schiller affirms, more actively than Kant, the need for Reason to employ a phenomenal champion:

> Reason has accomplished all that she can accomplish by discovering the law and establishing it. Its execution demands a resolute will and ardour of feeling. If

Truth is to be victorious . . . she must . . . appoint some drive to be her champion in the realm of phenomena; for drives are the only motive forces in the sensible world.[27]

Reason calls upon the play-drive, but Schiller insists that this is not to say that Reason is subservient to its champion. Rather, Reason is the original creator of the play-drive, by means of the following performative utterance: "Let there be a bond of union between the form-drive and the material drive; that is to say, let there be a play-drive, since only the union of reality with form, contingency with necessity, passivity with freedom, makes the concept of human nature complete"[28] (103).

Transcendental Reason, itself inaccessible, finds imperfect expression, says Schiller, not only in taste but in the intellect (an effect of the form-drive). He takes care to note, however, that the truth we glimpse via the intellect is *experienced differently* than the truth we apprehend in the presence of beauty. In the former, he says, our "delight" is of a peculiarly analytical kind: "When we take such delight in intellectual knowledge, we distinguish very exactly between our perception and our feeling, and look upon the latter as something incidental." In contrast, in the presence of beauty, "no such succession of activity and passivity can be discerned; reflection is here so completely interfused with feeling that we imagine that the form is directly apprehended by sense" (187). Schiller makes this distinction as part of a larger strategy of defending aesthetics from the charge of having an inherently amoral character.

Schiller's notion of the aesthetic makes important contributions to the model of ethics with affect that I endorse. First, he makes a persuasive case for the ethical insufficiency of intellect. Recent history, in particular the French Revolution, had forced him to ponder the disturbing coexistence of rational enlightenment and ethical barbarism. Consider "all the light which philosophy and empirical science have kindled"! "Our age is Enlightened; that is to say, such knowledge has been discovered and publicly disseminated as would suffice to correct . . . our practical principles"! "The spirit of free inquiry has . . . undermined the foundations upon which fanaticism and deception had raised their throne"! But, asks Schiller, "how is it, then, that we still remain barbarians (49–51)?" We remain barbarians because we call upon intellect to carry more moral weight than it can bear. No matter how "forcibly" arguments convince us of moral truths, Schiller says, only a cultivated disposition can bridge the gap between "acceptance" of truth and the "adoption" of it (51). "The development of man's capacity for feeling is, therefore, the more urgent need of our age . . . precisely because it provides the impulse for bettering our insights" (53). Here, Schiller suggests that, even if by some miracle, a rational consensus concerning moral principles were to be achieved, the problem of barbarism would still haunt us.

I also endorse Schiller's attempt to assign a pointedly ethical role to bodily affect; he figures the aesthetic as a disposition.[29] Moreover, although we are born with the potential for the aesthetic, it is something that must be cultivated through a combination of self-inducement and cultural education. As Schiller puts it, the aesthetic disposition is "at once a state of our being and an activity we perform."[30] I follow Schiller in thinking of dispositions as distinctly disciplined forms of affect, as deliberate "modulation[s] of the psyche,"[31] as requiring something like what Foucault calls "technologies of the self," that is, the means by which humans effect "a certain number of operations on their own bodies and souls, thought, conducts, and way of being, so as to transform themselves in order to attain a certain state of happiness, purity, wisdom, perfection, or immortality."[32] Foucault and I both part company with Schiller, however, when he bestows upon this aesthetic ethics the power to harmonize or reconcile; for Schiller, a proper aesthetic education is morally indispensable because it alone can reconcile our "physical character" (which demands multiplicity and ceaseless change) with our "moral character" (which demands unity and "unconditional cause.")[33]

Schiller imagines a (meta)physics different from that of the enchanted materialism that I pursue. He shares what Gordon Michalson calls Kant's "background metaphysical trust" that "reality as a whole is the scene of an ongoing cooperative effort between humanity and God in the production of a moral universe."[34]

More overtly and confidently than Kant, Schiller[35] pictures the world as a benevolent order enchanted with divine will. His account of the aesthetic mood, for example, treats the longing for personal and social unity as a sign of a primordial harmony that was fully realized in the ancient Greek world but with which we now fail to maintain steady contact (31). Only while under the spell of the aesthetic mood can we again capture something of that harmony, and then only briefly. The aesthetic mood, while it lasts, achieves reconciliation. One receives physical pleasure from the closure heretofore restricted to the logical realm of the ideal; one no longer merely envisions a beautiful unity, one has come to embody it; one not only is pressed upon by the multiple specificities of matter, one experiences them as a perfect complexity. The aesthetic disposition thereby betokens the existence of a primordial harmony, both within human nature and between humans and the universe. It is a talisman or sign, Schiller notes:

> In the enjoyment of beauty, or aesthetic unity, an actual union and interchange between matter and form, passivity and activity, momentarily takes place, [and] the compatibility of our two natures, the practicability of the infinite being realized in the finite . . . is thereby actually proven (189).

In regretting the loss of the gold age of cosmological harmony, Schiller tells a disenchantment tale. The gods have retreated, he says, though there is a certain historical necessity to their departure and to the fragmentation of the self that it produces: "If the manifold potentialities in man were ever to be developed, there was no other way but to pit them one against the other"—"no other way in which the species as a whole could have progressed" (39, 41). Moreover, Kantian Reason has now filled the role vacated by a more directly involved divinity. Schiller retains Kant's notion of a transcendental Reason as the guarantor of morality even as he criticizes Enlightenment "reason" as a one-sided, cold abstract.

Schiller is well aware that in assigning such a important moral role to the aesthetic disposition, he must respond to the charge that the motivational power of the play-drive is indifferent to the ends to which it is put. Schiller acknowledges that there is some truth to this, but he says that the danger is greatly ameliorated by the natural affinity—a gratuitous gift of nature (191)—between the play-drive and Reason. Remember, the play-drive is the angel of Reason, its agent in the sensible world. Although the play-drive ought to be cultivated and refined, Elizabeth Wilkinson and L. A. Willoughby say that there is for Schiller an "irreducible basis of natural endowment without which even the best [aesthetic] . . . education is of no avail."[36]

According to Schiller,[37] "The step from the aesthetic to the logical and moral state (i.e., from beauty to truth and duty) . . . man can accomplish simply of his own free will. . . . But the step from brute matter to beauty . . . must first be facilitated by the grace of Nature" (163). We are graced with a "delight in semblance, and a propensity to ornamentation and play." This makes trusting the aesthetic disposition a whole lot easier.

Schiller's notion of "semblance" is another of his attempts to inscribe the aesthetic within the bounds of Reason. Beauty is that which "we love just because it is semblance, and not because we take it to be something better" (193). The aesthetic is an appreciation of beauty that acknowledges the inferiority of beauty to "the truth of morals" or the "real existence" of the inaccessible noumenal realm. The lover or maker of beauty must "scrupulously refrain" (197) from "dishonest semblance" and its "lying colours which mask the face of truth and are bold enough to masquerade as reality." He must instead engage only in that "honest" and "beneficent" semblance "with which we fill out our emptiness and cover up our wretchedness" (201). (Schiller's "beneficent semblance," which knows itself to have a purely palliative function, is akin to what Nietzsche will call a necessary illusion.)

Schiller's distinction between authentic "aesthetic play" and hedonistic "fantasy play" is also designed to link the aesthetic to the moral. Fantasy play is an activity of the imagination "which, without any reference to form, . . . simply delights in . . . a free association of images" (209). "With its wilful moods and unruly appetites," fantasy is

> uncultivated taste [which] seiz[es] . . . upon what is new and startling—on the colourful, fantastic, and bizarre . . . shunning nothing so much as tranquil simplicity. It fashions grotesque shapes, loves swift transitions, exuberant forms, glaring contrast, garish lights (211).

Aesthetic play, quite to the contrary, engages an "autonomous shaping power within" which "subjects the arbitrary activity of the imagination to its own immutable and eternal unity, introduces its own autonomy into the transient, its own infinity into the life of sense."[38]

Schiller's distinctions between beauty and truth, dishonest and beneficent semblance, and aesthetic and fantasy play are his attempts to keep the aesthetic within the bounds of a higher law, the absolute of a Reason that can never be known directly. He locates his affective ethics within a Kantian metaphysic that can not quite accommodate it in order to ward off the charge that he has exposed ethics to the whim and caprice of subjective taste and bodily appetite. Schiller himself names the "formidable argument" raised against him:

> The delights of the Beautiful can, in the right hands, be made to serve laudable ends. But it is by no means contrary to its nature for it to have, in the wrong hands, quite the opposite effect, and to put its soul-seducing power at the service of error and injustice.[39]

Schiller proclaims this objection to be "entirely right; for beauty produces no particular result whatsoever, neither for the understanding nor for the will. It accomplishes no particular purpose, neither intellectual nor moral."[40] Because it heals the self, however, the aesthetic nevertheless provides the essential precondition of the free exercise of the moral will. Schiller notes:

> The transition from a passive state of feeling to an active state of thinking and willing cannot . . . take place except via a middle state of aesthetic freedom . . . it is . . . the necessary pre-condition of our attaining to any insight or conviction at all. *In a word, there is no other way of making sensuous man rational except by first making him aesthetic.*[41]

Only in the aesthetic mood is one together enough to go about the difficult but utterly "free" business of willing. Only then, says Schiller, is one "enabled . . . to make of himself what he will— . . . the freedom to be what he ought to be is completely restored to him."[42]

Schiller's picture of a moral will that chooses truth without, in any way, being primed or conditioned sits uneasily with his own claims about the singular necessity of the aesthetic state. Over and over, Schiller finds himself making the paradoxical assertion of the aesthetic as *the amoral precondition of an unconditioned morality.* The aesthetic disposition frees us to will the universal law freely. The aesthetic modulation of the psyche conditions the exercise of the unconditioned moral will. Such formulations trip over themselves in trying to affirm a positive role for sensuous experience in morality while still defending a notion of morality as the pure act of an unconditioned will. Beauty surely does *not* "meddle in the business of either thinking or deciding"—it "merely imparts the power to do both, [having] . . . no say whatsoever in the actual use of that power."[43] The aesthetic is surely *not* "an aid to thought"—it "merely . . . furnish[es] the thinking faculty with the freedom to express itself according to its own laws." Schiller admits, however, that even this mere imparting and mere furnishing "presupposes that the freedom of the thinking powers could be inhibited, which seems to contradict the notion of an autonomous faculty."[44] For Schiller, as for Kant, the autonomous, affect-free will is treated as indispensable even though it appears to be impossible.

How then might one summarize Schiller's treatment of the aesthetic? First, the aesthetic is an existential possibility, one of the dispositions available to human beings given appropriate circumstances and education. Precisely because realization of this possibility engenders a feeling of harmony, the aesthetic disposition also functions as a sign of a designed universe. The aesthetic disposition is a special instance of the play-drive; the play-drive is a special tool of Reason's demand that the self seek unity; the demand for unity, responsible for our progression from savagery to civilization, is a gratuitous gift of nature. To the question, then, "What is the aesthetic?" Schiller answers that it is a gracious disposition and a divine sign.

The aesthetic, as a refinement of sensuous experience, is also presented as a precondition of moral action. Beautiful things, says Schiller, give sensuous pleasure. If this pleasure—and the sense-drive that participates in it— is progressively refined through an aesthetic education, then beauty can work in tandem with the moral will. And only then can the "soul-seducing power"[45] of beauty function to make us live according to the principles that we had hitherto merely believed in. Beauty will support both sound and unsound judgments, both kind and cruel principles—after all, willing the good cannot be the effect of any external condition for Schiller as for Kant. But, the harmony of self engendered at the moment of exposure to the beautiful is nonetheless the condition of possibility of any willing at all, good or ill. In short, in response to the question, "What does the aesthetic do?" Schiller replies that it heals the self and thus enables the free will to exercise itself morally.

Schiller's model of "ethics-with-aesthetics" surely has its problems. In addition to the assumption of cosmological harmony alloyed to it, many people today either find the notion of primordial drives untenable or understand them to be more complex than Schiller imagined. Despite this, I am unable to dismiss either his central claim about the ethical insufficiency of intellectuality or his intuition that "play" is somehow involved in the will to engage the other ethically. Schiller was unconvinced that ethics is solely a matter of a code, a set of rational criteria set out in advance of behavior to guide and judge it. *On the Aesthetic Education of Man* was Schiller's attempt to speak a word for "disposition" as an ethical entity. Dispositions are at least as much made as given, and their aesthetic education is as crucial to ethics as principles, reasons, and their assemblage into a moral code.

Here, Michel Foucault sides with Schiller. Although Schiller does not provide the details of his aesthetic pedagogy, Foucault gives considerable attention to the "micropolitics" of ethics, to the techniques for building an aesthetic-ethical sensibility.

Schiller to Foucault: Micropractices of Ethics

Kant officially bars sensuous affect from the agency side of pure morality, but it seems to keep leaking back in. Schiller gives more weight to the aesthetic in morality, but he jeopardizes the purity of moral reason in providing this supplement. Is there another problematic that can compete with these two possibilities credibly in thinking about the relation of aesthetics to ethics?

Also a partial critic of Enlightenment, Foucault believes with Schiller that a code is morally inadequate: "For an action to be 'moral,' it must not be reducible to an act or a series of acts conforming to a rule, a law, or a value. . . . There is . . . no moral conduct that does not [also] call for the forming of oneself as an ethical subject; and no forming of the ethical subject without 'modes of subjectivation' and an 'ascetics' or 'practices of the self' that support them."[46] Making principled assertions is a part of ethics, but one must also ask "what is the work which I must effect upon myself so as to be capable and worthy of *acceding* to the truth?"[47] In *Use of Pleasure*, Foucault examines one time and place where great attention was paid to this latter task. Whereas today "the main emphasis is placed on the [ethical] code, on its systematicity, its richness, its capacity to adjust to every possible case," in Greek and Greco-Roman antiquity "the strong and dynamic [ethical] element is to be sought in the forms of subjectivation and the practices of the self."[48] In this model of ethics, "the necessity of respecting the law and the customs—the *nomoi*—was very often underscored, [but] more important than the content of the law and its conditions of application was the attitude that caused one to respect them."

The real challenge in thinking about ethics, then, is to "keep in mind the distinction between the code elements of a morality and the elements of ascesis, neglecting neither their coexistence, their interrelations, their relative autonomy, nor their possible differences of emphasis."[49]

Both Schiller and Foucault insist upon the intimacy of the ethical and the aesthetic, where the latter describes a sensibility formed in part by self-conscious craft. The ethical dimension of Foucault's last works comes to the fore most sharply, I think, when placed in the ethical tradition of Schiller. One can now hear Foucault's "aesthetics of existence" as a rejoinder to Schiller's call to work on the self so as to bind the body's "ardour" to an ethical code. Many of Foucault's neo-Kantian critics fail to note this connection, perhaps because they distance morality further from its somatic energies than even Kant did and further from aesthetics than Schiller did.

Foucault speaks of technologies of the self, or the means through which humans effect "a certain number of operations on their own bodies and souls, thoughts, conducts, and way of being, so as to transform themselves in order to attain a certain state of happiness, purity, wisdom, perfection, or immortality."[50] That formulation exhibits a precise ambiguity with regard to the question of who or what is directing these elaborations and operations, and what ends they serve. Is the transformation of self a matter of socially imposed normalization? Or are techniques "of" the self-normalizing pressures internalized by the self and applied to itself? Or do such technologies afford opportunities for reflective modification of the self by the self? Foucault believes it impossible to discern exactly the relative weights of these three in the formation of any given self. His early work accentuated the first two modalities of self-formation; for example, the discussion of "bio-power" in *Discipline and Punish* sensitized readers to the normalizing power of disciplinary practices that, like Schiller's aesthetic education, write the law right into the body. Hence, Foucault speaks of subjectivation rather than education. Eagleton makes a Foucaultian point when he warns that Schiller's attempt to conjoin reason with sentiment has the effect of inscribing power "in the minutiae of subjective experience,"[51] and that it participates in the larger historical trend whereby "power is shifting its location from centralized institutions to the silent, invisible depths of the subject itself."[52] But, that is just one side of Foucault, a side he never dismissed but nonetheless complicates.

Foucault's later work affirms a project of aesthetic inscription—sensibility appears as susceptible, to some uncertain degree, to self-conscious craftsmanship. Here, Foucault foregrounds the last modality of self-formation, that is, the reflective modification of the sensibility of the self by the self. If the point of his early genealogies was to expose individualism as a ruse of power and to disrupt our association of self-discipline with freedom, the point of his later work is to enunciate the more complex thesis that there is no self without discipline, no discipline that does not also harbor opportunities for arts of the self, and no effective ethics without such an aesthetic project. A moment of freedom survives within subjectivity after all, at least when it is not reduced to a purely intellectual formation.

What kind of freedom can coexist with ubiquitous, productive power? Foucaultian freedom is surely not the Kantian idea of an autonomous rational will; neither is it Schiller's romantic revision of Kant wherein an aesthetic modulation of the psyche allows the rational will fully to engage. Like Schiller, Foucault refuses to reduce ethics to a matter of reason; but unlike Schiller, Foucault proceeds further to pluralize the notion of "reason":

> I think that the central issue of philosophy and critical thought since the eighteenth century has been, still is, and will, I hope, remain the question, *What* is the Reason that we use? What are its historical effects? What are its limits, and what are its dangers?[53]

Schiller and Foucault are both friendly critics of Enlightenment, though their concern with, respectively, disposition and subjectivation, does not exclude reason. Indeed, for both thinkers, such an exclusion cannot occur and must not be attempted. For Schiller, the relation between rationality and morality is an ontological necessity; for Foucault, it is a pragmatic one linked to the philosophical history of the west and to the linguistic element of ethical life. Schiller repeatedly ties the aesthetic disposition to the "imperious" voice of Reason; Foucault understands himself as "fortunately committed to practicing a rationality."

Foucault resignifies freedom by locating it in relation to a historically situated rationality and a recalcitrant body. He tries to find a way to speak of the moments of individual self-direction that persist inside disciplinary power and to do so outside of a Kantian vocabulary. To engage "the limits that are imposed on us" is, says Foucault, at the same time to "experiment with the possibility of going beyond them."[54] He refuses to define freedom in opposition to a system of external constraints; freedom is rather a reflective heteronomy. It is the recognition of one's implication in a web of social and physical relations within which reside vital opportunities for self-direction. Sometimes, the self-direction is direct; more often, it is by arts, techniques, and strategies applied by the self to a corporeal sensibility below the level of direct intellectual control. The experience of freedom is still possible; one can still experience the exhilaration of making a mark upon what one comes to be. But this liberatory self-naming is not a transcendence of power. It consists, rather, in tentative explorations of the outer edges of the current regime of subjectivity. These engagements with the frontier foreground the possibility of new configurations of identity. These novelties are themselves a function of an institutional matrix, they still are implicated in historically contingent practices of power, and they still contend with a body that never fully coincides with the subjectivity available to it. Kafka's ape made a similar point. Caught and caged for exhibition, Rotpeter decided to become human, for only then would he be let out. "Freedom," he says, "was not what I wanted. Only a way out; right or left, or in any direction; I made no other demand."[55] He seeks not unconditional freedom, only a way to transform his situation into a place with more room to exercise his potential for self-direction.

Foucault abandons Schiller's Kantian language of moral autonomy, but he shares some of Schiller's (and Kant's) faith in the transformative capacity of an ideal like freedom. He acknowledges that the very experience of freedom depends, again to some uncertain degree, on the ardent wish for individualized self-direction and on the dream of a beautifully designed subjectivity. Such efficacious fictions help to make the freedom there is to be had havable. Foucault, also, I think, retains a bit of romantic faith in beauty. Schiller linked beauty to goodness in this way: An aesthetic mood arises in the presence of a beautiful object in nature, and what is beautiful about it is the singularity of its very existence; as one becomes practiced in experiencing natural objects in their unique specificity, one, in turn, becomes more competent at recognizing other selves for their own sake; thus, the characteristic quality of the self under the sway of an aesthetic mood is an appreciation of the freedom (i.e., the self-determining potential) of others. Foucault never endorses such a theory, but his insistence on describing the arts of crafting a self as an *ethical* practice suggests that he too forges a link between respect for others and a refined aesthetic sensibility.

When Schiller experienced beauty, he glimpsed the harmony originally designed for us. In the enjoyment of beauty, he notes, "the practicability of the infinite being realized in the finite is . . . thereby actually proven."[56] Foucault does not share this vision of a designed or providential world but endorses a more Nietzschean picture. Kant's notion of the moral law as an "imperious demand" or command, which Schiller more or less adopts, holds no appeal for Foucault. He finds a morality based in transcendental command to be inimical to the spirit of ethical generosity and to be too blunt and harsh and too inattentive to the complexities of specific situations and possibilities. Perhaps he overplays that point—maybe a transcendental morality imbued with a spirit of generosity can be so attentive. Because Foucault rejects Schiller's metaphysics of harmony, he cannot use Schiller's solution to the problem of the moral indifference of affect, that is, the claim that one can distinguish clearly, in theory and in experience, between an aesthetic sensibility serving reason and a promiscuous fantasizing, between a lying semblance and a semblance understood to be for entertainment purposes only. How, then, might a non-Kantian respond to the idea that the motivational power of the aesthetic is indifferent to the ends to which it is put?

The Dangers of Aestheticization

Neo-Kantians and neo-Marxists together have raised the concern that to allow aesthetics to enter ethics is to pollute it with the arbitrariness of taste; an aestheticized ethics removes morality from the "realm of determinate truth and falsehood" and opens the door to "mystified national-aestheticist themes, including . . . Nazi cultural propaganda."[57] In aesthetics, what counts is dramatic effect, not ethical content; beauty and other affections divert attention from the principle of "respect for all rational nature as ends-in-themselves" in favor of "a dramaturgical model of conduct, in which action becomes meaningful solely qua performative gesture."[58] As Schiller describes the worry, the aesthetic tends toward the "new and startling— . . . the colourful, fantastic, and bizarre, the violent and the savage"; it valorizes "grotesque shapes, . . . swift transitions, exuberant forms, glaring contrasts, garish lights, and song full of feeling."[59]

How to respond to such concerns? One can begin by acknowledging that there is no way to guarantee that an aesthetic disposition will produce or even incline toward goodness, generosity, or social justice. Affect can join narcissism, beauty can serve violence, and enchantment can foster cruelty. These links are not inevitable, however, and an affective ethics does not automatically lead to frivolity, violence, or cruelty. It is also important to recall, as the critics often fail to do, that even rationality-based morality cannot determine what its ethical effects will be. Kant, for instance, was eventually compelled to come to terms with a propensity to evil in the will that the will might not be able to overcome by its own power. The source of the moral law (reason, nature, God) has never been definitively established or known with certainty by humans, and this uncertainty allows a wide variety of ethical effects. It can, as with Weber's Calvinists, provoke energetic attempts to enact an austere code. Or it can, as with the heirs of Blumenberg's nominalism, issue in a free-wheeling orientation of self-assertion.

There are, however, some positive ways to respond to the ethical indeterminacy of affect, though here, too, no cure exists. One can, for example, argue on behalf of a particular ethical use of affect or, in what is perhaps a more effective strategy, tell exemplary stories of such uses in the hope of enchanting bodies and inflecting imaginations toward them. One might wish for the means to make a more determinate or certain impact on ethical life, but no one has discovered them yet. Like my story of contemporary enchantments, Foucault's account of Greco-Roman practices of "care of the self," for example, is not simply an attempt to open the cultural imaginary to a wider range of ethical models. It is also a *call* to engage in the self-discipline necessary to assemble one's affects into an aesthetic sensibility and to render sense-perception sensitive to the amazing specificity of everything around us. This is, I think, what Nietzsche also meant to do when he said

> *One thing is needful.*—To "give style" to one's character—a great and rare art! It is practiced by those who survey all the strengths and weaknesses of their nature and then fit them into an artistic plan until every one of them appears as art and reason and even weaknesses delight the eye. Here a large mass of second nature has been added; there a piece of original nature has been removed—both times through long practice and daily work at it. Here the ugly that could not be removed is concealed; there it has been reinterpreted and made sublime. Much that is vague and resisted shaping has been saved and exploited for distance views; it is meant to beckon toward the far and immeasurable.[60]

One gives oneself style in order to become more self-content, more joyful, and ultimately more disposed toward generosity. Deleuze and Guattari's call to exercise caution and to proceed slowly in self-experimentation makes a similar point about the need to combine affective energies with deliberate disciplines. George Kateb, too, believes that though "the hostility . . . of aestheticism to morality often is . . . great," it is also possible "that a more deliberate aestheticism in one form or another may cooperate with morality or may be its good friend."[61]

But, again, it should be admitted that there is nothing inherently ethical about an artistry of the self and that something like cruelty or violence will be the object of a self-conscious aestheticization. To use an American example instead of the German one, the Pentagon has presented television images of annihilating weapons as sublime mushroom clouds against a desert sky, as a meteor shower of lights over Baghdad, as a sleek and elegant stealth bomber-bird. It is, however, both futile and oppressive to respond to such aestheticizations by attempting to eradicate the aesthetic dimension of ethics. As Schiller suggests, the organization of affect is crucial to the effectivity of ethics. So the attempt to sever ethics from aesthetics because of the dangers carried by the latter spells the probable defeat of ethics.

Also, it has been contended that an affective model of ethics, which posits desire as a powerful force in ethical life, subjects ethics to the tyranny of corporeal cravings, pleasurable emissions, and irrational obsessions. Ethics thus becomes a dangerous discourse of the body. Schiller was able to ward off the danger of hedonism by divorcing aesthetic play from fantasy play, but, if one rejects Schiller's metaphysical justification for this separation, what defense is there against the "wilful moods" and "unruly appetites" of the body?[62] Here, one good response consists in asserting the importance of discipline to aesthetics. A case also could be made that fantasy play itself performs an ethical function in that it calls the oppressiveness of symbolic law into question. Such a challenge can contribute to the emergence of a new, more generous ethos. Then, perhaps, one can defend Foucault's approach without conceding that ethics, properly understood, has nothing to do with fantasy play.[63]

Foucault's critics often miss that he assigns a central role to micropolitical self-discipline. Terry Eagleton, for example, conceives of the aesthetic as a discourse concerned with "the way reality strikes the body on its sensory surface."[64] Eagleton is right to link aesthetics to a sensuous, responsive body, but his juxtaposition of the body to a reality that *strikes* it figures the body as a reactive receptor; the aesthetic self is treated as only a consumer of beautiful things. By figuring bodily responsiveness as a kind of reflex, Eagleton's formulation obscures the possibility of an experimentally cultivated responsiveness to others. He obscures the way arts of the self are integral to ethics. Eagleton overlooks a third term, *sensibility*, residing between a striking reality and a stricken body.

Sensibility, a refinement or new assemblage of sensible primordia, is culturally encoded and temperamentally delimited, but it is still educable to some uncertain degree. Like the code dimension of ethics, techniques of sensibility-formation are concerned with governing and refining behavior. The difference is that these techniques respond to subtle norms of admirable behavior and thought; they address the question of which modes of perception and which styles of comportment, and not simply which actions, are most laudable. It even might be said that this makes for a more resilient and careful approach to ethics. Codes are crude things, and much behavior of ethical significance—that is, with the potential to do violence to others—slips between the cracks. "What struck me about Antiquity," says Foucault, "is that the points around which reflection is most active regarding sexual pleasure are not at all the points which represented the traditionally received forms of prohibition. On the contrary, it was where sexuality was the least restricted that the moralists of antiquity questioned themselves with the most intensity and where they succeeded in formulating the most rigorous doctrines."[65]

Another danger commonly associated with an affective model of ethics is the privatization of the practice of ethics, or the reservation of these private arts to a small cultural elite. Stephen Best and Douglas Kellner put the point in Marxist terms. Those who reject "traditional rationalist politics based on ideology critique, the overcoming of false consciousness, the subordination of art to politics, and a pragmatic concern with the serious business of seizing power," can respond to our libidinal manipulation by a capitalist order only with the feeble attempt to stylize self-perception.[66] Best and Kellner view the aesthetic turn not as an attempt to harness affective energies but as a retreat from ethics and politics. Alex Callinicos concurs:

> Foucault . . . asks why "everyone's life couldn't become a work of art?" The answer, of course, is that most people's lives are still . . . shaped by their lack of access to productive resources and their consequent need to sell their labour-power in order to live. To invite [these people] . . . to make a work of art of their lives would be an insult—unless linked to precisely the kind of strategy for global social change which . . . poststructuralism rejects.[67]

Of course, it is not clear whether neo-Marxism itself possesses a viable "strategy for global social change" or whether it has done enough to cultivate a sensitivity to the impositions and violences engendered by such an ambitious project. One might also reply that the failure to focus on the economic dimensions of ethics is not a dismissal of their importance. Why would someone *choose* to focus on the micromaterialism of sensibility?[68] Perhaps because she judged that the obstacles to social justice included not only a lack of knowledge about economic oppression or a lack of the means to mitigate them, but also a lack of willingness to employ the knowledge and means available. Such an affective model of ethics would endorse Schiller's insight that any political response to our barbarisms depends, in part, on the cultivation of a somatic will to combat them. Upon what fund of ethical energy do critics of this model draw?

The macromaterialist critics insist that only the quest for a "politics of alliances" and "coalition building"[69] counts as an ethical response to injustice. Attempts to cultivate an generous disposition simply do not qualify. Eagleton says as much when he reduces Foucault's project to a desire to perfect one's personal style: "Foucault's vigorously self-mastering individual remains wholly monadic. Society is just an assemblage of autonomous self-disciplining agents, with no sense that their self-realization might flourish within bonds of mutuality."[70] But, Foucault does not have a monadic conception of the self. Rather, he insists on the impossibility of being outside a regime of power—a regime that both functions as the condition of possibility of any subjectivity and is incapable of preventing the emergence of political movements that disrupt the regime. Foucault does not reject "bonds of mutuality," though he does oppose the notion of "self-realization": he finds the quest for self-realization to be indulgent and implicated in an arbitrary project of normalization, as demonstrated in his study of the nineteenth-century hermaphrodite Herculine Barbin. But, there is no reason that an "aestheticized" self cannot engage in collective practices of mobilization for reasons other than self-realization. As Schiller might say, an aesthetic education can be one of the means through which we improve the quality and generosity of our connectedness to others.[71]

If one examines the contemporary concern about the aestheticization of ethics, what seems to cause the most alarm is the refusal to define ethics primarily in terms of a code or "prescriptive ensemble" of values, rules of action, and criteria of judgment. Many models of ethics are based on the undemonstrated presumption that if one does not endorse a *command* ethics one can have no ethics at all, that only a code-centered model can ensure a care for others. These models acknowledge some value to Schiller's aesthetic modulation of the psyche, *but not in the sphere of reason, ethics, or politics.* In contrast, those who focus on the "manner in which one ought to form oneself as an ethical subject acting in reference to the prescriptive elements that make up the code,"[72] do so because they concur with Foucault and Schiller that ethics must not fail to address the question of barbarism in an age of reason.

The aesthetic dimension of ethics is clearly susceptible to misuse, but so is the commitment to moral command or to the scientific method or to the exercise of authority. The unavoidable question is whether dispositions and sensibilities are ethically dispensable. To state the hypothesis boldly, command moralities have lost their hold on many people today, and they secure it for others only by recourse to forms of fundamentalism that are violent and exclusionary in character. "The idea of a morality as obedience to a code of rules is now disappearing," writes Foucault. "To this absence of a morality, one responds, or must respond, with a research which is that of an aesthetics of existence."[73] Foucault and Schiller together press critics of "aestheticization" to acknowledge how the perspective they endorse needs the aesthetic element that they want to expunge; they critically examine the sufficiency of the model of ethics as a code; and they ask us to think again about the relation of intellectual rationality to barbarism.

Language and the Code Dimension of Ethics

Richard Flathman's approach to ethics is not Kantian, Romantic, or Foucaultian; it is not grounded in rational imperatives or concerned with developing techniques for building an ethical sensibility. It focuses, instead, on the role that language plays in ethics, in particular, on how it ensures that the translation of principles into practical rules always will be imperfect and the gap between ethical rules and ethical outcomes never will be fully bridged. Rules cannot "themselves determine the conduct of those to whom they apply," says Flathman, because rules are made up of words, and the signification of words is inherently multiple and fluctuating.[74] Language is porous and contextually contained, and, as the context shifts, the rules always fail to keep pace.[75]

Flathman's critique of ethical rule-making as insufficient to ethical conduct is convincing to me. He speaks effectively against those who find principles and rules sufficient to the ethical life, but his account of language underplays its somatic character. For language is not only a matter of significations and failures of signification ("indeterminacy"), it is also about sound, noise, and differential intensities or affects. Isn't there, as Deleuze and Guattari suggest, a "sonority" to language? Sonority refers to the aural effectivity that living, moving, snorting, weeping, laughing bodies possess. Sonority does not represent, for it does not operate via images or in the visual mode; it is, rather, a "block that opposes the visual memory."[76] Kafka's stories are filled with enactments of such sonority:

> The receiver gave out a buzz of a kind that K. had never before heard on a telephone. It was like the hum of countless children's voices—but yet not a hum, the echo rather of voices singing at an infinite distance—blended by sheer impossibility into one high but resonant sound which vibrated on the ear as if it were trying to penetrate beyond mere hearing.[77]

This sonorous buzz is neither the form nor the content of expression; it is "pure and intense"; it is "always connected to its own abolition—a deterritorialized musical sound, a cry that escapes signification, composition, song, words . . . " (6).[78]

Now, sonority is a property of bodies-in-space. The sonority that K. heard was the emission of an assemblage of bodies, some technological, some metallic, some electric, some microbiological, some human. Moreover, each of these bodies, by itself, can be sonorous. Take, for example, a singular human body—its teeth grind and chatter, its lips smack and whistle, its tongue says, "Ahhh." Deleuze and Guattari go so far as to say that to use the mouth for speaking is to "deterritorialize" the mouth from its more primitive, sonorous function. Language-use steals the mouth from sound, including those sounds that accompany eating:

> [L]anguage always implies a deterritorialization of the mouth, the tongue, and the teeth. The mouth, the tongue, and the teeth find their primitive territoriality in food. In giving themselves over to the articulation of sounds, the mouth, tongue, and teeth deterritorialize. Thus, there is a certain disjunction between eating and speaking, and even more, despite all appearances, between eating and writing [because] . . . writing goes further in transforming words into things capable of competing with food. . . . To speak, and above all to write, is to fast (20).

"To speak is to fast." Language deterritorializes the mouth, tongue, teeth; in speech, sonority recedes in favor of signification (and the regular failure of signification). Language steals the mouth from eating/sonority and tries to make it pronounce/mean; language bends the sense of taste into the sense of meaning. But, some sonority manages to attach to language-use nonetheless. Words harbor cries, moos, meows, buzzes, mutterances, laughter, etc. These disruptive sounds contribute to the spell-binding effect of stories told aloud, the enchanting power of chants. Deleuze and Guattari note that

> children are well-skilled in the exercise of repeating a word . . . in order to make it vibrate around itself. . . . Kafka tells how, as a child, he repeated one of his father's expressions in order to make it take flight on a line of non-sense: "end of the month, end of the month" (21).

Sonority can distract humans from the sense of what someone is saying and propel them to idiosyncratic associations and thoughts—to engage in something like what Flathman calls an idiolect. Idiolects—speech acts that "make use, willfully . . . of the argot of a social and cultural *sous-monde*" (28)[79]—are polyglot, hybridizing ways of talking that disclose the singular character of those whose mouths employ them. My sense, however, is that the effects of such sonority are only weakly captured by the terms determinacy or indeterminacy.

To acknowledge both the semantic and the sonorous dimensions of language is to see that ethical codes also include these two elements. Flathman is right that rules are inherently ambiguous, and right to point out that rules do not function without "acceptance, commitment, or subscription." But these acts of will themselves require a certain mobilization of bodily energies by sonorous and other linguistic-affective means. Ethical commitments, for example, must overcome somatic inertia if they are to become ethical acts, and that overcoming requires an organization of affective intensities. In rejecting the overconfidence in rules evinced by neo-Kantians, Flathman inadvertently brings out how important arts of the self are to the sensitive ethical life.

At times, Flathman moves toward this terrain himself, for example, when he says that "if rules and rule following take us to or away from any destination they do so by the elbow not by the throat" (50). The point that Flathman intends to make here is that the power of rules is the polite and noncoercive kind rather than the crude and aggressive kind. But his rhetoric also marks a point where rule-following moves from a state of mind and a problem of signification to a matter of elbows, throats, postures, comportments, arts, and disciplines. It points to the somatic dimension of "rule-ing" and gestures toward the material tactics through which ethics proceeds.

Why are such moments relatively rare in Flathman's thinking? Why not experiment with the sonority of rules and the how of ethical conduct? For some theorists, this reluctance issues from a metaphysical imaginary within which earthly life and animal behavior are denigrated. Flathman clearly does not project a supersensible realm. His eschewal of affect seems to issue, rather, from a healthy aversion to moralism (i.e., the eager desire to impose one's own standards of faith, belonging, sexuality, etc., on others in the name of God, universality, or civilization). Flathman fears that to focus theoretical attention on how ethics works on the body is to support attempts to manipulate and homogenize individual behavior. He likes rules to be slippery so that people can elude the coercive traps set by them. From his perspective, the gap between rules and conduct is an opportunity to be exploited, for the failure of rules to self-enact can be part of a project to

> diminish the incidence of rote, mechanical, mimetic, or otherwise submissive behaviors. To the extent that individuals and groups . . . recognize that interpreting and judging are necessary to rules and rule following, attentive and self-critical thinking and acting will be legitimated and otherwise encouraged (56).

Flathman locates ethical agency in the "willful individual," though he acknowledges that this self is contextually circumscribed (90). An enchanted materialism goes a bit further. If humans are bodies-in-space among other bodies-in-space, and if agency is the (differentially distributed) capacity to make a difference in the world without knowing quite what you are doing, then there might be multiple sites of agency. An enchanted materialism embraces the possibility that differential degrees of agency reside in the intentional self, the inherited temperament of a self, a play-drive, molecules at far-from-equilibrium states, nonhuman animals, social movements, political states, architectural forms, families and other corporate bodies, sound fields. And, if there are multiple sites and degrees of micro- and macro-agency, then it becomes ethically important for humans to listen to subintentional forces within the self (e.g., side perceptions, wayward thoughts, the voice of "stress," the urge to play or to categorize). For these voices and forces could be shaping one's disposition in ways that are at odds with one's noble intentions, and it might be possible to work on some of these unruly elements by tactical means—to render them, for example, more amenable to a generous disposition. Flathman is right that an ethical theory concerned with moral sensibility risks becoming moralistic. But a focus on the energetics of ethics also enables more reflective arts of the self and more creative uses of the lines of flight opened up by the gap between the semantic and sonorous dimensions of linguistic forms. Tactics of the self are not only essential to the cultivation of responsiveness toward the singularity of other bodies, human and nonhuman, they are also needed to cultivate the singular individuality prized by Flathman.

Flathman himself goes a little way down this path when he notes the importance of an "adverbial" kind of social discipline, wherein rule followers "are associated with one another not by agreement in objective or purpose but . . . by their subscription to . . . do whatever they do in certain (civil) ways or manners . . . " (95). Here, the aim is not to authorize one set of ethical pursuits but to govern the performative style or "personae" of "self-chosen actions." How are such personae formed? Flathman says little about the mechanism of this, but we know it entails discipline. The adverbial requirement marks the need to restrict the imagination of "substantive satisfactions" to those aims capable of being enacted "*politely, temperately,* and *fastidiously; resolutely, candidly,* and *forthrightly; morally, legally,* and *civilly*" (99). One notes, however, that it is precisely because many enactments are not performed civilly (but rather belligerently, cruelly, stingily, crudely, or violently) that one must enter the dangerous terrain of ethical work on the self.

The Ethics of Enchanted Materialism

As Flathman points out, principles are more indeterminate than one might wish, and rules are insufficient to the principles they serve. Also, as Schiller and Foucault point out, neither principles nor rules are *self*-motivating. Even Kant seems to suggest, by his assignment of a moral role to a special set of "sentiments," that ethics involves intermediaries between the reception of a command and the mobilization of the will to abide by it. I have been making a case, through my readings of these theorists, for a model of ethics as a complex interplay of code and sensibility. Sensibility provides an impetus to enact the code and also sometimes reveals the need to revise it. Just how does an enchanted sensibility make it more likely that ethical principles will be enacted as ethical practices? Any response to this question must be somewhat experimental. The one that I am playing out is basically this: Enchantment is a feeling of being connected in an affirmative way to existence; it is to be under the momentary impression that the natural and cultural worlds *offer gifts* and, in so doing, remind us that it is good to be alive. This sense of fullness—what the Epicureans talked about in terms of *ataraxy* (contentment with existence)—encourages the finite human animal, in turn, to give away some of its own time and effort on behalf of other creatures. A sensibility attuned to moments of enchantment is no guarantee that this will happen, but it does make it more possible. Any sensibility is an orchestrated arrangement of affections, but affective energies are unruly and protean forces and tend to wander from the musical score. Thus, the link between them and an ethical sensibility is tenuous and unstable and requires repeated acts of discipline and retuning. I do not think that there is any way around this fragility or the effort it takes to respond to it.

Foucault agrees, at least up to a point. He names four tasks of an ethic. Each ethic identifies those *parts of the self* that are of particular moral concern (overt behavior, secret beliefs, dreams, inarticulate urges); a set of *exercises* (musical, gymnastic, meditational, liturgical) to install the ethical code on the body[80]; a *rationale* for obedience to ethical principles and exercises; and an *ideal of the self* to which the ethical person aspires.[81] That list of ethical tasks addresses first the sensibility dimension of ethics and then the code dimension. But Foucault himself said little about the latter—about what principles he endorsed, what moved him to pursue them, and what was the content of the ethical ideal toward which he was drawn. He refused to comment on these because "the role of an intellectual is not to tell others what they must do. By what right would he do so? And remember all the prophecies, promises, injunctions and plans intellectuals have been able to formulate in the course of the last two centuries and of which we have seen the effects."[82]

I think Foucault is right that ethical theorists have no special moral standing, but to remain silent about one's ethical vision because one lacks special standing is also problematic. If the claim is that ethical codes work only in tandem with sensibilities, then one needs to take the risk of articulating pieces of both elements so that the relationship between them can be explored. One needs to describe a set of ethical ideals and to offer an account of why they motivate, even if this description and this account are inherently contestable. One needs, in short, to enter the fray without special standing.

What is the content of my ethic of enchanted materialism, and what are the sources upon which it draws? The content, in important respects, is Thoreauian. Its appreciation of nonhuman, as well as human, sites of vitality—of what might be called its hyperecological sense of interdependence[83]—proceeds from and toward the principle of treading lightly on the earth. This is not to rule out or demonize technological engagements with it but, rather, to temper them with the modesty that comes from acknowledging the independent vitality of nonhuman forms and from admitting corollary limits in the capacities of human agents to know exactly what they are doing when they manipulate the world in which they participate. Related to this task is the need to discern more subtly the sensuous singularity of all things, natural and artifactual. By becoming more responsive to other material forms with which one shares space, one can better enact the principle of minimizing harm and suffering.

The source or rationale for this ethic is more difficult to articulate. Why ought enchanted materialists tread lightly, be humble, remember interdependencies, pay attention to details? Why work to discipline affect into a sensibility of generosity? There are many different reasons; there is no single rationale from which all human beings could be expected to draw. The terms *reasons* and *rationale* do not even apply equally well to all of the motivational sources. Some people are moved by the experience of divine command, some by divine love, some by humanistic sympathy, some by Kantian duty, some by a sense of correspondence between beauty and justice, and some by the enchantments of contemporary life.[84] My sense, however, is that all of these, in different ways, tap into a subintentional disposition in favor of life. For me, this disposition, akin to what Schiller spoke of in terms of the "gift" of a play-drive, is the fundamental ethical source. I am not sure if it is true that the other sources identified by other people derive from this one—for here is where modesty is most called for in every ethical theory—but I offer this story:

> There is, for most humans, a subdispositional attachment to the abundance of life that is deeply installed in their bodies. This attachment provides a positive energetics from which some try to cultivate a stance of presumptive generosity. But, this attachment also can be absent or killed by abuse, disease, or terrible misfortune. And then ethical theories of any sort become deactivated or moot. This is a tragic element within a world of enchanting matter. Attachment to this world is the contingent source of receptivity and generosity toward other bodies.[85] In the hem of this matrix, ethical principles, rules, ideals, and sensibilities are born. A variety of macro- and micro-agents act as midwife.

8

Attachments and Refrains

> Every new thought that wishes to make a differ-
> ence, even from one's previous thought, involves a
> new creation story, a new conception of origins,
> history, mind, body, world, and cosmos.[1]
> (*John Docker*)

DURING the time that it has taken to write this book, thousands of trage-
dies and horrors—thousands of specific acts of cruelty, madness, violence,
and suffering—have entered the world and come to my attention. Some
are the result of accident or other forces beyond human control, and some
are deliberate or political effects; most, it seems, are a combination of
the two. These instances have come to me through newspapers, radio,
television, films, and more personal and direct forms of experience. There
is no need to list examples; everyone has their own that readily come to
mind, for suffering is an affective condition difficult to ignore. For most
people, and especially at initial exposure, the suffering of others and the
prospect or experience of one's own suffering make an impression. This
physio-psychic fact is exploited by the contemporary news media, which
courts its audience by keeping it in a constant state of alarm: A plane has
crashed! A hurricane is brewing! Your water supply might be contami-
nated! Two men gunned down on the West side last night; killers still at
large! A new virus hits the U.S.! The number of dangers against which we
are warned every day has increased with the number of hours of broadcast
of the news. Insofar as the news media give prominence to the most sensa-
tional or dramatic forms of disaster, they both encourage a sense of fatalism
and divert attention from more everyday, structural forms of suffering,
such as grinding poverty and poor education.

How can someone write a book about enchantment in such a world?
This is a question that I have repeatedly asked myself. Several thoughts
emerge in response. One is an appeal to experience. Enchantment does
coexist with despair; somehow, it remains an existential actuality. Enchantment, that energizing and unsettling sense of the great and incredible fact
of existence, reflects a stubborn attachment to life that most bodies seem
to possess. To be enchanted is, in the moment of its activation, to assent
wholeheartedly to life—not to this or that particular condition or aspect

of it but to the experience of living itself. Moreover, these momentary experiences, as they accumulate, can have salutary effects on the background sense of being that informs daily life. I give voice to the minor chords of enchantment and seek to amplify what the more insistent sounds of suffering might mask. I see this task as worthy, partly because the more aware of wonder one is—and the more one learns to cultivate it—the more one might be able to respond gracefully and generously to the painful challenges posed by our condition as finite beings in a turbulent and unjust world. An enchantment tale disrupts the apocalyptic tenor of the news and the despair or cynicism that it breeds.[2] Because the news media cultivate a crisis mentality, it is important to heighten awareness of our profound—and empowering—attachment to life. For such attentiveness can help to transform shock at tragedy into a political will to reform painful social structures.

The background experience of enchantment can be brought out only by condensing and exaggerating its presence and force.[3] I have done this, but I also acknowledge that the power of enchantment to induce the graceful stance that I seek is limited and, for the most part, indirect. It is also important to note that the mood of enchantment is but one component, even if an underacknowledged one, of ethical life. The Kantian moral sentiments of duty and respect also can be a source of ethical concern. So can the experience of suffering, insofar as it fosters pathos or the recognition of our common liability to (physical, emotional, social, existential) pain. Adorno identifies suffering as "the unrest that makes knowledge move"[4]; suffering can also propel ethical action. Stephen K. White notes how, for Sheldon Wolin, it is "the common experience of 'misery' that 'creates the basis' and trajectory of a radical democratic political force."[5] My own sense is that the ethical and political potential within suffering is more likely to be realized if one's attention to suffering is infused by or remixed with the en-couraging experience of wonder.

Enchantment as a Weak Ontology

Another way to position my story of contemporary enchantments within the field of political and ethical theory and to summarize the themes that have emerged therein is to describe it as a *weak ontology*. This is the name that White gives to an emerging genre of social theory that develops its political analyses in conjunction with a set of contentions about the fundamental character of human being and the world. The practitioner of weak ontology believes that "such conceptualizations of self, other and world are necessary or unavoidable for an adequately reflective ethical and political life."[6] What distinguishes a weak ontologist from a traditional metaphysician is that the former emphasizes the necessarily speculative and contestable character of her onto-story and thus does not try to demonstrate its truth in any strong sense.[7]

I share White's sense that an ontological imaginary is an important part of political and ethical theorizing. Even more intriguing to me is his suggestion that the "ontological turn" encourages theorists to articulate a positive political and ethical vision. The idea here is that an onto-picture provides a more convivial setting for normative affirmations than does a discourse that strives to be postmetaphysical. How does a weak ontology encourage affirmative theorizing? I would augment White's work by suggesting that it does so by providing a kind of ground for theoretical claims. Theory that includes an onto-tale can link its specific contentions and critiques to a larger picture of the onto-possibilities, thus placing them in a richer and broader context. Thus situating its ethical and political commitments, a weak ontology enables a theory's audience to make better sense of why the theory singles out for criticism this (rather than that) political structure, why it identifies this (rather than that) ideology as the chief political danger, why it advocates this (rather than that) set of institutional reforms. A weak ontology bestows upon such choices and judgments a status that is more than subjective but less than objective: they are not as rhetorically thin as an individual preference or as dogmatically heavy as a generalizable truth—not too skinny and not too fat. . . .

Thus it is that onto-stories might give political theory an extra dose of normative courage. They might also enhance the aesthetic and rhetorical, hence persuasive, power of a theory. Think, for example, of what Donna Haraway's cyborg ontology did for (and to) her feminist socialism. Or of how the onto-story of the disenchantment of modernity supported the political agendas of Weberians and Marxists. White puts the point this way: Though a weak ontology cannot "determine categorically" political or moral judgments, it can help "engender certain dispositions toward ethical-political life that alter the affective and cognitive direction one takes into specific issues."[8] White takes seriously, as do I, the idea that affects are politically and ethically relevant, and one of the things an onto-story can do is inflect affective energies in one way rather than another. A metaphysical imaginary is always engaged in political interpretations, and this imaginary works indirectly at the level of affect. To render it explicit is to make it more available as a rhetorical strategy.

White understands the ontological turn in contemporary theory as a response to the criticism that critical theory (in its generic sense) has devoted too much effort to negative critique and not enough to elaborating an affirmative political response to the moral dangers and political injustices it exposes. (Such was the gist of my complaint with Horkheimer and Adorno.) White both notes a recent move in the direction of more

affirmative theorizing and puts pressure on the theorists whom he engages
to develop that dimension further: "I want to shift the intellectual burden
here from a preoccupation with what is opposed and deconstructed, to an
engagement with what must be articulated, cultivated and affirmed in its
wake."[9] For example, White chides the philosopher Judith Butler for ges-
turing toward, but failing to articulate more specifically, her commitment
to " 'fundamentally more capacious, generous, and "unthreatened" bear-
ings of the self.' "[10] The kind of articulation that White is looking for is a
demonstration of how this possibility resides within the ontological condition as Butler sees it. White presses Butler both to say more about the
normative vision propelling her critical work and to identify those dimensions of her ontology that would have to be cultivated in order to enact
the more generous model of self that she admires. What is it about being
as she conceives it that can be drawn upon as a resource for more capacious
identities?

There are, of course, reasons to resist White's call for a more explicit
onto-story. A theory might, for example, understate its moral ideals and
underdraw its nature-picture in order to forge a political coalition between
groups with widely divergent metaphysical imaginaries. Or, normative ret-
icence might reflect a normative commitment to secularism, liberal individualism, or moral skepticism. *The Enchantment of Modern Life* does,
however, heed White's call; it experiments with the possibility that human
generosity can be enhanced by an onto-picture of a vibrant, quirky, and
overflowing material world. It offers an account of the world that highlights its capacity for inspiring wonder, and its sometimes fanciful descrip-
tions aspire to augment our actual attachments to the world. The fanciful
and the real, like the virtual and the actual, are incestuous partners—
we have no choice about them being connected; what counts is how we
mobilize the connections. These connections do not assume the form of
a tight argument, and they have contingency built into them. They are
affective affinities that move from wonder to attachment and attachment
to generosity.

White's thinking about weak ontology helps me to articulate and defend the style of theorizing pursued in this book. This is the case even
though we have differing images of what constitutes ontological terrain.
For White, weak ontologies articulate *human* being and *its* world. He
conceives of ontology along the model of what Charles Taylor calls philosophical anthropology, and he shares the early Heidegger's view that "the
analysis of being . . . has to be done through an existential analysis of
human being (*Dasein*). Ontological reflection thus becomes inextricably
entangled with distinctive characteristic of human being . . . "[11] While I
agree (who could not?) that ontological reflection is human reflection,
White's framing of ontology tends to understate the shared materiality of

humans and nonhumans. An onto-story, I think, is as much about a physics or nature-picture as it is a depiction of the fundamental character of human identity, agency, will, and mortality. In my alter-tale, the two imaginaries are presented as integral to each other. My story differs from White's by only a few degrees, but these can make a difference in the ethos that is (to use White's term) *prefigured* by them.

Regarding the matter of agency, for example, I emphasize how human agency is essentially bound up with nonhuman manifestations of it—how, as Latour puts it, what defines the anthropos are the alliances and exchanges between "technomorphisms, zoomorphisms, phusimorphisms, ideomorphisms, theomorphisms, sociomorphisms, psychomorphisms."[12] I pursue an ethics that applies to cross-species as well as interhuman relations. I first broaden the sense of what agency means to cover the ability to make a difference in the world without knowing exactly what you are doing, and I project this agency as distributed, to varying degrees, to atoms that move, plants that engage their environment, and animals that communicate, as well as humans that write onto-stories, protest war, engage in hate speech, and so forth. Humans, among other things, are bodies in space amidst other bodies in space. In the ontological imaginary that guides White's metatheoretical account of the ontological turn, nonhuman matter does not seem to be alive, and human bodies pretty much have a lock on vitality. Both my and White's ontological assumptions are, we would agree, contestable.

That human distinctiveness is central to White's onto-story is perhaps best illustrated by his list of the themes that a good weak ontology will consider:

> Weak ontologies do not proceed by categorical positing of, say, human nature or telos. . . . Rather, . . . they offer . . . figurations of human being in terms of certain existential realities, most notably language, morality or finitude, natality and the articulation of "sources of the self." These figurations are accounts of what it is *to be* a certain sort of creature: first, one entangled with language; second, one with a consciousness that it will die; third, one which, despite its entanglement and limitedness, has the capacity for radical novelty; and, finally, one which gives definition to itself against some ultimate background or "source," to which we find ourselves always already attached, and which evokes something like awe, wonder, or reverence.[13]

Linguistic entanglement ("language"), recognition of one's mortality ("finitude"), the capacity to receive and provoke surprises ("natality"), and articulating the larger background against which the individual positions herself ("sources of the self") is an excellent list of the preoccupations proper to political theory done in the weak ontology mode, but it is too restrictive. It excludes those onto-pictures wherein humans figure as crossspecied, as well as intersubjective, beings. It is a little too conceited about humans, and it thereby underplays the many ways in which we are implicated in, or inspired, overwhelmed, and moved by, forces inside and outside us. How sharply ought the line between humans and nonhumans be drawn? White wants to keep the distinction in constant sight, in part, because he wants to defend "the political" as a distinctive space. "It would be hard," he writes, "to maintain a claim of adequacy for a conception of the political that does not contain figurations marking the distinctiveness of human beings as the peculiar subjects of self-fashioning commonality."[14] It does seem to me that the claim to a distinctively political realm is dependent on a claim about the uniqueness of the human creature. But, my sense is that both claims have been inflated and that some of our disappointments with the lived world might flow from this inflation.

White favors a conception of self that is, in contrast to the "Teflon" self of some versions of liberalism, a "sticky" self situated in time, space, society, and biography.[15] But, even this self is still not sticky enough for those, like me, who figure the human individual as a particularly complex body within assemblages of other bodies of varying degrees of complexity. Thus, human-animal and organism-machine relations, in addition to intersubjective relations, appear as constitutive of the self, and the sometimes significant differences between humans and nonhumans are treated as matters of degree more than kind. I agree with William E. Connolly:

> [R]adical divisions posed in the past between humans and non-humans have now either become highly contestable or devolved into differences of degree. The soul, language, the will, reason, culture, and so on no longer mark the human species as unique. The Kantian idea is that everything else in nature is subordinated to persons as the only beings who are ends. We need to become more special with respect to each other and less so with respect to putative divisions between us and the rest of nature.[16]

On my view, then, nonhuman activity is as much an "existential reality" as is language, finitude, natality, and sources of the self. Why, for example, restrict one's definition of language so that only humans can have it? Birds communicate, too, and, as the examples at the end of this chapter suggest, so do ants and plants. Once attention is paid to the phenomena of nonhuman languages, the sonorous and affective dimension of human speech also comes to the fore. Indeed, within human relations themselves there are affective modes of communication operating below the threshold of the most conceptually sophisticated modes of intersubjectivity.

White further suggests that if you do not focus on finitude, you are probably slacking on the onto-job. But, again, maybe the centrality of such a theme is less a function of ontology per se than the effect of a particular ontological imaginary. What if you, like Deleuze or Lucretius, imagine the world in terms of an overabundance of forms or plenitude—as a place where, although individual humans and individual objects are surely mortal, the matter of which they are made is not. This world is pictured as both finite and infinite, both short of resources and abundantly full, both temporally bound and ever ongoing. The molecular assemblages formed by matter (you, me, the table) are temporary and frail, but the process of becoming goes on and on and on. It is not finite.

White names a concern with finitude as crucial to ontology because in his onto-picture, humans are placed at the center of things. He thus tends to equate human mortality with ontological finitude. This is not to say that onto-stories should not try to come to terms with the fact that one's subjection to death is a crucial and troubling issue, but only to say that different metaphysical pictures have located that fact differently. Some philosophers, such as Heidegger, Levinas, and Critchley, give it center stage; others, including Epicurus and sometimes Socrates, work to distract attention from it. Even others, such as Nietzsche, focus on it precisely in order to enhance the ability to recognize the plenitude of matter.

In a thoughtful section criticizing Butler's tendency to understate the stickiness of identity, White argues that an onto-story that emphasizes human finitude is better able to engender care for others than one that does not. To focus on the point that all mortals have a limited number of becomings allotted to them is to be more likely to treat their attachment to any given identity with respect. "How careful will I really be in interpretive encounters," asks White, "if at heart I take the other's particular identity formations to be just so much congealed potentiality which needs to be loosened up? In a certain sense, I just won't see the point of carefulness in my engagement with the other's identity."[17] I think White, like Critchley, is right to say that a focus on finitude is one way to foster ethical generosity. White is also right in calling attention to the relevance of this issue to Butler's philosophy. However, when the concentration on finitude is linked to White's other criteria for onto-reflection, the range of possible responses to the issue of finitude is unduly restricted. There are multiple ways to engage finitude, even if none of them perfectly achieves its aim: one might strive to transcend the finitude of a disenchanted world through the pursuit of eternal life in the hereafter; one might seek to incorporate eternal life into this world by reinvigorating a medieval Christian model of enchantment; one might seek to become resigned to a disenchanted world in which death is oblivion; one might look to a recuperated Romanticism in order to teach oneself how better to accept the meaninglessness of existence; or one might seek to overcome resentment over the fact of mortality by cultivating attachments to a world that allows numerous links to human, animal, material, technical, and artificial bodies. In the last instance, one would work to dislodge the fact of finitude a few degrees from the central position that it tends to acquire in the other orientations. I am not saying that this short list of orientations to human finitude is exhaustive or that the orientation I pursue is the one everyone should adopt. I am saying that it is a valuable orientation to consider for those who resist both disenchanted and purposive images of the world.

Crucial to my onto-story is what White calls natality, that is, the capacity to give and receive surprises, a capacity Deleuze described as becoming-otherwise. My onto-tale discerns this capacity in (and to some extent bestows it upon) matter per se rather than the matter of humanity alone. Using White's vocabulary, I would say that the material cosmos functions as a source of the self, that is, an "ultimate background . . . to which we find ourselves always already attached, and which evokes something like awe, wonder, or reverence."[18] Perhaps now is a good time to say a bit more about that source or larger network, within which I position myself and from which I draw sustenance. In previous chapters, I draw on Thoreau, Latour, Lucretius, Prigogine, and Kafka to sketch that cosmos; I now augment it with the sound-imagery of Deleuze and Guattari.

The Sonorous Cosmos

Among the numerous self-designations that Deleuze and Guattari audition in *A Thousand Plateaus*, their claim to be "cosmic" philosophers is especially intriguing to someone thinking about onto-stories and the enchantment and disenchantment of the world. Their "cosmos" does not name the largest or most encompassing unit of analysis, as in the progression individual-society-earth-cosmos. Rather, cosmos names a dimension of being within all conceptual and experiential strata; it is that energetic aspect of things, thoughts, matter, which has not (yet) crystallized into a place of knowing or belonging. The cosmos consists of "fuzzy aggregates,"[19] or "forces, densities, intensities" that "are not thinkable in themselves."[20] This sphere of lively primordia (to switch to Lucretian terms) cannot serve as a locus of transcultural identification (as in the cosmopolitanism of, say, Kant), for it is too mobile and protean. The cosmos of Deleuze and Guattari entails a materialism akin to the one invoked by my tale of modern enchantments.

Also relevant to that tale is Deleuze and Guattari's claim that sounds—specifically, repetitive sounds like chants and refrains—provide sensory access into the cosmological (i.e., energetic and rumbling) dimension of things. To sing or hum or otherwise enter into a musical refrain is to get into a groove—your torso sways side to side, your chin nods north and south, your toes tap up and down, your chest dips down and out. But what is distinctive about this groove is that it is not wholly smooth; each of its repetitions never exactly repeats its predecessor. One's postural (spiral) repetitions mimic the audible repetitions of the refrain, which itself reenacts the (spiral) motility of cosmos.

Let us examine more closely how the refrain opens an onto-window, how it reveals the cosmological energetics operative within and amidst the self. Deleuze and Guattari[21] describe a three-step dynamic induced by the refrain. The first is the production of a sense of "shelter," as when an infant cries in repeating waves of sound, or when "a child in the dark . . . comforts himself by singing under his breath," or when a frightened adult repeats the mantra "keep calm, it'll be okay, it'll be okay." In such cases, the refrain fixes "a fragile point" (312), and "is like a rough sketch of a calming and stabilizing . . . center in the heart of chaos" (311). The second effect of the refrain is to organize a space of home around that central point, thus pushing disorder back beyond a borderline: "The forces of chaos are kept outside. . . . This involves an activity of selection, elimination and extraction . . . , a wall of sound" (311). Deleuze and Guattari believe that the experience of "having a place" is not simply spatial but is also sonorous—to be on a territory rather than lost, to be somebody rather than nobody, is to be moving into a more orchestrated arrangement of sound. You find yourself at a loss or disoriented, swirling around amidst the youthful, scrambling energies of cosmos, and so you enter into a sonorous stream of repetition in order to compose yourself.

The effects of the refrain do not end with this comforting organization. For even as the refrain is building up a little house, it is also making overtures toward the no-man's land—the not exclusively human land—beyond it. This is the third effect of the refrain, a slight twinge or tic of dissonance. The refrain tosses a note or two into the uncharted territory beyond the wall that it has just built—"one launches forth, hazards an improvisation . . . , ventures from home on the thread of a tune," grafts "a breakaway" (311–12). Although the home formed via the refrain has a certain stability to it, that stability is, like that of the sounds—and the cosmos—"vibratory." According to Deleuze and Guattari:

> Every milieu is vibratory, in other words, a block of space-time constituted by the periodic repetition of the component. . . . Every milieu is coded, a code being defined by periodic repetition, but each code is in a perpetual state of transcoding or transduction (313).

In other words, even the home locale ("milieu") is alive with movement and change—and how could it not be, given the shimmering, shimmying quality of its sounds (indeed, of the energetic onto-matter of the world)? Even sounds that line up as a refrain include some that step out of line, flip out of the groove, and fly off. "It is a question of elements and particles, which do or do not arrive fast enough to effect a passage. . . . [T]here

are always elements that do not arrive on time" (255)—and these tardy
bits mean that lines of possible connection are constantly being formed
and reformed between entities.

Such breakaway vibrations put your body in contact with the other potential refrains humming around it. These spiraling sounds come out of
the mouths of nonhumans as well as humans. You whistle a song started
by a bird; you shudder in the wake of the cawing of a crow; a cricket
chirps louder as the echo of your footsteps recedes. Sometimes, as that
last example suggests, refrains do not come from "mouths" at all: "Birds
are still . . . important, yet the reign of birds seems to have been replaced
by the age of insects, with its much more molecular vibrations, chirring,
rustling, buzzing, clicking, scratching, and scraping." Such sounds, too,
enact a "diagonal" into the cosmos (308–9).

What Deleuze and Guattari here refer to as the breakaway dimension
of the refrain, they elsewhere refer to as a line of flight. In their onto-
picture, humans are surrounded by "a continuous line of borderlines
(*fiber*). . . . A fiber stretches from a human to an animal, from a human or
an animal to molecules. . . . A fiber strung across borderlines constitutes
a line of flight" (249). Humans thus appear as essentially nonhuman as
well as human, a fact that they will best sense when they are en-chanted
by a refrain:

> The refrain is a prism. . . . It acts upon that which surrounds it . . . , extracting
> from it various vibrations, or decompositions, projections, or transformations.
> The refrain also has a catalytic function: not only to increase the speed of the
> exchanges and reactions in that which surrounds it, but also to assure indirect
> interactions between elements devoid of so-called natural affinity . . . (349).

Through sound, through the various refrains we invent, repeat, and catch
from nonhumans, we receive news of the cosmic energies to which we
humans are always in close, molecular proximity. Deleuze and Guattari
are authors of an enchantment tale. They imagine a world so overflowing
with entities, creations, and forces that mutual infection is inevitable. My
story explores the possibility that this ontological susceptibility to contagion could be rendered into a more sympathetic and generous relationship
with one's cohabitants.

Attachment as a Gift

If all goes well, children seem to be born with a capacity for enchantment,
and most adults retain something of this power. The onto-story of Deleuze and Guattari, with its infectious vibrations and energetic morphing
within and across assemblages, provides one explanation for this profound

and apparently primordial attachment to being. There are also other ways to conceive of it—as a biological will to live or a survival instinct, as the effect of random electric surges in the brain, or as the presence of God. In an essay titled, "The Overwhelming Force," Clement Rosset reflects on this attachment to life, this capacity for enchantment, which he terms *beatitude*:

> Other terms would probably work just as well: joie de vivre, gladness, jubilation, pleasure of existence, adhesion to reality, and still others. The word is not important; what counts here is the idea or intention of an unconditional allegiance to the simple and unadorned experience of the real.[22]

I agree with Rosset that moments of "unconditional allegiance" do exist, even while I resist the description of this experience as "simple and unadorned." In my onto-story, the network of affects, postures, and ideas required for enchantment is not simple, and enchantment can also result from carefully staged circumstances and aesthetically educated senses. Yet, Rosset does put his finger on how enchantment (like disenchantment) is never fully under one's control—on the way in which it requires something like what Schiller called a "fortuitous gift of nature." If the attachment to life, the basis of both pathos and enchantment as affective resources for ethics, is absent (as in some people with affective disorders or in so-called sociopaths), then there might not be any way to instill it or to create it. The unknowability and unmanufacturability of this ethical ground find their parallels in the way that enchantment hits one as if from out of the blue, without warning. You can prepare for it, try to cultivate a receptivity toward it, but it is never only or fully the product of will or intention. For Rosset, the "bolstering effect" of beatitude is "an 'extraordinary intervention' "; it arrives unexplained and sometimes against all odds; it is "the mystery inherent in the zest for life" that Hesiod refers to when he writes that " 'the gods have hidden what keeps men alive.' "[23]

Plants, Ants, Robopets, and Other Enchanting Things

This book explores several sites of enchantment in contemporary life and stages encounters with phenomena that surprise, fascinate, disturb, and provoke wonder. I try to point to those kinds of places where enchantment, at least for some of us some of the time, seems to hang out—the border between humans and animals and between organisms and machines, as well as those places where one confronts a perplexing, almost overwhelming, degree of complexity. I also discuss, as examples of minor experiences of wonder, the persistent belief in a "supersensible" world of one kind or another; the occasional, weird outbreak of original thinking amid pressures toward conformity; the swerve, or "decisionism," of molecules at far-from-equilibrium states; the sublimity of Mount Ktaadn; the agile mobility of khakis in a commercial advertisement. Many other minor experiences could have been chosen, as I have learned from almost everyone with whom I share my reservations about the story of modernity as disenchanted.

There is, for example, the encounter with plants that, in response to an overabundance of aphids on their leaves, call ladybugs to their rescue by means of a language of chemical scents. Such behavior turns out to be but one of the many ways in which plants make their mark on the world, and it suggests that even plants possess a kind of agency.[24] Plants participate in interpreting their environment at a level well below that of human interpretations but in a way that nevertheless bears a family resemblance to it, thus belying our claims to uniqueness. Or, consider the amazing ant, whose ability to navigate around obstacles and to work collectively provides a model for computer scientists seeking to design Internet, telephone, and air traffic routing systems:

> Ants cope with traffic jams by planning ahead. As they march, they deposit a trail of chemicals called pheromones for other ants to follow. But a few ants stray from the path and explore other options, also depositing pheromones as they go. So where there is a blockage, ants have immediate information about other routes. Scientists have devised "virtual ants"—snippets of computer code that zoom around the network to monitor traffic and potential backup routes. Instead of dropping chemical pheromones, virtual ants leave bits of electronic information to enlighten other ants that may be passing through later.[25]

Just as intriguing as the events of interspecies communication and of animal language is the encounter with our intrabody communication system.[26] The human body possesses an astonishing network of relays between, for example, thoughts and arteries. Evidence of this network is provided by the placebo effect, as employed in the recent return to "sham surgery":

> In 1939, long before high-tech drugs came along to treat the chest pain known as angina, an Italian surgeon named Fieschi devised a simple technique. Reasoning that increased blood flow to the heart would ease his patients' pain, he made tiny incisions in their chests and tied knots in two arteries. The results were spectacular. Three quarters of all patients improved. One third were cured. Two decades later, the National Institutes of Health paid a young cardiologist in Seattle, Dr. Leonard A. Cobb, to conduct a novel test of the Fieschi technique. Dr. Cobb operated on 17 patients. Eight had their arteries tied; the other nine got incisions, nothing more. In 1959, the *New England Journal of Medicine*

published his findings: the phony operations worked just as well as the real thing.[27]

Some surgeons are today advocating sham surgery, even as others raise concerns about the ethics of tricking patients, even if to deploy the healing power of their illusions.

The natural world, it seems, continues to function as a reservoir of enchantment. This is especially true regarding those dimensions of nature that until recently had escaped human notice or operated below the threshold of human perception. "Mere" plants, ants, and ideas turn out to have a degree of complexity and material efficacy that humans have hitherto ignored or underestimated. New scientific practices and instruments render these capacities sensible to us, and we are both charmed and disturbed by them.[28]

Nature enchants, but so do artifacts. Man-made complexities also can provoke wonder, surprise, and disorientation. Take, for example, the exciting and slightly unnerving power that personal computers can wield over their owners, as when one finds it difficult to pull oneself away from the screen after playing around on the Internet too long. Chris Chesser suggests that the personal computer provides an outlet for the human desire for magic (i.e., for a means by which to transform wish into reality). He refers to this as the "invocational power" of computer use. By typing in a word or string of words, one is able to invoke or conjure up one's object of desire, to make it appear on the screen. Clicking on a link is a lot like saying "Open sesame!" "The metaphor of invocation is useful," says Chesser, "because it stresses not the devices called computers, but the capacities with which they endow users. . . . Invocation is a form of quasi-magical language act made possible by data infrastructures. Computer discourse conveys power: commands, entries, queries, searches, visualisations."[29]

Personal computers hold us in their sway and carry us away, and this could, under the right circumstances, induce in us a joyful sense of the synchronicity of desire and reality. But, here, more readily than in the case of nature-enchantment, we become aware of the kinship between enchantment and enthrallment. How disturbing that an inanimate machine, or an advertisement for jeans, is allowed to function as an active agent! This combination of wonder and concern is displayed in an article about Sony Corporation's 1999 release of its robot-pet product. Greg Allen, proud new owner of "the world's first home robot to benefit from artificial intelligence," responds with wonder to his robot-puppy:

> Allen sat spellbound as Astro wobbled to its shiny feet, cocked its magnesium alloy head and fixated its diode eyes on a pink ball. 'He's looking at his pink ball, he's following it with his head and he's wagging his tail!' enthused Allen,

as Astro took his first tentative steps. . . . The Sony robodogs bark, play, respond, watch, see, learn, remember. They wander forward to meet guests, independently navigate their environments, perk up when praised, recoil when scolded.[30]

A scientist who develops artificial pets in Kyoto then gives voice to the troubling dimension of this techo-enchantment: " 'I've been reading about the people who built the atomic bomb because I profoundly identify with them,' de Garis told *The New York Times Magazine* this month. They knew what they were doing and where it would lead, and I worry about where this will lead.' His fear notwithstanding, the possibilities now being presented by artificial intelligence and robotics science have sparked interest across the planet."[31]

Another category of minor experiences of wonder consists in those that are neither natural nor, exactly, technical. This is the realm of the cultural—of film, art, music, sport. There is, for example, the game of baseball, which Andrew Seligsohn sees as expressive of a profound attachment to life and as capable of engendering the kind of energy necessary for ethics:

> To the extent that the disenchantment of the world is attributed to the world's increased technicity, we have here a counter-example. Through the roughly 150 years of its history, baseball has become more and more technically sophisticated, but rather than producing disenchantment, this has only further enchanted the fans, whose rooting is interwoven with an ever-increasing array of strategic possibilities and an ever-increasing body of knowledge with which to analyze them. In addition, baseball's enchantment persists despite its embroilment in economic relations of the most crass variety.[32]

Seligsohn shows how the enchantment of baseball occurs at numerous sites of crossing.

In closing, I offer Wim Wenders's 1986 film, *Wings of Desire*, written in collaboration with Peter Handke, as a cinematic site of enchantment. It is the story of embodied life as seen through the eyes of two guardian angels. The angels are depicted as middle-aged men in overcoats who have thus far spent eternity witnessing but not experiencing human and other material forms of life. Their distanced, aesthetic perspective allows the viewer to see the creaturely side of humans—people appear as fascinating animals. The angels make notations in their small books when they witness peculiar (and, to us, endearing) activities, for example, the woman who closed her umbrella and let herself get drenched. "It's great to live only by the spirit, to testify day by day for eternity only to the spiritual sides of people," says one angel. "But sometimes I get fed up with my spiritual existence. Instead of forever hovering above, I'd like to feel there's some weight to me, to end my eternity and bind me to the earth. At each step, each gust of wind, I'd like to be able to say, 'Now,' and 'now' and 'now' and no longer say 'since always' and 'forever.' " This wistful angel wants to be an ordinary human and to feel that extraordinary attachment to life. This attachment both inhabits humans and is something that, because of their daily routines, humans are less likely than angels to discern. Wenders's film challenges what Rosset describes as the "long philosophical tradition from Plato to Heidegger which has believed . . . that there is no joy truly accessible to humanity unless one 'goes beyond' the simple joy of life, distancing oneself from any object situated in existence."[33]

In one scene, the angel comes across a man about to die on the street after a motorcycle crash. To comfort him, the angel begins listing the very particular things about life that this man has loved. To the man these thoughts come as if from nowhere. Together, they slowly speak the following words:

the fire on the cattle range,
the potato in the ashes,
the boathouse floating in the lake,
the Southern Cross,
the Far East,
the Great North,
the Wild West,
the Great Bear Lake,
Tristan de Cunha,
the Mississippi Delta,
stromboli,
the old houses of Charlottenburg,
Albert Camus,
the morning light,
the child's eyes,
the swim in the waterfall,
the stains from the first raindrops,
the sun,
the bread and wine,
hopping,
Easter,
the veins of the leaves,
the color of stones,
the pebbles on the stream bed,
the white tablecloths outdoors,
the dream of a house inside the house,
the loved one asleep in the next room,
the peaceful Sunday,

the horizon,
the light from the room shining in my garden,
the night flight,
riding a bicycle with no hands,
the beautiful stranger,
my father,
my mother,
my child . . .

When I gather together the animals, arguments, molecules, suggestions, forces, interpretations, sounds, people, and images of this study, one theme emerges. The modern story of disenchantment leaves out important things, and it neglects crucial sources of ethical generosity in doing so. Without modes of enchantment, we might not have the energy and inspiration to enact ecological projects, or to contest ugly and unjust modes of commercialization, or to respond generously to humans and nonhumans that challenge our settled identities. These enchantments are already in and around us.

Notes

Chapter 1
The Wonder of Minor Experiences

1. Milan Kundera, *The Unbearable Lightness of Being* (Harper & Row, 1984), 39.

2. My project overlaps with and draws inspiration from the work of other theorists exploring the intersection of politics, ethics, and aesthetics. See Romand Coles, *Rethinking Generosity: Critical Theory and the Politics of Caritas* (Cornell University Press, 1997); William E. Connolly, *Why I Am Not a Secularist* (Minnesota University Press, 1999); Kimberly Curtis, *Our Sense of the Real: Aesthetic Experience and Arendtian Politics* (Cornell University Press, 1999); John Docker, *1492: The Poetics of Diaspora* (Cassells/Continuum Press, 2001); Thomas L. Dumm, *A Politics of the Ordinary* (New York University Press, 1999); Kennan Ferguson, *The Politics of Judgment: Aesthetics, Identity, and Political Theory* (Lexington Books, 1999); Moira Gatens, *Imaginary Bodies: Ethics, Power and Corporeality* (Routledge, 1996); Melissa Orlie, *Living Ethically, Acting Politically* (Cornell University Press, 1997); Morton Schoolman, *Reason and Horror: Aesthetic Individuality, Democracy and Critical Theory* (Routledge, forthcoming 2001); Michael J. Shapiro, *Cinematic Political Thought: Narrating Race, Nation, and Gender* (New York University Press, 1999).

3. I offer my tale of ethics and enchantment as one response to Stephen White's criticism that while "poststructuralist and postmodern thought . . . carries a persistent utopian hope of a 'not yet,' " it too often "remains blithely unspecific about normative orientation in the here and now." See Stephen White, *Affirmation in Political Theory: The Strengths of Weak Ontology* (Princeton University Press, 2000), 90. White makes this charge in the context of his thoughtful examination of the ontological turn in political theory. I discuss his project and my relationship to it in chapter 8.

4. Philip Fisher, *Wonder, the Rainbow, and the Aesthetics of Rare Experiences* (Harvard University Press, 1998), 131. Fisher links wonder to visuality and then explanation or the "poetics of thought." The mood I am calling enchantment has much in common with Fisher's wonder, though the former's closest link is to sound rather than sight. Fisher offers an interesting account of wonder's role in motivating acts of understanding—what interests him most is wonder's "drive toward intelligibility." I emphasize how wonder marks the vitality and agency of a world that sometimes bestows the gift of joy to humans, a gift that can be translated into ethical generosity. Despite these differences, we share an interest in the affective dimension of ethical and intellectual life.

5. Quoted in Lorraine Daston and Katharine Park, *Wonders and the Order of Nature: 1150–1750* (Zone Books, 1998), 113.

6. Ibid., 13, states: "Descartes called wonder the first of the passions, 'a sudden surprise of the soul which makes it tend to consider attentively those objects which seem to it rare and extraordinary.' "

7. Ibid., 16.

8. Deleuze and Guattari, *Thousand Plateaus*, 349.

9. Franz Kafka, *The Trial* (Schocken Books, 1974), 10.

10. On the cusp of this change, Rousseau dreams of a modern form of community governed by a civil religion and a general will; Hegel then imagines a state that would allow citizens to recover their implication in a larger ethical order without sacrificing modern individuality; Marx rejects Hegel's cure but affirms the diagnosis of alienation—later, alienated workers will become subjects of *anomie* and *gesellschaft* (i.e., a "rationally developed mechanistic type of social relationship characterized by impersonally contracted associations between persons"); finally, Weber collects these various claims under the banner of "the disenchantment of the world."

11. These three senses of disenchantment are linked—to live in a dead world with linear forms of thought is likely to depress the spirits.

12. Max Weber, "Science as a Vocation," in Weber, *From Max Weber: Essays in Sociology*, ed. H. H. Gerth and C. Wright Mills (Oxford University Press, 1981), 140.

13. Ibid., 139.

14. Jackson Lears, *Fables of Abundance: A Cultural History of Advertising in America* (Basic Books, 1994), 19.

15. J. K. Gibson-Graham, *The End of Capitalism (As We Knew It)* (Blackwell Publishers, 1996), ix.

16. Voltaire, *Candide*, trans. Robert M. Adams (W. W. Norton, 1991), 8–9.

17. Ibid., 9.

18. Wendy Brown, *State of Injury* (Princeton University Press, 1995), 55, makes a similar point about the value of forgetting when she inquires into those places where a marginalized group's investment in "its own history of suffering . . . come[s] into conflict with the need to give up these investments, to engage in something of a Niezschean 'forgetting' of this history, in the pursuit of an emancipatory democratic project."

19. Thomas Moore, *The Re-Enchantment of Everyday Life* (HarperCollins, 1996), 128, draws a sharp distinction between enchantment and idealism, "the former keeping us charmed as we live our ordinary earthly lives, the latter focusing our attention away from the ordinary and the human." Moore's project of re-enchantment is framed by the disenchantment tale: he seeks ways to overcome the loss of meaning caused by speedy and materialistic modes characteristic of modernity, and he equates disenchantment with secularization and the de-souling of society. His perspective also differs from mine in its focus on re-spiritualizing contemporary life. But Moore and I share an interest in the minor experiences of wonder in everyday life.

20. Ibid., 108.

21. Immanuel Kant, *Critique of Judgment*, trans. Werner Pluhar, Hackett, 1987, 66 (hereafter cited as *CJ*; page numbers refer to those of the *Akademie* edition of Kant's works and appear in the margins of the Pluhar translation).

22. Ibid., 65.

23. Ibid., 66.

24. Ibid., 72.

25. Lucretius, "De Rerum Natura," in *The Epicurean Philosophers*, ed. John Gaskin (Everyman Library, 1995), Book I, no. 1021.

26. Friedrich Nietzsche, *Thus Spoke Zarathustra*, trans. Walter Kaufmann, (Penguin, 1976), "On the Pitying," pt. II, 3.

27. One notable exception here is William Connolly; see *The Augustinian Imperative* (Sage 1993) and "Reworking the Democratic Imagination," *Journal of Political Philosophy* 5, no. 2 (June 1997), 194–202.

Chapter 2
Cross-Species Encounters

1. "Edward Lorenz, the discoverer of deterministic chaos in weather systems, produced the first computer image of a strange attractor . . . and . . . it looks something like a butterfly. . . ." From Harriett Hawkins, *Strange Attractors: Literature, Culture and Chaos Theory* (Prentice-Hall, 1995), 127.

2. Paul Patton, "Power in Hobbes and Nietzsche," in *Nietzsche, Feminism and Political Theory*, ed. Paul Patton (Routledge, 1993), 155, offers a parallel argument about the role of the *feeling* of power in Nietzsche. The contrast he draws is between thinking of power in terms of affect concomitant with certain activities and thinking of it as a possession. "Nietzsche proposes a conception of human agency as governed not simply by the drive to increase power but by the drive to maximize the *feeling* of power. . . . Given the self-conscious, interpretive element in every human act of will, it follows that humankind is the one animal in which the feeling of power is divorced from any direct relation to quantity of power."

3. Donna Haraway, "Manifesto for Cyborgs: Science, Technology, and Socialist Feminism in the 1980's," *Socialist Review* 15, no. 2, 1985, underplays the aesthetic dimension of her imagery, perhaps because it would reveal, within the cyborg, a nostalgia for childhood. And cyborg is an identity designed precisely to ward off nostalgia for origins. For a further discussion of this, see my "Primate Visions and Alter Tales," in Jane Bennett and William Chaloupka, *In the Nature of Things* (Minnesota University Press, 1993).

4. Michel Tournier, *Friday* (Pantheon, 1966), 73.

5. Ibid., 203. Friday reminds us of Nietzsche's tragic optimist, who expresses his Dionysian-Apollinian nature by exclaiming: "Everything that exists is both just and unjust, and equally justified in both. What a world!" See *The Birth of Tragedy*, sec. 9.

6. Ibid., 194–95.

7. Gilles Deleuze, "Michel Tournier and the World without Others," in *The Logic of Sense*, trans. Mark Lester (Columbia University Press, 1990), 319.

8. Tournier, *Friday*, 189.

9. Ibid., 180.

10. Franz Kafka, "A Report to an Academy," in Franz Kafka, *The Complete Stories* (Schocken, 1971).

11. My reading of Kafka's stories as experiments of movement clashes with the dominant interpretation of Kafka as a no-way-out prophet of protototalitarian stasis. A good example of this reading is a humorous piece in *The New York Times Book Review* that speculates about what Kafka's home page on the Web might look like: "Franz Kafka: It should by now be clear to you that my home page can offer little in the way of happiness or sustenance, only as much *unadulterated suffering* as one could hope for. Yet the only 'home' I have ever known is this virtual one. . . . At the very least my advice to you would be to flee immediately and find a real home. . . . Admittedly, it is far from clear how ever to escape the Web; very likely you will find yourself cast pitilessly down a labyrinth of endless links, condemned, as I am, to a lifetime of futile searching. . . ." (Bookend, "Virtual Authors: The Web Sites," *The New York Times*, Dec. 31, 1995, 19.) At the end of chap. 5, I challenge both the idea that we live in a disenchanted world and the idea that Kafka's stories are exemplary exaggerations of that alienated condition.

12. Irene Pepperberg, "Comprehension of 'Absence' by an African Grey Parrot: Learning with Respect to Questions of Same/Different," *Journal of the Experimental Analysis of Behavior* 50, no. 3 (1988): 559.

13. Ibid., 560–61.

14. Irene Pepperberg, "Numerical Competence in an African Gray Parrot," *Journal of Comparative Psychology* 108, no. 1 (1994): 36.

15. Ibid., 38. Monkeys, too, have numerical abilities, as reported by *All Things Considered*, Oct. 22, 1998: "[N]ew findings in this week's issue of *Science* magazine . . . show [that] . . . two rhesus monkeys were able to understand an abstract mathematical concept . . . " See http://search.npr.org/cf/cmn/cmnps05fm.cfm?SegID=33331.

16. Irene Pepperberg, Katherine Brese, and Barbara Harris, "Solitary Sound Play during Acquisition of English Vocalizations by an African Grey Parrot: Possible Parallels with Children's Monologue Speech," *Applied Psycholinguistics* 12, no. 2 (1991): 152.

17. Ibid., 156.

18. "Unlocking the Mystery: The Amazing Animal Mind," *Turning Point*, with Barbara Walters, Forrest Sawyer, and Diane Sawyer, ABC News, transcript. Oct. 10, 1996.

19. Pepperberg, Brese, and Harris, "Solitary Sound Play," 155.

20. Rene Girard, *Violence and the Sacred*, trans. Patrick Gregordy (Johns Hopkins University Press, 1972), 145. For a very useful discussion of Girard, see William E. Connolly, *The Ethos of Pluralization* (Minnesota University Press, 1995). Irene Pepperberg's research on vocal learning also confirms that Alex is a subject within an intersubjective, multispecied learning community. In one study, "Vocal Learning in Grey Parrots: Effects of Social Interaction, Reference, and Context," *The Auk* 111, no. 2 (1994): 300–313, Pepperberg used three different methods to teach juvenile parrots to do what Alex does. "Each bird experienced: (1) audiotaped tutoring that was nonreferential and noninteractive and did not demonstrate contextual applicability; (2) videotapes that provided reference and limited information about context but were noninteractive; and (3) live human tutors, who interactively modeled the meaning and use of the labels. The birds learned only from the live tutors."

21. One interesting foray into such an ethic is Robert Goodin, Carole Pateman, and Roy Pateman's "Simian Sovereignty," *Political Theory* 25, no. 6 (1997): 821–49. For additional fascinating accounts of the intelligence of birds, see Theodore Xenophon Barber, *The Human Nature of Birds* (Penguin, 1994).

22. Gilles Deleuze and Felix Guattari, "November 28, 1947: How Do You Make Yourself a Body without Organs," in Gilles Deleuze and Felix Guattari, *A Thousand Plateaus*, trans. Brian Massumi (University of Minnesota Press), 1987, 161.

23. My formulation here concurs with Homi Bhabha's sense, as quoted in "The Third Space," in Jonathan Rutherford, ed., *Identity: Community, Culture, Difference* (Lawrence and Wishart, 1990), 211, that "the importance of hybridity is not to be able to trace two original moments from which the third emerges, rather hybridity to me is the 'third space' which enables other positions to emerge. This third space displaces the histories that constitute it, and sets up new structures of authority, new political initiatives, which are inadequately understood through received wisdom."

24. For Deleuze and Guattari, *Thousand Plateaus*, a "plane of consistency" is a holding together of disparate elements in such a way as to construct an intensive state. "Every BwO is itself a plateau in communication with other plateaus on the plane of consistency. The BwO is a component of passage" (158). The book is divided into plateaus rather than chapters: "A plateau is reached when circumstances combine to bring an activity to a pitch of intensity that is not automatically dissipated in a climax" (Translator's Foreword, xiv).

25. Ibid., 157.

26. Ibid., 151.

27. See Norbert Elias, *The Civilizing Process, Volume One: The History of Manners* (Blackwell, 1994).

28. The "rule immanent to experimentation: injections of caution," in Deleuze and Guattari, *Thousand Plateaus*, 150.

29. Ibid., 163. With the possible exception of the masochist, Deleuze and Guattari introduce us to no positive exemplars of BwO; we do meet some negative models (e.g., its "emptied" and "cancerous" doubles).

30. Ibid., 162.

31. Ibid., 161.

32. Bhabha ("Third Space," 214) makes a related claim in his discussion of the Rushdie affair: "I think the case has also illustrated how within the Shi'ite sect . . . there are a number of other positions. Now it is true that those positions are not dominant at the moment but it has raised—and this is where I think I would make a . . . practical claim, for a kind of hybridisation which exists no matter whether you keep on asserting the purity of your own doctrines—it has raised more graphically than before the notion of religious law versus secular law, and the presence of a kind of . . . enunciative aperture through which, whether you like it or not, your 'fundamentalist' credo is going to have to pass. . . . [I]f we advance out positions a few years and then look back, we'll see how that even within the apparently intractable 'fundamentalist' position, a number of incommensurabilities has emerged (not at the level of theological interpretation, but at the level of effectivity. . . ."

33. Deleuze and Guattari, *Thousand Plateaus*, 155–56.

34. "Actually existing, structured things live in and through that which escapes them. . . . This side-perception may be . . . localized in an event. . . . But it is also continuous like a background perception that accompanies events, however quotidian." From Brian Massumi, "The Autonomy of Affect," in *Deleuze: A Critical Reader*, ed. Paul Patton (Blackwell, 1996), 229.

35. "That there are other ways, other procedures than masochism, and certainly better ones, is beside the point; it is enough that some find this procedure suitable for them." From Deleuze and Guattari, *Thousand Plateaus*, 155.

36. Ibid., 154–55.

37. "Desire" might not be the most perspicuous category through which to think about assemblages, crossings, passages, flows. It is both too vague and too confined to sexuality. Although it has the advantage of insisting upon the role of body, affect, aesthetics, it can also limit thinking about the kinds of techniques one might experiment with in pursuit of BwO.

38. I am grateful to Anne Brown for helping me to think about the relation among enchantment, compulsion, and masochism.

39. Deleuze and Guattari, *Thousand Plateaus*, 161.

40. Ibid., 161.

41. Lears, *Fables of Abundance*, 47. For Lears, "the desire for a magical transfiguration of the self was a key element in the . . . carnivalesque advertising tradition, and an essential part of consumer goods' appeal in nineteenth century America. The origins of that dream were complex and obscure; certainly it drew . . . from ancient folk myths . . . as well as Protestant conversion narratives" (43). Lears's project is quite parallel to mine: he wants to show how pockets of "animistic countertendencies" remain within advertising and its commodity culture; I want to identify sites of enchantment that reside within modernity and its calculable world. Advertising is not one of the sites of enchantment I explore here, although after reading Lears, I think it surely counts as one. I am grateful to Melissa Orlie for leading me to Lears's work.

42. I take this term from Kathy Ferguson's excellent study of it in *The Man Question: Visions of Subjectivity in Feminist Theory* (University of California Press, 1993).

43. See, to name only a few, Pnina Webner and Tariq Modood, eds., *Debating Cultural Hybridity* (Zed Books, 1997); Talal Asad, *Genealogies of Religion* (Johns Hopkins University Press, 1993), 239–68; Alan Sinfield, "Diaspora and Hybridity: Queer Identities and the Ethnicity Model," *Textual Practice* 10, no. 2 (1996), 271–93; Stuart Hall, "Cultural Identity and Diaspora," in *Identity: Community, Culture, Difference*, ed. Jonathan Rutherford (Lawrence & Wishart), 1990, 222–37; Homi Bhabha, *The Location of Culture* (Routledge, 1994); Paul Gilroy, *The Black Atlantic* (Verso, 1993). I am grateful to Ann Curthoys and John Docker for helping me think through the differences between my project and a related one as pursued in post-colonial studies.

44. For a nuanced treatment of the relevance of a geographical imaginary to such a project, see Michael J. Shapiro, *Violent Cartographies: Mapping Cultures of War* (Minnesota, 1997): "to produce a critical political approach to the ethics of the present, it is necessary to oppose the dominant stories of modernity and the

institutionalized, geopolitical versions of space, which support existing forms of global proprietary control, for both participate unreflectively in a violence of representation" (174). Shapiro also presents a fascinating account of how Arab-Jew relations might have been narrativized as a "hybridity" rather than "a geopolitically based antagonism" (199).

45. Bruno Latour, *We Have Never Been Modern* (Harvard University Press, 1993), 115.

46. Daston and Park, *Wonders and Order*, 209.

47. See ibid., 27, 56–57.

48. In the case of human clones, the fear seems to be that too much of one's own "self" would be around. Although here, too, it's the diversity of the world that they seem to threaten.

49. See "The Third Space," 211.

50. The way out here, suggests Massumi, is to think the relation as external to its terms. I do think, also, that even the language of hybridity might be inflected toward the Deleuzean sense that Massumi and I affirm. See Brian Massumi, "Which Came First? The Individual or Society? Which Is the Chicken and Which Is the Egg? The Political Economy of Belonging and the Logic of Relation," in *Anybody*, ed. Cynthia C. Davidson (MIT Press, 1997), 175–88.

51. Marsha Rosengarten, "A Pig's Tale: Porcine Viruses and Species Boundaries," in Alison Bashford and Claire Hooker, eds., *Contagion: Historical and Cultural Studies* (Routledge, forthcoming). The explosive political debate of the late 1990s concerning genetically engineered crops raises a similar set of concerns. For a good account of these issues, see L. Levidow, "Whose Ethics for Agricultural Biotechnology," in V. Shiva and I. Moser, eds., *Biopolitics: A Feminist and Ecological Reader on Biotechnology* (Zed Books, 1995), 175–90.

52. For Bhabha, "Hybridity is precisely about the fact that when a new situation, a new alliance formulates itself, it may demand that you should translate your principles, rethink them, extend them." See "Third Space," 216.

Chapter 3
The Marvelous Worlds of Paracelsus, Kant, and Deleuze

1. Giovanni Dondi, *De Fontibus Calidis Agre Patavini Consideratio*, 2, c. 1382, cited in Daston and Park, *Wonders and Order*, 135.

2. Haraway, *Primate Visions*.

3. Chapter 4 examines these different renditions of the story of disenchantment.

4. In short, in a world construed as disenchanted, it is easy for liberals and communitarians alike to lose faith in the distinction between power and legitimate authority. And when this happens, political cynicism is not likely to be far behind. For a good account of cynicism and how it functions in American politics, see William Chaloupka, *Everybody Knows: Cynicism in America* (Minnesota University Press, 1999).

5. Daston and Park, *Wonders and Order*, define *preternatural* in this way: "Between the commonplace and the miraculous lay the large and nebulous domain of the marvelous. . . . Medieval natural philosophers . . . had largely excluded such

marvels . . . as neither regular but demonstrable. Many . . . neo-Aristotelians continued to hold this position, but they were increasingly challenged by a new type of philosopher, whom we will call the 'preternatural philosophers' " (159–60). "These men not only reclaimed wonder as a philosophical emotion, but also rehabilitated wonders as useful objects of philosophical reflection" (137).

6. On the peculiar Christianity of Paracelsus, see Walter Pagel, *From Paracelsus to Van Helmont*, ed. Marianne Winder (Variorum Reprints, 1986), 327. Writes Pagel: "Religious motives pervade the thought and work of Paracelsus. It is Christian, rather than humanistic, motives which serve him as justification for the physician's art and craft, prescribe the ends to which it is to be devoted, enter into the very structure of his medical doctrines, and form the background to his empirical and experimental attitude. Paracelsus' was a Christian occult philosophy . . . which in no way excluded magical practices . . . "

7. Paracelsus, *Selected Writings*, ed. Joland Jacobi (Princeton University Press, 1979), 121. For Paracelsus, God was immanent in nature: " . . . for the Holy Ghost and nature are one, that is to say: each day nature shines as a light from the Holy Ghost and learns from him, and thus this light reaches man, as in a dream" (181). Human redemption, that is, the realignment with divine will made necessary by Adam's fall, was to be achieved by reading the signs of nature wisely. Paracelsus read them by means of the careful naturalist observation and laboratory experimentation that he called magic and the scholarly tradition of divination and interpretation that he called the cabala: "If we would know the inner nature of man by his outer nature; if we would understand his inner heaven by his outward aspect: if we would know the inner nature of trees, herbs, roots, stones by their outward aspect, we must pursue our exploration of nature on the foundation of the cabala. For the cabala opens up access to the occult, to the mysteries; it enables us to read sealed epistles and books and likewise the inner nature of men" (133).

8. It is surely possible to discern elements of divine will in nature, but it will never be fully transparent. For a good discussion of this subject, see Michel Foucault, *The Order of Things* (Vintage, 1973), chap. 2. Walter Pagel, perhaps underestimating the sophistication of the textual strategies that Paracelsus brought to bear on the Book of Nature, describes him as having a view of nature as "a visible reflection of the invisible work of God . . . , [who has] graced us with glimpses into His secret wisdom." (Walter Pagel, *Paracelsus: An Introduction to Philosophical Medicine in the Era of the Renaissance*, 2nd rev. ed. [Karger, 1982], 53–54.)

9. Paracelsus, *Selected Writings*, 122–23.

10. Pagel, *Paracelsus*, 51.

11. Daston and Park, *Wonders and Order*, 40, make a similar point when they argue that Augustine "made of wonder a serious and sobering emotion, dissolving its links with the . . . sorts of pleasure rooted in the experience of novelty and stressing instead its affinity with religious awe."

12. I discuss this habit in terms of the Thoreauian practice of "microvision" in Jane Bennett, *Thoreau's Nature: Ethics, Politics, and the Wild*, rev. ed. (Rowman and Littlefield, 2001). What provoked enchantment for Paracelsus was God *as He was mediated through nature or scripture*. Paracelsus encountered God at a remove from His frightening omnipotence, and this distance might be crucial to the enchantment effect. Here, one can see how what I call enchantment resembles the

sublime of Burke and Kant. This affinity also can be seen in my account in chap. 5 of Thoreau and "Ktaadn."

13. Paracelsus, *Selected Writings*, 21.

14. As Pagel, *Paracelsus*, 60, explains, for Paracelsus the fact that Scammonea is a purgative means that "there is 'scientia' in the herb which teaches it how to purge—just as there is internal 'scientia' in the pear tree which teaches it how to grow pears. . . . It is this 'scientia' which we should try to catch. 'When you overhear (*ablauschen*) from the Scammonea the knowledge which it possesses, it will be in you just as it is in the Scammonea. . . .' "

15. Ibid., 112, "Iliaster is a kind of primordial matter, but not matter in the ordinary corporeal sense. It is rather the supreme pattern of matter, a principle that enables coarse visible matter and all activity of growth and life in it to develop and exist."

16. Gilles Deleuze, *Difference and Repetition*, trans. Paul Patton (Columbia University Press), 211, insists that there is also an important difference between the two. It is the difference between the "possible" and the "virtual." In Deleuzean terms, Iliaster "is opposed to the real; the process undergone by the possible is therefore a 'realisation.' By contrast, the virtual is not opposed to the real; it possesses a full reality by itself. The process it undergoes is that of actualisation." Deleuze adds, "Every time we pose the question in terms of possible and real, we are forced to conceive of existence as a brute eruption, a pure act or leap which always occurs behind our backs and is subject to the law of all or nothing"—but the virtual field is no void, but is as warm with vitality (211). Finally, the "possible" participates in the logic of resemblance: it is "an image *of* the real. . . . The actualisation of the virtual, on the contrary, . . . breaks with resemblance as a process. . . . Actual terms never resemble the singularities they incarnate. In this sense, actualisation . . . is always a genuine creation. . . . For a . . . virtual object, to be actualised is to create divergent lines which correspond to—without resembling—a virtual multiplicity" (212). I return to Deleuze's notion of the virtual field at the end of this chapter.

17. Pagel, *Paracelsus*, 228; see also Paracelsus, *Selected Writings*, 17.

18. Daston and Park, *Wonder and Order*, 161; Pagel, *Paracelsus*, 104–5.

19. Deleuze, *Difference and Repetition*, 1. A singularity is a virtual potentiality that has begun to actualize, or, as John Landau puts it, "a possibility that escapes compression into actualization" (Landau, <http://cs.art.rmit.edu.au/deleuzeguattarionary/s/pages/singularity.html>>). One could say that singularities emerge from the "limbus."

20. Deleuze, *Difference and Repetition*, 21.

21. See Ben Bova, *Immortality* (Avon Books, 1998), 80–81.

22. Gilles Deleuze, *Cinema 2: The Time Image* (University of Minnesota Press, 1989), 129, acknowledges "the dangers of citing scientific propositions outside their own sphere. It is the danger of arbitrary metaphor or of forced application. But perhaps these dangers are averted if we restrict ourselves to taking from scientific operators a particular conceptualizable character that itself refers to nonscientific areas and converges with science without applying it or making it a metaphor. It is in this sense that we can talk . . . of quantum spaces in Robbe-Grillet, . . . of crystallized spaces in Herzog. . . ." See also Paul Patton's discussion of Deleuze's

use of "language adapted from Nietzsche's remarks on physics," in Patton, *Deleuze and the Political* (Routledge, 2000), 52–53.

23. Gilles Deleuze and Felix Guattari, *Kafka: Toward a Minor Literature* (Minnesota University Press,1986), 21. I discuss this "sonorous" element of language further in chap. 7.

24. Foucault, *Order of Things*, 23.

25. J. Cardan, *De la Subtilite* (French trans., Paris, 1656), 154, quoted in ibid., 24.

26. Foucault, *Order of Things*, 17.

27. *CJ*, 422.

28. Ibid., 383, note 46.

29. See William Connolly, *Political Theory and Modernity* (Basil Blackwell, 1988), 78–80.

30. *CJ*, 374. "An organized product of nature is one in which everything is a purpose and reciprocally also a means" (376). Water, air, and earth are not for Kant organisms (see 425).

31. William Connolly, *Why I Am Not a Secularist* (University of Minnesota Press, 1999), chap. 7, reads *Critique of Judgment* alongside Hannah Arendt, *Lectures on Kant's Political Philosophy* (University of Chicago Press, 1982), in order to expose the central role the ideal of purity plays in both thinkers.

32. *CJ*, 401.

33. Ibid., 406, my emphasis.

34. But, again, Kant is careful to say that this concept too is a subjective necessity: We must not be "so bold as to posit a different, intelligent being above nature as its architect, since that would be presumptuous." (Ibid., 383.)

35. Ibid.

36. Ibid., 268. I hesitate over whether to describe it as a "subjective" necessary or as a "rational" one, and Kant does seem to use them differently—the latter seems somehow to have more necessity, perhaps because reason has a dual residence, both in the concrete human subject and in supersensible.

37. See Werner Pluhar, "Translator's Introduction," *CJ*, lxxi–lxxii.

38. *CJ*, 379. See also Kant's claim, 383, "We are not trying to introduce [into physics] a special causal basis, but are trying to introduce only another method for our use of reason in investigating."

39. Perhaps this is why it is Paracelsus and not Kant who extensively explores cases of human madness or sickness, instances where the "universal" structure of human nature breaks down. It would be most uncomfortable for Kant to dwell on such instances: Kant needs the mind as a place of stability and cross-personal uniformity more than Paracelsus does. See, for example, Paracelsus, "The Diseases that Deprive Man of His Reason . . . ," in *Four Treatises of Theophrastus von Hoheheim Called Paracelsus*, trans. C. Lillian Temkin, George Rosen, and Gregory Zilboorg (Johns Hopkins University Press, 1941).

40. *CJ*, xxxvi. The Imagination is the power of "reflection," or of an active sensibility that responds to objects by picturing or "reflecting" them back to itself. The Understanding is the power of "concepts"; "a concept groups together many instances (of things or events) in terms of attributes they share as instances of the same kind."

41. Ibid., 230.

42. Ibid., 204. Taste "does not contribute anything to cognition, but merely compares the given presentation in the subject with the entire presentational power, of which the mind becomes conscious when it feels its own state."

43. Ibid., 205.

44. Ibid., 211.

45. Ibid., 290.

46. Ibid., 292.

47. See Gilles Deleuze, *Kant's Critical Philosophy: The Doctrine of the Faculties*, trans. Hugh Tomlinson and Barbara Habberjam (University of Minnesota Press, 1984), 60.

48. It is particularly easy to see how Paracelsus—who routinely mingled natural science with God— failed to respect the last of these divides. In physics, says Kant, we must "abstract entirely from the question as to whether natural purposes are purposes *intentionally* or *unintentionally* . . . [and] . . . settle for regarding natural purposes as objects that are *explicable* solely in terms of natural laws . . . conceived of by using the idea of purposes . . . , and that are even internally *cognizable* only in this way. . ." (*CJ*, 383)

49. Kafka, "Great Wall of China," 235. I return to this story in chap. 5, as part of a discussion of social complexity as a site of enchantment.

50. Latour, *We Have Never Been Modern*, 137. I am indebted to Latour . . . and other theorists as I try to articulate the enchanting dimension of hybrids and to specify what is responsible for their peculiar power to carry one to the other world always there behind one's back. See Donna Haraway, *Primate Visions* (Routledge, 1989); Thom Kuehls, *Beyond Sovereign Territory* (University of Minnesota Press, 1996); and Tim Luke, "Cyborg Subjectivities," *Theory and Event* 1, no. 1 (January 1997).

51. Kafka, *Complete Stories*, 426–27.

52. I take the phrase from Fisher, *Wonder*, 31.

53. Deleuze and Guattari, *Thousand Plateaus*, 273.

54. Ibid., 274.

55. Its task "is not to direct . . . a thought which pre-exists in principle and in nature," but to "create," to "bring into being that which does not yet exist." (Deleuze, *Difference and Repetition*, 147.)

56. Ibid., 131.

57. Ibid., 147

58. Ibid., 139.

59. "The reason of the sensible, the condition of that which appears, is not space and time but the Unequal in itself, *disparateness* as it is determined and comprised in difference in intensity. . . ." (Ibid., 222–23.)

60. Ibid., 237.

61. Ibid., 276.

62. Ibid., 277. Ants long have been a source of wonder and fascination: "The Dutch naturalist Jan Swammerdam, for example, thought the humble ant deserved as much admiration as God's largest and gaudiest creations, on account of 'its care and diligence, its marvelous force, its unsurpassed zeal, and extraordinary and inconceivable love for its young." (Daston and Park, *Wonders and Order*, 323.)

63. Deleuze and Guattari, *Thousand Plateaus*, 308–9.

64. Daston and Park, *Wonders and Order*, 360, quote Schiller's poem as follows:

> Feeling not the joy she bids me share,
> Ne'er entranc'd by her own majesty,
> Knowing her own guiding spirit ne'er,
> Ne'er made happy by *my* ecstacy,
> Senseless even to her Maker's praise,
> Like the pendule-clock's dead, hollow tone,
> Nature Gravitation's law obeys
> Servilely,—her Godhead flown.

Chapter 4
Disenchantment Tales

1. Max Weber, *From Max Weber: Essays in Sociology*, ed. H. H. Gerth and C. Wright Mills (Oxford, 1981), 347.

2. Ibid., 331.

3. Ibid., 282.

4. Max Weber, "Science as a Vocation," in ibid., 155.

5. Ibid., 139.

6. Weber, *From Max Weber*, 350.

7. Weber, "Science as a Vocation," 140.

8. Ibid., 138.

9. Weber, *From Max Weber*, 345.

10. Gilbert G. Germain says that the progressive emptying of magic from the world functions as Weber's philosophy of history. See his *A Discourse on Disenchantment: Reflections of Politics and Technology* (SUNY Press, 1993), 28.

11. Weber, *From Max Weber*, 331.

12. Weber, "Science as a Vocation," 139.

13. Weber, *From Max Weber*, 293, describes these different senses of rationalization.

14. Max Weber, *The Protestant Ethic and the Spirit of Capitalism*, trans. Talcott Parsons (Charles Scribner's Sons, 1958), 105. See also Frederic Jameson, "The Vanishing Mediator; or Max Weber as Storyteller," in Jameson, *Ideologies of Theory, Essays 1971–1986*, vol. 2, *The Syntax of History* (University of Minnesota Press, 1988), 26. Daston and Park, *Wonders and Order*, chap. 3 and 4, discern the same kind of nonlinearity in late medieval/early modern conceptions of wonder. Demagification was pursued rigorously by the Scholastic philosophical writers, but the "preternatural philosophers" who followed them by over two hundred years made wonder and wonders central to natural philosophy.

15. Weber, *From Max Weber*, 281.

16. Weber, "Science as a Vocation," 141, my emphasis.

17. Ibid., 139. My thanks to Barry Hindess for pointing out the importance of the "in principle" in Weber's writing.

18. Alan Sica, *Weber, Irrationality, and Social Order* (University of California Press, 1988), 168.

19. In chap. 5, I consider challenges to this choice of ideal by those who conceive matter as containing an irreducible element of incalculability.

20. Weber, *From Max Weber*, 282.

21. Charles Taylor, *The Malaise of Modernity* (House of Anansi Press, 1991), 3.

22. Arthur Mitzman, *The Iron Cage: An Historical Interpretation of Max Weber*, (Knopf, 1970), 220.

23. Anthony J. Cascardi, *The Subject of Modernity* (Cambridge, 1992), 19.

24. Lawrence Scaff, *Fleeing the Iron Cage: Culture, Political and Modernity in the Thought of Max Weber* (University of California Press, 1989), 224.

25. Weber, "Science as a Vocation," 152. According to Sheldon Wolin, "Legitimation, Method and the Politics of Theory," in *Legitimacy and the State*, ed. William E. Connolly (Basil Blackwell, 1984), 81, significance "becomes the crucial concept in Weber's politics of knowledge. It symbolizes the moment of freedom for the social scientist when he registers his affirmations, when he exchanges the settled routines of inquiry for the risks of action. It is akin to a form of momentary and secular salvation for it creates meaning in an otherwise meaningless world." Jameson, "Vanishing Mediator," 6–7, sees not resentment but "ennui" as the state that Weber is seeking to avoid: the "experience of the divorce of means from ends that has its objective embodiment in rationalization . . . finds its subjective expression in ennui." Jameson distinguishes ennui from "the Romantic despair" of the early years of the nineteenth century, when the beautiful aristocratic world was losing sway. In response to this very specifiable loss, the romantic sufferer "withdraws completely from the world," but does so dramatically, for the prospect of return is still high enough to warrant that kind of expenditure of creative energy. But whereas the romantic mood was "a coming to consciousness of some fundamental loss in shock and rage, a kind of furious rattling of the bars of the prison, a helpless attempt to recuperate a lost being by posing and assuming one's fatality in 'interesting' ways," ennui sets in after the object of one's longing is long gone, historically speaking. Rage is now replaced by a mood of passivity or boredom. He who suffers from ennui "can no longer remember a situation qualitatively different from his own and assumes, naturally enough, that all life is thus empty." The world is starting to seem not merely denuded of life, but inherently dead. Jameson also distinguishes ennui "from that affect most characteristic of our time, namely anxiety." Anxiety "is an active principle [that] . . . results from a sudden awareness of the self as the unjustified source of all values and of all action, an awareness that can arise only in the moment of choice and not in a situation of generalized inactivity." Romantic despair, ennui, and anxiety can be seen as three moments in the historical process of demagification, "in which the soul, having first registered its shock and distress at the new and barren world in which it finds itself, begins with a kind of paralyzed detachment to take an inventory of its surroundings, before [concluding] . . . that it is itself the very ground of the latter's bustling agitation." For Jameson, then, Weber's tale of rationalization and demagification is the tale of the increasing humanization of the world.

26. Weber, "Science as a Vocation," 139, says that science "belongs" to the process of disenchantment "as a link and motive force."

27. Scaff, *Fleeing Iron Cage*, 224, argues that "the world" that is disenchanted refers for Weber to the *cultural* sphere, to "the temporal course of everyday affairs, the space of action and appearance, the humanly constructed environment of the life-world and culture." I argue instead that disenchantment occurs in the story at the psychic, social, and natural levels.

28. Weber, "Science as a Vocation," 138.

29. Ibid., 140.

30. Weber, *From Max Weber*, 294.

31. Ibid., 283.

32. Weber, *From Max Weber*, 281. According to Mitzman, *Iron Cage*, 220–21, this two-world metaphysic, in conjunction with a theology that disenchants the mundane world, eventually leads to the "emancipation of rational thought from all religious beliefs" and to "the abandonment of any notion of an inherent meaning in worldly affairs."

33. Ibid., 290.

34. Ibid., 291.

35. Ibid., 281.

36. Weber, "Science as a Vocation," 155.

37. Weber, *From Max Weber*, 282. Also, Weber, "Science as a Vocation," 147, 152, states that science plainly admits that it cannot decide between competing values or ultimate priorities: " 'Scientific' pleading is meaningless in principle because the various value spheres of the world stand in irreconcilable conflict with each other. . . ." Or again, "so long as life remains immanent and is interpreted in its own terms, . . . the ultimately possible attitudes toward life are irreconcilable, and hence their struggle can never be brought to a final conclusion." This means that the individual, not the scientist, is called upon to "make a decisive choice."

38. Ibid., 345.

39. Max Weber, "Religious Reflections," as quoted in Mitzman, *Iron Cage*, 222.

40. Weber, *From Max Weber*, 345.

41. Weber, "Science as a Vocation," 155.

42. Ibid., 139, states: "One need no longer have recourse to magical means in order to master or implore the spirits, as did the savage, for whom such mysterious powers existed. Technical means and calculations perform the service."

43. Germain, *Discourse on Disenchantment*, 5.

44. Weber, *Protestant Ethic*, 181.

45. Hans Blumenberg, *The Legitimacy of the Modern Age* (MIT Press, 1983).

46. Ibid., 137. The challenge to Scholasticism and its "spiritual system [of] creation as 'providence' " receive much more attention in Blumenberg's text than does Scholasticism itself. In Weber's disenchantment tale, the lost alternative was figured as a system of magic, contrasted to science and to religions of the "ethical" type. In the antisecularist version (the version that Blumenberg specifically contests), the object of loss is pictured as a medieval Christian cosmology.

47. For Nietzsche and Epicurus, who affirm a one-world metaphysic, the "things of this world" include *every* thing there is. But in the two-world meta-

physic of the secularization thesis, the (experiential) world is but a tiny fragment of reality, a drop in the ontological bucket.

48. Blumenberg, *Legitimacy*, 147.

49. Ibid., 153. Nominalism's rejection of the idea that things are conceivable as particulars of a universal here forms an uncanny alliance with Deleuze's critique of the Kantian image of thought in favor of a notion of spiral repetition. See discussion in chaps. 3 and 6.

50. Ibid.

51. Daston and Park, *Wonders and Order*, 118, reveal how the notion of a purpose in nature need not be paired with a notion of a wondrous world. Both teleologist and wonder-theorists (who Daston and Park describe as the "preternatural philosophers") pictured a world in which humans could feel relatively secure as parts of a larger order. But whereas a wonder-filled world required careful attention to sensuous particulars, to the singularity of things, the teleological cosmos of the Scholastics repudiated such an empirical focus in favor of philosophical reflection on universals. See their wonderful and nuanced discussions, chaps. 3, 4.

52. Blumenberg, *Legitimary*, 169.

53. Ibid., 159.

54. E. Ann Kaplan speaks of documentary film as performing a similar witnessing role. See Kaplan, "Trauma, Cinema, Witnessing," in Rosanne Kennedy and Jill Bennett, eds., *World Memory: Personal Trajectories in Global Time* (Sydney University Press, 2001).

55. Good examples of the latter include Robert Bellah, *Habits of the Heart* (University of California Press, 1996), and Richard Madsen, William Sullivan, Ann Swidler, and Robert Bellah, *The Good Society* (Vintage, 1992), but also Paul Virilio's work on speed and politics, including *The Art of the Motor* (University of Minnesota Press, 1995) and *Open Sky* (Verso Books, 1997). For a good summary, see James DerDerian, "Virtually Wagging the Dog," *Theory & Event* 2:1, at http://muse.jhu.edu/journals/theory_&_event/toc/archive.html#2.1.

56. Foucault describes them as "ethical problematizations" (i.e., those practices and domains of life that come to be seen as in need of special care, attention, or discipline). See Michael Foucault, *The Use of Pleasure* (Random House, 1985), especially the Introduction and Part IV, chap. 1, "A Problematic Relation."

57. Simon Critchley, *Very Little . . . Almost Nothing: Death, Philosophy, Literature* (Routledge, 1997).

58. Ibid., 85–86. The subtleties of Critchley's recuperation of romanticism deserve more extensive inquiry. I am merely identifying some of the ethical themes that he extracts from Jena romanticism: (1) its acknowledgment of death as a meaningless finality; (2) its attempt to cope with the banality of the everyday by means of imagination; (3) its use of the literary form of the fragment as a synecdoche of the human self; and (4) its valorization of skepticism as promoting humility in the face of the other.

59. Ibid., 97. "We are inheritors of . . . a *romantic modernity.* . . . romanticism provides the profile for a modernity in which we are both unable to believe, but which we are unable to leave."

60. Kafka, *Complete Stories*, 456. Although Kafka's stories might, as this one does, illustrate elements within the disenchantment tale, I argue throughout the

book and especially at the end of chap. 5 that they are not themselves contained by that narrative.

61. Lucretius, "De Rerum Natura."

62. Ibid., II, 308. "The primordia of things cannot be perceived with the eyes" (I, 265); the nature of the primordia themselves "lies far away from our senses, below their purview" (II, 308).

63. Epicurus, "Letter to Herodotus," in Gaskin, *Epicurean Philosophers*, 19.

64. Lucretius, "De Rerum Natura," I, 311.

65. B. C. Crandall, "Molecular Engineering," in *Nanotechnology: Molecular Speculations on Global Abundance*, ed. B. C. Crandall (MIT Press, 1966), 1.

66. Ibid.

67. Ibid., 14–16, my emphasis.

68. Richard Crawford, "Cosmetic Nanosurgery," in Crandall, *Nanotechnology*, 62–63.

69. Ted Kaehler, "In Vivo Nanoscope and the 'Two Week Revolution,' " in Crandall, *Nanotechnology*, 50.

70. John Markoff, "Tiniest Circuits Hold Prospect of Explosive Computer Speeds," *The New York Times*, July 16, 1999, A1, C17.

71. Crandall, "Molecular Engineering," 5.

72. Epicurus, "Letter to Herodotus," 15.

73. Deleuze and Guattari, *Thousand Plateaus*, 274.

74. Stephen K. White, *Sustaining Affirmation: The Strengths of Weak Ontology in Political Theory* (Princeton University Press, 2000), 91. On this point, see also discussion by Connolly, *Why I Am Not a Secularist*, chap. 6.

75. Epicurus, "Letter to Menoeceus," in Gaskins, *Epicurean Philosophers*, 45.

76. Ibid., 45.

77. The Epicurean says not to fear death because it is only oblivion, and then suggests that you work on yourself to accept death as oblivion, for then you will be less likely to be resentful in your relations with others in life. You might augment the Epicurean perspective by saying that the end of life involves above all the loss of others you love and the disappearance—in some cases forever—of memories that deserve to be stored. The struggle is to come to terms with these losses without resenting the world for not overcoming them and without allowing all of life to be colored by the inevitability of such losses, without allowing nature and life to become disenchanted because of that.

78. Deleuze and Guattari, *Thousand Plateaus*, 150.

79. See Massumi, "Autonomy of Affect," 217–39.

80. Crandall, "Molecular Engineering," 193–94.

Chapter 5
Complexity and Enchantment

1. Good examples of the ecospirituality position can be found in Thomas Moore, *The Re-Enchantment of Everyday Life* (HarperCollins, 1996); Michael Tobias and Georgianne Cowan, eds., *The Soul of Nature: Celebrating the Spirit of the Earth* (Penguin, 1996); Catherine L. Albanese, *Nature Religion in America:*

From the Algonkian Indians to the New Age (University of Chicago, 1990); Wade Sikorski, *Modernity and Technology: Harnessing the Earth to the Slavery of Man* (University of Alabama, 1993). The writings of Wendell Berry and Barry Lopez might also be classified as such. Morris Berman, *The Reenchantment of the World* (Cornell, 1981), 16, focuses on the social ills issuing from the fact that "from the sixteenth century on, mind has been progressively expunged from the phenomenal world." Erazim Kohak, *The Embers and the Stars: A Philosophical Inquiry into the Moral Sense of Nature* (University of Chicago, 1984), emphasizes the moral more than the ecological dangers of a disenchanted world.

2. Matthew Fox, "Creation Spirituality," in Tobias and Cowan, *Soul of Nature*, 207.

3. See, for example, Barry Lopez, "Apologia," in Tobias and Cowan, *Soul of Nature*.

4. For example, Moore, *Re-enchantment of Everyday Life*, x, writes that enchantment "can give a sensation of fulfillment that makes life purposeful and vibrant. In an enchanted life . . . , we do have frequent, even daily opportunities to enter a . . . level of experience that has more charm than practicality."

5. I use the term *arboreal* to describe an environmentalism, like that of the ecospiritualists, that imagines nature to be an organic whole: "The tree and root inspire a sad image of thought that is forever imitating the multiple on the basis of a centered or segmented higher unity. . . . It is odd how the tree has dominated . . . Western thought . . . : the root-foundation, *Grund, racine, fondement*." From Deleuze and Guattari, *Thousand Plateaus*, 16–18.

6. Network is, says Latour, *We Have Never Been Modern*, 3, "more supple than the notion of system, more historical than the notion of structure, more empirical than the notion of complexity."

7. Isabelle Stengers and Ilya Prigogine, "The Reenchantment of the World," in Stengers, *Power and Invention* (University of Minnesota, 1997), 34.

8. Henry Thoreau, *The Writings of Henry David Thoreau V: Excursions and Poems* (AMS Press, 1968), 205.

9. Stanley Cavell, *The Sense of Walden* (North Point Press, 1981), 28. To say that Thoreau "inflected" nature is different from claiming that he considered it to be a fiction. The language of "social construction" or "linguistic production" was not available to Thoreau, but it is unlikely that he would have endorsed it. That is because those ways of marking nature's internal relation to artifice overstate the earth's pliability; they tend to write nature as inert matter without a will of its own. Thoreau, in *The Writings of Henry David Thoreau: A Week on the Concord and Merrimack Rivers*, ed. Carol Hovde (Princeton University Press, 1980), 325, insists to the contrary that "of pure invention, such as some suppose, there is no instance. To write a true work of fiction even, is only to take leisure and liberty to describe some things more exactly as they are."

10. Thoreau, *Writings of Thoreau: Week on Concord and Merrimack*, 340.

11. Henry Thoreau, *The Writings of Henry Thoreau: Walden*, ed. J. Lyndon Shanley (Princeton University Press, 1973), 25, refers to this as the power of the "They." He first became aware of its overbearing presence when he asked his tailor for a certain style coat and was told that "they" don't make them anymore. Writes

Thoreau: "When I hear this oracular sentence, I am for a moment absorbed in thought, emphasizing to myself each word separately that I may come at the meaning of it, that I may find out by what degree of consanguity *They* are related to *me*, and what authority they may have in an affair which affects me so nearly. . . ."

12. Henry Thoreau, *The Writings of Henry David Thoreau: Journal*, vol. 8, ed. Bradford Torry and Francis Allen (Houghton Mifflin, 1949), 43–44.

13. Henry Thoreau, *The Writings of Henry David Thoreau: The Maine Woods*, ed. Joseph Moldenhauer (Princeton, 1972), 70. Ktaadn reveals the presumptuousness of his Edenic expectations: "This ground is not prepared for you," says the mountain. "Is it not enough that I smile in the valleys? I have never made this soil for thy feet, this air for thy breathing . . . " (64).

14. Ibid., 71.

15. Henry Thoreau, *The Writings of Henry David Thoreau: Journal*, vol. 4, ed. Leonard Neufeldt and Nancy Craig Simmons (Princeton, 1992), 382.

16. Thoreau, *Writings of Thoreau: Walden*, 100.

17. Ibid., 325.

18. Thoreau, *Writings of Thoreau: Week on Concord and Merrimack*, 339.

19. "It does seem as if mine were a peculiarly wild nature, which so yearns toward all wildness." In Henry Thoreau, *The Writings of Henry David Thoreau: Journal*, vol. 1, ed. John Broderick (Princeton, 1981), 344.

20. Foucault, *Use of Pleasure*, 28.

21. Latour, *We Have Never Been Modern*, 10–11, says, " 'Translation' creates . . . hybrids of nature and culture . . . [;] 'purification' creates two new entirely distinct ontological zones: . . . human beings [and] . . . nonhumans. . . . Without the first . . ., purification would be . . . pointless. Without the second, . . . translation would be . . . limited, or even ruled out. . . ."

22. Ibid., 12.

23. Here, I draw upon Wade Sikorski's fascinating account of psychoneuroimmunology in *Infected with Difference: Healing Dis/Ease in the Body Politic*, 1999, available at Fatbrain.com.

24. Latour, *We Have Never Been Modern*, 41, states, "We've never been modern" because "we've" never been what "we" officially proclaim ourselves to be (i.e., single-minded purifiers). "The link between the work of purification and the work of mediation has given birth to the moderns, but they credit only the former with their success."

25. Ibid., 27–28. According to Latour, the decision to ignore hybridity officially was the result of a compromise worked out between Robert Boyle and Thomas Hobbes. As a way of settling their dispute over who would draw the new, scientific picture of the world, each agreed to exclusive rights over one sector of a partitioned reality. Hobbes's sector was culture and the social sciences, and Boyle's was nature and the experimental sciences. Together, they formalized a world "in which the representation of things through the intermediary of the lab is . . . dissociated from the representation of citizens through the intermediary of the social contract. . . . [T]he representation of nonhumans belongs to science, but science is not allowed to appeal to politics; the representation of citizens belongs to politics but politics is not allowed to have any relation to the nonhumans produced and mobilized by science and technology."

26. Ibid., 36–37.

27. Ibid., 39.

28. Ibid., 124. It is also hardly a reason to define modernity as the qualitatively superior victor in the great battle with the Ancients. "Modern is thus doubly asymmetrical: it designates a break in the regular passage of time, and it designates a combat in which there are victors and vanquished" (10). For a good discussion of the egalitarianism expressed by Latour's criticism of asymmetry, see David Berreby, ". . . That Damned Elusive Bruno Latour," *Lingua Franca*, September/October 1994, 22–32.

29. Ibid., 115. Latour, *We Have Never Been Modern*, 115. Latour sees modernists, antimodernists, and postmodernists as sharing a commitment to this story: "The antimoderns firmly believe that the West has . . . transformed the premodern cosmos into a mechanical interaction of pure matters. But instead of seeing these processes as the modernizers do—as glorious, albeit painful conquests—the antimoderns see the situation as an unparalleled catastrophe. . . . The postmoderns . . . accept the idea that the situation is indeed catastrophic, but they maintain that it is to be acclaimed rather than bemoaned! (123)

30. Ibid., 115.

31. Ibid., 142.

32. "Cyborgs are about particular sorts of breached boundaries that confuse a specific historical people's stories about what counts as distinct categories crucial to that culture's natural-technical evolutionary narratives," in Donna Haraway, Foreword, *The Cyborg Handbook*, ed. Chris Hables Gray (Routledge, 1995), xvi. For an interesting account of the links between cyborg identities and the liberal tradition, see Timothy W. Luke, "Liberal Society and Cyborg Subjectivity: The Politics of Environments, Bodies and Nature at Century's End," *Alternatives: A Journal of World Policy*, XXI (1996), 1–30.

33. Latour, *We Have Never Been Modern*, 137.

34. Michel Serres, *Hermes: Literature, Science, Philosophy*, ed. Josue Harari and David Bell (Johns Hopkins University Press, 1982), 101–2.

35. Ilya Prigogine, *The End of Certainty: Time, Chaos, and the New Laws of Nature* (Free Press, 1997), 55.

36. Ilya Prigogine and Isabelle Stengers, *Order Out of Chaos: Man's New Dialogue with Nature* (Bantam Books, 1984), 13, say that nonequilibrium "may in fact be taken as the very basis of the definition of a biological system."

37. A fluctuation is a small change in the parameters of a system, for example, in the humidity, pH, salt concentration, light, or nutrients of an ecosystem. See ibid., 167.

38. Ibid., 180–81. See also ibid., 14, in which the authors claim that far from equilibrium, matter "begins to be able to perceive, to 'take into account,' in its way of functioning, differences in the external world (such as weak gravitational or electric fields)."

39. Ibid., 162.

40. Prigogine, *End of Certainty*, 68.

41. Prigogine and Stengers, *Order Out of Chaos*, 6.

42. Prigogine, *End of Certainty*, 72.

43. Prigogine and Stengers, *Order Out of Chaos*, 13.

44. Ibid., 143.

45. Ibid., 146, say that the notion of reversible and determinist trajectories "does not belong exclusively to classical dynamics. It is found in relativity and in quantum mechanics" as well. For example, in the model of the atom wherein "each orbit is characterized by a well-determined energy level in which electrons are in steady, eternal, and invariable movement. . . . The orbits are defined as being without interaction with each other or with the world. . . ." This is the case even though other aspects of quantum mechanics are at odds with this Leibnizian model; electrons are also pictured as able to "jump from one orbit to anther. . . . It is here that quantum mechanics . . . does not define the determinist and reversible description as being complete."

46. See Prigogine and Stengers, "A Question of Style," in Serres, *Hermes*, 150; "a dynamic description is only determinist if the description of its initial state is completely accurate. . . . [While] no description actually produced will be perfectly determinist . . . determinism stands out as a limit. . . ."

47. Ibid.

48. Ibid., 152, say, "It is of no use to increase the level of precision or even to make it *tend toward* infinity; uncertainty always remains complete—it does not diminish as precision increases."

49. Ibid., 152.

50. See Prigogine and Stengers, *Order Out of Chaos*, 18: the aim is to "emphasize the conceptual creativeness of scientific activity and the future prospects and new problems it raises. In any case, we now know that we are only at the beginning of this exploration. We shall not see the end of uncertainty or risk. Thus we have chosen to present things as we perceive them now, fully aware of how incomplete our answers are."

51. Ibid., 73.

52. Ibid., 177.

53. Ibid., 187.

54. Ibid.

55. Isabelle Stengers, *Power and Invention* (University of Minnesota Press, 1997), 9.

56. Prigogine, *End of Certainty*, 189, says, "What is now emerging is an 'intermediate' description that lies somewhere between the two alienating images of a deterministic world and an arbitrary world of pure chance. Physical laws lead to a new form of intelligibility as expressed by irreducible probabilistic representations."

57. Ibid., 17.

58. Franz Kafka, *The Castle* (Schocken, 1967), 235–36.

59. Sigmund Freud, in *Standard Edition of the Complete Psychological Works*, trans. James Strachey, vol. 17 (Hogarth Press, 1953–1974), 225, arrives at this understanding of the uncanny etymologically: "the word '*heimlich*' is not unambiguous, but belongs to two sets of ideas . . . : on the one hand it means what is familiar and agreeable, and on the other, what is concealed and kept out of sight." Freud notes that encounters with things that confound established conceptual boundaries are likely to have an uncanny effect. We know that Kafka's stories are filled with such transgressions—of the animal-human line in *The Metamorphosis*,

"Jackals and Arabs," "Josephine the Mouse Singer," and "A Report to the Academy" and of the organism-machine line in *In the Penal Colony* and in "The Bucket-Rider." Kafka also regularly confounds distinctions between rational and irrational, the clear and the mysterious, and waking and dream states.

60. The story opens with a description of the wall's peculiar method of piecemeal construction, which guarantees that there will always be gaps in it. The purpose of the wall is to protect the settled peoples of China from the nomads in the north. So why build it in discontinuous sections of 1,000 yards by two teams working at opposite ends? Because, this way, the masons could gain a (false) sense of completion–the border was too vast to enclose completely within "even the longest lifetime." (Kafka, *Complete Stories*, 152.)

61. Ibid., 173.

62. Ibid., 167.

63. If there is something to this thesis, then attempts to render the channels of bureaucratic authority more visible and overt, and more democratically accountable, must pay greater attention to the strange hold that complexity has over us.

64. Ibid., 150.

65. Ibid., 172–73.

66. Deleuze and Guattari, *Kafka*, 41.

67. Kafka, *The Castle*, 237.

68. Ibid., 297.

Chapter 6
Commodity Fetishism and Commodity Enchantment

1. T. Richards, *The Commodity Culture of Victorian England: Advertising and Spectacle, 1851–1914* (Verso, 1991), 11. (Cited in John Jervis, *Exploring the Modern: Patterns of Western Culture and Civilization* [Blackwell, 1998], 95.)

2. Michael McCadden, quoted in Stuart Elliott, "The Media Business: Advertising; The Latest Music Dorm to Find Resurrection by Mainstream Marketers Is Swing, in All Its Glory," *The New York Times*, Jan. 18, 1999.

3. My thanks to Bill Chaloupka for helping me to develop this description of the ad and for his thoughts about the limits and insights of a Marxian reading of commercial culture.

4. Franz Kafka, "The Bucket Rider," in *Complete Stories*, 412–13.

5. Franz Kafka, "Cares of a Family Man," in *Complete Stories*, 428.

6. See Bruno Bettelheim, *The Uses of Enchantment* (Vintage, 1989), and Sigmund Freud, "The Uncanny," in *The Standard Edition of the Complete Psychological Works of Sigmund Freud*, vol. 17 (Hogarth, 1954–1974).

7. Ackbar Abbas, "Cultural Studies in a Postculture," in *Disciplinarity and Dissent in Cultural Studies*, eds. Cary Nelson and Dilip Parameshwar Gaonkar (Routledge, 1996), 291–92.

8. Grant McCracken, *Culture and Consumption* (Indiana University Press, 1988), xv.

9. Frank DeCaro, "Millennium a Go-Go: Frugging to 2000," *The New York Times*, Apr. 18, 1999, sec. 9, 1.

10. See, for example, Allan Schnaiberg and Kenneth Alan Gould, *Environment and Society: The Enduring Conflict* (St. Martin's Press, 1994.)

11. These themes are developed in Michael Best and William E. Connolly, *The Politicized Economy* (D.C. Heath, 1976); William E. Connolly, *The Ethos of Pluralization* (University of Minnesota Press, 1995), ch. 4; Fred Hirsch, *Social Limits to Growth* (Harvard University Press, 1976); John Buell, *Democracy by Other Means: The Politics of Work, Leisure and the Environment* (University of Illinois Press, 1995).

12. See E. F. Schumacher, *Small Is Beautiful: Economics as if People Mattered* (Harper Perennial, 1989).

13. Might the fear that changing the infrastructure of consumption would entail the end of pleasure in consumption be one source of cultural resistance to the adoption of more ecofriendly ways of life?

14. Jervis, *Exploring the Modern*, 98.

15. See Wendy Brown, *States of Injury* (Princeton University Press, 1995), especially pp. 59–60. I share Brown's concern to mitigate the role of *ressentiment* in contemporary politics; for me, enchantment is an important counter to resentment, as affective states predispose their bearers for or against a particular existential state, as well as a political program.

16. Deleuze and Guattari, *Thousand Plateaus*, 216, 226.

17. Marx, *Capital*, vol. II., 952.

18. Ibid., vol. II, 953.

19. Ibid., vol. I, 166.

20. Michael Taussig, *The Devil and Commodity Fetishism in South America* (University of North Carolina Press, 1983), 25–26.

21. Frederick Jameson, *Postmodernism, or the Cultural Logic of Late Capitalism* (Duke University Press, 1991), 233, refers to this as "the mystery of the equivalence of radically different things."

22. Marx, *Capital*, vol. I, 953.

23. Taussig, *Devil and Commodity Fetishism*, 4.

24. Marx, *Capital*, vol. I, 163–65.

25. Karl Marx, "The Leading Article in No. 179 of the *Kolnische Zeitung*," in Karl Marx and Frederick Engles, *Collected Works*, vol. 1, *Karl Marx: 1835–43* (Lawrence and Wishart, 1975), 189.

26. *The Compact Edition of the Oxford English Dictionary* (Oxford University Press, 1971), s.v. "fetish." Jean Baudrillard, *The Consumer Society* (Sage, 1998), 26, in his Marxist incarnation, puts the point this way: In their "splendour and profusion," we forget that commodities are "*the product of a human activity* and are dominated not by natural ecological laws, but by the law of exchange-value."

27. My thanks to John Docker (Docker to author, e-mail, June 9, 1999) for these points. For Docker, "perhaps what Marx and modernists like Adorno and Horkheimer share is a messianic desire to effect total change in modern society by punishing the people for their reversion to paganism and permitting themselves to be seduced (made passive, as if female?) by the commodity or advertising fetish." See also John Docker, *Postmodernism and Popular Culture* (Cambridge University Press, 1994).

28. Michael Hardt and Antonio Negri, *Empire* (Harvard University Press, 2000), 62, for example, emphasize the Marx for whom the "multitude" is less a primitive than a protean, vital force: "The multitude is the real productive force of our social world, whereas Empire is a mere apparatus of capture that lives only off the vitality of the multitude—as Marx would say, a vampire regime of accumulated dead labor that survives only by sucking off the blood of the living." For Hardt and Negri, the "teleology" of the multitude "consists in the possibility of directing technologies and production toward its own joy and its own increase of power." Moreover, (industrial, intellectual, aesthetic, communicative) laborers "cannot be completely subjugated to the laws of capitalist accumulation—at every moment they overflow and shatter the bounds of measure" (396–97). Here, Hardt and Negri discern in Marx a conception of power closer to that of Deleuze and Guattari than Horkheimer and Adorno.

29. Richards, *Commodity Culture*, 11.

30. Norman D. Livergood, *Activity in Marx's Philosophy* (Martinus Nijhoff, 1967), 3.

31. Karl Marx, "Difference between the Democritean and Epicurean Philosophy of Nature" (doctoral dissertation), in Marx and Engles, *Collected Works*, vol. 1, 42–43.

32. Ibid., 49.

33. C. J. McFadden, *The Philosophy of Communism* (Benziger Bros., 1939), 27; quoted in Livergood, *Activity in Marx's Philosophy*, 3.

34. Marx, "Difference," 49.

35. Livergood, *Activity in Marx's Philosophy*, ix.

36. Marx, "Difference," 50.

37. Ibid., 50–51. *Ataraxy* is the state of the sage who has attained inner freedom through knowledge of nature and deliverance from fear of death. (See Marx and Engles, *Collected Works*, vol. 1, 21n, 736.)

38. Ibid., 70.

39. Ibid., 72.

40. George F. McCarthy, *Marx and the Ancients: Classical Ethics, Social Justice and Nineteenth Century Political Economy* (Rowman & Littlefield, 1990), 30–31.

41. Ibid., 40–41.

42. Ibid., 45.

43. Karl Marx, "Notebooks on Epicurean Philosophy," in Marx and Engles, *Collected Works*, vol. 1, 416.

44. McCarthy, *Marx and Ancients*, 25.

45. Max Horkheimer and Theodor Adorno, *Dialectic of Enlightenment*, trans. John Cumming (Herder and Herder, 1972).

46. Ibid., 126. This sense of the systemic quality of the culture industry is presented in more semiotic terms by Baudrillard, *Consumer Society*, 27. For Baudrillard, consumption takes the form of a "chain of *signifiers*. . . . [O]bjects are never offered for consumption in absolute disorder. They . . . are always arranged to . . . orientate the purchasing impulse towards *networks* of objects in order to captivate that impulse and bring it . . . to the limits of its economic potential. Clothing, machines and toiletries thus constitute object *pathways*, which establish inertial constraints in the consumer. . . . He will be caught up in a *calculus* of objects, and

this is something quite different from the frenzy of buying and acquisitiveness to which the simple profusion of commodities gives rise."

47. What is the standard of art against which Horkheimer and Adorno, in *Dialectic of Enlightenment*, 31, judge and find wanting the culture industry? It is an art that self-negates (i.e., displays its own inability to reconcile its transformative aspirations with its dependence on the status quo). It is an art cognizant of the fact that what "enables it to transcend reality . . . is to be found in those features in which discrepancy appears; in the necessary failure of the passionate striving for identity." Adorno develops this theme more fully in *Negative Dialectics* (Seabury Press, 1973) and *Aesthetic Theory* (Routledge, 1983). As Morton Schoolman puts it, art becomes "the only form of thought able to convey the nonrepresentational character of nature, nature's nonidentity, and to expose the illusion of any aesthetic impersonation of being." See Morton Schoolman, "Towards a Politics of Darkness: Individuality and Its Politics in Adorno's Aesthetics," *Political Theory*, February 1997, 57–92.

48. Horkheimer and Adorno, *Dialectic of Enlightenment*.

49. This is not to deny that GAP, Inc., contributes to economic injustice. According to the Wetlands Preserve Environmental and Social Justice Activism Center (http://www.wetlands-preserve.org), GAP was one of eighteen U.S. clothing companies named in a lawsuit accusing them of using indentured labor—predominantly young women from Asia—to produce clothing on the island of Saipan.

50. Horkheimer and Adorno, *Dialectic of Enlightenment*.

51. Ibid., 136, state, "Demand has not yet been replaced by simple obedience." Baudrillard, *Consumer Society*, 175, makes a related point when he writes that "the whole system of values rests on this: there is in the consumer an absolute instinct which inclines him by essence towards his preferential ends—the *moral* myth of consumption which is the direct heir to the idealist myth of man as naturally inclined towards the Beautiful and the Good. . . ."

52. Horkheimer and Adorno, *Dialectic of Enlightenment*, 127.

53. Ibid., 134.

54. Ibid., 124.

55. Ibid., 126, state, "The totality of the culture industry . . . crushes . . . insubordination and makes [it] . . . subserve the formula. . . . The whole world is made to pass through the filter of the culture industry."

56. Ibid., 134–35, state: "The universal triumph of the rhythm of mechanical production and reproduction promises that nothing changes."

57. Docker, *Postmodernism and Popular Culture*, 43, makes a similar point when he says that the Culture Industry essay assumes "a smooth fit between aesthetic forms, images, representations and non-aesthetic realms, . . . as if the capitalist world was a smoothly functioning totality, without divergence, disjunction, conflict, contradiction, questioning, challenge, reversal, inversion, messiness, inexplicability, enigma."

58. For Horkheimer and Adorno, *Dialectic of Enlightenment*, 131, contemporary culture is merely the highest form, the realization, of a leveling tendency inherent in culture per se: "[T]oday aesthetic barbarity completes what has threatened the creations of the spirit since they were gathered together as culture and neutralized. . . . Culture as a common denominator already contains in embryo

that schematization . . . which bring[s] culture within the sphere of administration."

59. Ibid., 166–67.

60. Deleuze, *Difference and Repetition*, 57, states, "*Re*-petition opposes *re*-presentation: the prefix changes its meaning, since in the [latter] . . . case difference is said only in relation to the identical, . . . in the other it is the univocal which is said of the different. [Spiral] repetition is the formless being of all differences, . . . which carries every object to that extreme 'form' in which its representation comes undone. The ultimate element of repetition is the disparate [*dispars*], which stands opposed to the identity of representation."

61. Horkeheimer and Adorno, *Dialectic of Enlightenment*, 144, state: Amusement "is possible only by insulation from the totality of the social process, by desensitization . . . [to] the . . . claim of every work . . . to reflect the whole. . . ."

62. Ibid., 143.

63. Ibid., 144.

64. Ibid.

65. Daston and Park, *Wonders and Order*, 66–67, show how the wondrous and the commodified have had a long history of cohabitation. As far back as the twelfth century, Europeans "craved direct contact with wonders. . . . In addition to being textual objects—things to think about and think with—natural wonders were also things in and of themselves: gems with marvelous properties, exotic plants and animals, and even human beings of unusual or unfamiliar appearance. . . . [T]he value of such mirabilia sprang in part from their scarcity in the European market. As a result, wonders were also commodities: to be bartered, bought, sold, collected, and sometimes literally consumed."

66. Horkheimer and Adorno, *Dialectic of Enlightenment*, 154–55, state: "In the culture industry the individual is an illusion not merely because of the standardization of the means of production. He is tolerated only so long as his complete identification with the generality is unquestioned. Pseudo individuality is rife: from the standardized jazz improvisation to the exceptional film star whose hair curls over her eye. . . . The bourgeois whose existence is split into a business and a private life, whose private life is split into keeping up his public image and intimacy, whose intimacy is split into the surly partnership of marriage and the bitter comfort of being quite alone, at odds with himself and everybody else, is already virtually a Nazi, replete both with enthusiasm and abuse. . . ."

67. Ibid., 147.

68. Ibid., 148, state: "Anyone who doubts the power of monotony is a fool."

69. As James Schmidt, "Language, Mythology, and Enlightenment: Historical Notes on Horkheimer and Adorno's *Dialectic of Enlightenment*," *Social Research* (Winter 1998), 811, 820, shows, after the completion of (the collection of fragments called) *The Dialectic of Enlightenment*, "Horkheimer and Adorno turned their attention to . . . the manuscript's sequel: a 'positive theory of dialectics' that would explain how the 'rescue of enlightenment' might be accomplished." Schmidt also notes that "none of the material that was said to have been completed has yet been found."

70. Adorno might realize this in his other texts, especially *Negative Dialectics*, but, even so, he does not apply it to consumption.

Chapter 7
Ethical Energetics

1. Elaine Scarry, *On Beauty and Being Just* (Princeton University Press, 1999), 81.

2. My understanding of affect has been influenced by Brian Massumi's work in this area. "Affect," he says, "is most often used loosely as a synonym for emotion. But . . . emotion and affect—if affect is intensity—follow different logics and pertain to different orders." (See Massumi, "Autonomy of Affect," 221.)

3. See also Paul Saurette, "Kant's Culture of Humiliation," *Philosophy and Social Criticism* 27 (forthcoming, 2001), for a fascinating account of how Kant unofficially deploys arts of cultivation that threaten the explicit divisions between the sensible and the suprasensible and between politics and morality.

4. Scarry, *On Beauty*, 33. Scarry pursues a project related to mine, though perhaps closer to Schiller's in its focus on the soothing quality of beauty, rather than the charming-disturbing affectivity of enchantment, and closer to Kant in its identification of the "cognitive act" as the ultimate source of the wonder of beauty. The "material world constrains us . . . to see each person and thing in its time and place. . . . But mental life doesn't so constrain us. It is porous, open to the air and light, swings forward while swaying back . . . (48)."

5. There is another reading of Kant, focused around the *Critique of Pure Reason*, that translates what seems to me to be his complex revision of traditional two-world metaphysics into a version of the "two-aspect" model. While Stuart Hampshire and Gilles Deleuze support the suprasensible-sensible interpretation of Kant (and then try to revise it in the direction of a new materialism), Paul Redding, *The Logic of Affect* (Melbourne University Press, 1999), explores the strengths of the two-aspect model as a reading of Kant. This is a plausible rendering of the *Critique of Pure Reason*. But, I think it becomes less plausible when one adds in the Kant of *A Critique of Practical Reason* and *Religion within the Limits of Reason Alone*. Then the indispensability of the suprasensible dimension to Kant's moral philosophy shines through. I focus my discussion on Kant's *Religion within the Limits of Reason Alone* because Kant allows the affective bits of morality to come close to the surface in that book, perhaps because they are especially difficult to avoid when talking about good and evil. The power of Deleuze's *Kant's Critical Philosophy* is that it addresses the three *Critiques* together and shows how each makes room for the others.

6. Immanuel Kant, *Religion within the Limits of Reason Alone*, trans. Theodore Greene and Hoyt Hudson (Harper Torchbooks, 1960), 55.

7. Ibid., 23, my emphasis.

8. It might be that the law "engenders" respect at the very instant one hears the deep, commanding voice of the law. Or that the law "provides" respect in that respect is an organic part of law. Or that the law "enjoins" respect in that respect, while exterior to the law, is always its accompaniment.

9. Kant, *Religion*, 19.

10. Ibid., 44, my emphases.

11. Ibid., 45.

12. Ibid. Kant again complicates his own distinction between noumena and phenomena when he says that the moral law, as an injunction to obey, is one "incentive" alongside others vying for attention from the will (*Willkur*). (*Willkur* refers to the will insofar as it is a radically free capacity for choice—it is the site of the decision, made anew prior to each and every act, as to which incentive to incorporate into one's maxim.) Though the law participates in the status of an "incentive," it differs from all other incentives, says Kant, in that it "commands us potently, yet without making either promises or threats. . . ." (44) Here, Kant asks us to wrap our minds around the difficult idea of an injunction-that-works-without-threats and an incentive-whose-force-is-independent-of-promises. His discussion of miracles reinforces this point: Miracles are not a vital part of the structure of moral motivation, for "commands primordially engraved upon the heart of man through reason" are "incentive" enough. (79).

13. That we have an original "predisposition" to good means that the conditions of being into which we are thrown—survival instinct, sociality, and capacity for respect—themselves conduce to morality; that we have a "propensity" to evil refers to our unrenounceable freedom to deviate from the moral law.

14. Kant, *Religion*, 50.

15. Disposition, like *Willkur*, is an aspect of the will, but it refers to the enduring pattern of intention, the general strategic character of the will as opposed to the tactical choices of *Willkur*.

16. Kant, *Religion*, 57.

17. Ibid., 54, my emphasis.

18. Ibid., 56.

19. Ibid., 77.

20. The moral law is itself an archetype, as Kant reveals when he says that "the bare *idea* of conformity to law, as such, should be a stronger incentive for the will than all the incentives whose source is personal gain." Evil, as self-incurred perversity of will, "can be overcome only through the *idea* of moral goodness in its entire purity, together with the consciousness that this idea really belongs to our original predisposition. . . ." (Ibid., 78, my emphases.)

21. See Coles, *Rethinking Generosity*, 224n. 6.

22. The category of "moral sentiment" seems to be what Romand Coles describes as a "functional equivocation" in Kant. My reading of Kant on moral motivation highlights his struggle to articulate the slippery and complicated relation between mind and body. Coles pursues a similar interpretive strategy in his fascinating account of the "activeness" within Kant's definitionally "passive" and merely "receptive" faculty of sensibility. See Coles, chap. 1, especially 28–32.

23. *CJ*, no. 205.

24. Ibid., no. 242–43. For Kant, aesthetic judgment is "as free of 'interest' as the pure moral act is free of 'motive,' [it is] . . . characterized by disinterested pleasure even as the other is characterized by disinterested duty." Elizabeth Wilkinson and L. A. Willoughby, "Introduction," in Friedrich Schiller, *On the Aesthetic Education of Man*, ed. and trans. Elizabeth Wilkinson and L. A. Willoughby (Oxford University Press, 1967), xxiii.

25. Schiller, *On Aesthetic Education*, 97. There occurs within the play-drive a "reciprocal action" between the sense-drive and the form-drive "of such a kind

that the activity of the one both gives rise to, and sets limits to, the activity of the others, and in which each in itself achieves its highest manifestation by reason of the other being active."

26. Ibid., 46.

27. Ibid., 49.

28. Ibid. Reason demands this unity because "it is its nature to insist on perfection and on the abolition of all limitation, and because any exclusive activity on the part of either the one drive or the other leaves human nature incomplete and gives rise to some limitation within it."

29. According to Schiller, the aesthetic is a middle disposition: in experiencing something as beautiful, we are neither dominated by feeling nor ruled by principle; it is a state where neither duty nor inclination, neither impulse nor reason, neither intuition nor speculation reigns.

30. Schiller, *On Aesthetic Education*, 187. In the aesthetic mood our capacity for "receptivity" (the passive perception of matter) is engaged, even while our "formative" powers (which actively organize matter into objects of knowledge) are also exercised.

31. Ibid., 161.

32. Michel Foucault, "Technologies of the Self," in *Technologies of the Self*, ed. Luther Martin, Huck Gutman, and Patrick H. Hutton (University of Massachusetts Press, 1988), 18.

33. Schiller, *On Aesthetic Education*, 177. Aesthetic education is a matter of making our sensuous life "conformable to laws" and our intellectual life more "dependent upon sense-impressions." An aesthetic education brings "into being a third character which . . . might prepare the way for a transition from the rule of mere force to the rule of law, and which, without in any way impeding the development of moral character, might on the contrary serve as a pledge in the sensible world of a morality as yet unseen" (15). Kant, in another complication of his theory, concurs that moral gymnastics are needed to prepare the sensibility and receive the moral dictates brought to it by a will itself energized by nonsomatic means.

34. Gordon Michalson, *Fallen Freedom* (Cambridge, 1990), 18.

35. During that golden age, "however high the mind might soar, it always drew matter lovingly along with it; and however fine and sharp the distinctions it might make, it never proceeded to mutilate." (Schiller, *On Aesthetic Education*, 31.)

36. Wilkinson and Willoughby, "Introduction," lvi.

37. Schiller, *On Aesthetic Education*, 163. In other words, while "it is character that must set bounds to temperament" (93), "the favour of fortune alone can unloose the fetters of that first physical stage and lead the savage towards beauty" (191).

38. Ibid., 209. Earlier in the text, before Schiller introduces the notion of fantasy play, he explains hedonism as the result of a subaesthetic manifestation of the play-drive, characteristic of children and primitive peoples. The play-drive is the product of Reason's powerful demand for the Absolute, for that which is changeless, total, and unlimited; but if one is too dominated by bodily life, the call of the Absolute will be heard not as a beckoning to "ascend out of a limited reality into the realm of ideas (175)" but as an urge to absolutize *bodily* existence.

39. Ibid., 65.

40. Ibid., 147.

41. Ibid., 161. Schiller makes the point on the same page in this way: "The purely logical form, namely the concept, must speak directly to the understanding, [and] the pure moral form, namely the law, [must speak] directly to the will. But . . . for such a thing as a pure form to exist for sensuous man at all, this, I insist, has first to be made possible by the aesthetic modulation of the psyche."

42. Ibid., 147. I read the "enabling" power of Schiller's aesthetic as residing in the psychological tranquillity afforded as the fragments of the self fall into place and the opposing elements within cease fire. For Terry Eagleton, *The Ideology of the Aesthetic* (Blackwell, 1990), 106–9, the morally activating ingredient in Schiller's aesthetic disposition is best described not as the harmony of sense and reason but as their mutual "canceling out."

43. Schiller, *On Aesthetic Education*, 161.

44. Ibid., 131. According to Josef Chytry, *The Aesthetic State* (University of California Press, 1989), 149, Schiller "does not identify the moral with the aesthetic. Schiller fully recognizes the dangers of untrammeled aestheticism, but he interprets these pitfalls a resulting from an *inadequate* experience of beauty. The free play of faculties characteristic of aesthetic awareness ought to lead to awareness of the power of reason and the notion of a moral law, and any equation of this free play with the moral law itself reflects a serious misunderstanding of the experience.

45. Schiller, *On Aesthetic Education*, 65.

46. Michel Foucault, *Use of Pleasure*, 28. Foucault's comment about the Familistere at Guise illustrates his point about the importance of disposition. The building "manifested the power of ordinary workers to participate in the exercise of their trade" and so could be an "important sign and instrument of autonomy for a group of workers"; but because "no one could enter or leave the place without being seen by everyone," it "could be totally oppressive." What determines which of these potential effects comes into being is the sensibility of those who inhabit it: The Familistere "could only be oppressive if people were *prepared to use* their own presence in order to watch over others." (Michel Foucault, "An Ethics of Pleasure," in *Foucault Live*, trans. John Johnston and ed. Sylvere Lotringer [Semiotext(e), 1989], 266, my emphasis.) For Foucault, as for Schiller, becoming "prepared" to enact a possibility is a complicated aesthetic exercise, a matter of great skill involving complex practices of discipline.

47. Michel Foucault, "On the Genealogy of Ethics: An Overview of Work in Progress," in *The Foucault Reader*, ed. Paul Rabinow (Pantheon, 1984), 371, my emphasis.

48. Foucault, *Use of Pleasure*, 29–30.

49. Ibid., 31.

50. Foucault, "Technologies of Self," 18.

51. Eagleton, *Ideology of Aesthetic*, 20.

52. Ibid., 27.

53. Foucault, "Ethics of Pleasure," 269.

54. Foucault, "What is Enlightenment?" in *Foucault Reader*, 50.

55. Kafka, "Report to Academy," 253–54.

56. Schiller, *On Aesthetic Education*, 189.

57. Christopher Norris, *Uncritical Theory* (Lawrence and Wishart, 1992), 166–67.

58. Richard Wolin, *The Terms of Cultural Criticism* (Columbia University Press, 1992), 192.

59. Schiller, *On Aesthetic Education*, 211. Richard Wolin, "Foucault's Aesthetic Decisionism," *Telos* 67 (1986), 85, puts it this way: Because "provocative actions, gestures or spectacles" are the telos of aesthetics, Foucault's ethical universe will be "a Hobbesian state of nature . . . with a flair for style."

60. Friedrich Nietzsche, *The Gay Science*, trans. Walter Kaufmann (Vintage, 1974), 232, aphorism no. 290.

61. George Kateb, "Aestheticism and Morality: Their Cooperation and Hostility," *Political Theory*, February 2000, 5–37. Kateb beautifully articulates a "democratic aestheticism" whose goal is to be receptive and responsive "to as much of the world as possible" (20) while also "assert[ing] morality's supremacy" over aesthetics and seeking to "educate the sense of beauty and sublimity so that it serves morality rather than . . . [harm] it" (32). Kateb's treatment of the "undeniably complex" (6) relationship between ethics and aesthetics is subtle and fair-minded and persuasive. Perhaps because it sees the aesthetic disposition as in the first instance a "craving," it does not does adequately address, I think, the question of the *energetics* of ethics or consider the possibility that aesthetic moods might provide the impetus for ethical enactments.

62. Schiller, *On Aesthetic Education*, 211.

63. My thanks to Linda Zerilli for this point.

64. Eagleton, *Ideology of Aesthetic*, 13.

65. Foucault, "The Concern for Truth," in *Foucault Live*, 297.

66. Stephen Best and Douglas Kellner, *Postmodern Theory: Critical Investigations* (Guilford, 1991), 290. See also Eagleton, *Ideology of Aesthetic*, 17.

67. Alex Callinicos, *Against Postmodernism* (Polity Press, 1989), 91. Eagleton, *Ideology of Aesthetic*, 386, also charges Foucault with an indifference toward the poor.

68. Foucault is a materialist, too. He sees every social formation, including the construction of the self, the structure of work, the forms of the law, as a materialization. What Foucault denies is that one set of practices is material and fundamental, whereas others rest on top of them as effects.

69. Best and Kellner, *Postmodern Theory*, 290.

70. Eagleton, *Ideology of Aesthetic*, 393.

71. William Connolly has made this case eloquently in "Beyond Good and Evil: The Ethical Sensibility of Michel Foucault," *Political Theory*, August 1993.

72. Foucault, *Use of Pleasure*, 26. Foucault also refers to arts of the self as the processes through which one becomes the moral subject of one's own actions. (See Foucault, "On Genealogy of Ethics," 352.)

73. Foucault, "An Aesthetics of Existence," in *Foucault Live*, 311.

74. Richard Flathman, *Reflections of a Would-Be Anarchist* (University of Minnesota Press, 1998), 55.

75. Ibid., 54. Drawing upon Thomas Hobbes to explain why this is so, Flathman says that "the marks that we invent and use, 'besides the signification of what we imagine of their nature, have a signification also of the nature, disposi-

tions, and interest of the speaker.' " Here, Hobbes could be taken to say that language works in tandem with "disposition," and that dispositions are the result of a complex set of linguistic, habitual, gestural, and other corporeal practices. To alter a disposition, then, would be to alter several of these zones in relation to the others. Flathman, however, focuses solely on the matter of the "unintelligibility" of words; he presents the gap between rules and conduct as essentially a problem of *signification*.

76. Deleuze and Guattari, *Kafka*, 5.

77. Kafka, *Castle*, 197–98.

78. Deleuze and Guattari, *Kafka*.

79. Flathman, *Reflections*.

80. Ought one, for example, to engage in a long effort of learning, memorizations? Or seek a sudden and irreversible change in behavior? Or try to root out, down to the last hidden form, all forms of suspect desire?

81. See Foucault, "On Genealogy of Ethics," 355.

82. Foucault, "Concern for Truth," 305–6.

83. My thanks to Chris Falzon for this formulation.

84. "You can see," says Foucault, "On Genealogy of Ethics," 354, "that the way the same rule is accepted . . . [can be] quite different. And that's what I call the *mode d'assujettissment*." Foucault, *Use of Pleasure*, 27, also says that, in one mode of subjection, for example, obedience might be grounded upon divine law; in another, in a natural or cosmological order; in another, in a rational principle. Or one might strive to conform "because one acknowledges oneself to be a member of the group that accepts it," or "because one regards oneself as an heir to a spiritual tradition that one has the responsibility of maintaining or reviving," or because it gives "one's personal life a form that answers to criteria of brilliance, beauty, nobility, or perfection." This last rationale forms an important part of the Greco-Roman ethic examined in Foucault, *Use of Pleasure*, and Foucault's positive portrayal of it is perhaps most responsible for earning him the epithet "aestheticizer."

85. Thinkers in the classical tradition who have pursued this include Epicurus, Spinoza, Nietzsche. An excellent example in contemporary theory is George Kateb, *The Inner Ocean* (Cornell University Press, 1992).

Chapter 8
Attachments and Refrains

1. John Docker, "Creation Stories: Moses, Spinoza, and Freud," in *Demoralizing Theory, Regenerating, Micropolitics*, ed. Jane Bennett and Michael Shapiro (New York University Press, forthcoming).

2. Matthew Solan, *Men's Fitness*, December 1999, 45, says: "The right kinds of sounds—from smooth jazz to classical to world beat to easy listening—have been shown to create neurological and endocrine enhancements. Stop listening to the evening news, says alternative health guru Andrew Weil, M.D., because its long-term effect may produce a sense of helplessness and hopelessness. Read the paper instead, and add some background music. . . ."

3. The mood of enchantment is itself an exaggeration or intensification of perception.

4. Adorno, *Negative Dialectics*, 203.

5. Stephen K. White, "Three Conceptions of the Political: The Real World of Late Modern Democracy," in Aryeh Botwinick and William Connolly, *Democracy and Vision: Sheldon Wolin and the Vissicitudes of the Political* (Princeton University Press, 2001), 5.

6. White, *Affirmation*, 8.

7. Weak ontologists do, of course, seek to persuade others of the value or meaningfulness or benefits of their onto-tales.

8. White, *Affirmation*, 91.

9. Ibid., 8.

10. Ibid., 93. Butler is one of the four weak ontologists examined in White's book. George Kateb, Charles Taylor, and William Connolly are the others.

11. Ibid., 4.

12. Latour, *We Have Never Been Modern*, 137.

13. White, *Affirmation*, 9.

14. White, "Three Conceptions," 16.

15. White, *Affirmation*, 9–10.

16. William E. Connolly, "Rethinking *The Ethos of Pluralization*," *Philosophy and Social Criticism* 24, no. 1 (1998), 97.

17. White, *Affirmation*, 97.

18. Ibid., 9.

19. Deleuze and Guattari, *Thousand Plateaus*, 346–47.

20. Ibid, 342–43, state: "Whereas romantic philosophy still appealed to a formal synthetic identity ensuring a continuous intelligibility of matter . . . , modern philosophy tends to elaborate a material of thought in order to capture forces that are not thinkable in themselves. This is Cosmos philosophy."

21. Deleuze and Guattari, *Thousand Plateaus*.

22. Clement Rosset, *Joyful Cruelty: Toward a Philosophy of the Real* (Oxford University Press, 1993), 25.

23. Ibid., 18–19.

24. "Flowering Plants," *Morning Edition*, National Public Radio, July 9, 1999, transcript. Dr. Robert Raguso of the Department of Biology, University of Michigan, was featured in the broadcast. "My research," says Raguso, "focuses on the ecological role(s) of floral scent as a mode of chemical communication between plants and their insect pollinators. . . . I am interested in the roles played by plant volatiles . . . and the diversity of physiological and behavioral responses of animals, whether pollinators or opportunistic predators, to these chemical signals."

25. Sue Goetinck, "Electronic Ants to Roam the Internet," *The Baltimore Sun*, Dec. 5, 1998, 2A.

26. I am poised between believing the themes that I develop here about animal, plant, and molecular life and experimentally adopting them to see what happens to the world and to my own belief structure when one acts upon them.

27. Sheryl Gay Stolberg, "Ideas & Trends: Sham Surgery Returns as a Research Tool," Sunday Week in Review, *The New York Times*, Apr. 25, 1999. Some surgeons in 1999 again advocated sham surgery, and "experts estimate that 30 percent of all patients getting placebo treatment today improve."

28. The co-presence of wonder with unease is also expressed when the provocation for enchantment is a macro-natural phenomenon (e.g., Mount Ktaadn). This example is but one from within a rich discourse of "the sublime" in nature. In the presence of sublime nature, it is the exteriority of nature, its foreignness, its givenness, that is responsible for our sense of insignificance and for the fear that accompanies being assigned such a small place in the world. There, a dark sense of uneasiness comingles with an exhilarating sense of wonder. Perhaps this is what Kant was getting at when he said that it is the very externality of the voice of conscience that provokes in us a sense of awe and respect.

29. Chris Chesser, "Digitising the Beat: Police Databases and Incorporeal Transformations," *Convergence: The Journal of Research into New Media Technologies* (http://www.luton.ac.uk/Convergence). Chesser's article describes not only the appeal or enchantment of computer invocation but also its political dangers, in particular, those associated with the criminal profiling encouraged by centralized police databases.

30. Quoted in Vinay Mono, "Techno-pup: Smart Toy Heralds Robotic Future," *The Toronto Sunday Star*, Aug. 15, 1999, A1, A8.

31. Ibid., A8.

32. Andrew Seligsohn, e-mail correspondence with author, Nov. 9, 1998.

33. Rosset, *Joyful Cruelty*, 12, 14–15. As evidence for his claim that "simple existence is in itself a source of rejoicing," Rosset points to the importance people assign to recounting accurately the past events of their lives: "The smaller one's investment in what was happening in the past when one was participating in the events, the more one now refuses to hear that artichokes were served that day when in fact one remembers excellent asparagus. . . . This fastidious character of remembrance can only be interpreted as the mark of recognition. . . with respect to existence as such, of the inherent interest of all existence whatever it may be. . . ."

Index

46464003R00134

Made in the USA
Lexington, KY
05 November 2015